T0290467

Is It Okay to Sell the Monet?

Is It Okay to Sell the Monet?

The Age of Deaccessioning in Museums

Edited by Julia Courtney

ROWMAN & LITTLEFIELD
Lanham • Boulder • New York • London

Published by Rowman & Littlefield
A wholly owned subsidiary of The Rowman & Littlefield Publishing Group, Inc.
4501 Forbes Boulevard, Suite 200, Lanham, Maryland 20706
www.rowman.com

Unit A, Whitacre Mews, 26-34 Stannary Street, London SE11 4AB

British Library Cataloguing in Publication Information Available

Library of Congress Cataloging-in-Publication Data
Names: Courtney, Julia Hollett, editor.
Title: Is it okay to sell the Monet? : the age of deaccessioning in museums / edited by Julia Courtney.
Description: Lanham : Rowman & Littlefield, 2018. | Includes bibliographical references and index.
Identifiers: LCCN 2018018060 (print) | LCCN 2018020792 (ebook) | ISBN 9781442270831 (Electronic) | ISBN 9781442270817 (cloth : alk. paper) | ISBN 9781442270824 (pbk. : alk. paper)
Subjects: LCSH: Museums— Deaccessioning. | Museums—Deaccessioning—Case studies.
Classification: LCC AM133 (ebook) | LCC AM133 .I8 2018 (print) | DDC 069—dc23
LC record available at https://lccn.loc.gov/2018018060

∞™ The paper used in this publication meets the minimum requirements of American National Standard for Information Sciences—Permanence of Paper for Printed Library Materials, ANSI/NISO Z39.48-1992.

Printed in the United States of America

Contents

Part III: The Use of Proceeds: Ethics and the Role of Professional Associations

Part IV: Case Studies

Acknowledgments

Many thanks to contributing editor Katherine E. Lewis, for her impeccable editing support on this publication and for the recruitment of several of the essayists and to Mark Gold, a content specialist who assisted with many aspects of this volume. In fond memory of Gil Whittemore, a dedicated art law attorney and friend whom I had the pleasure of studying with at Harvard University.

Finally, this book recognizes the museum professionals, collectors, art law attorneys, boards of trustees, volunteers, and museum communities who, through best practices in their fields, work to ensure the safety and care of art and artifacts, and sustainability of museums, enabling them to continue to preserve the culture of the past. These efforts strengthen museums as a whole, securing their future, which ultimately benefits the communities they serve.

Introduction

Can We Save the Art and the Museum?

Julia Courtney

On a frigid day in mid-December 2017, the sidewalk near the Peabody Museum on the campus of Harvard University was buzzing with bundled protestors from Pittsfield, Massachusetts, a community in the Berkshires. Carrying signs and wearing bright red and black buttons on their lapels that read "Save the Art," the protestors rallied against the most recent round of controversial deaccessioning in an American museum—this time art from the Berkshire Museum was on the auction block. Inside museum professionals, board members, and volunteers from museums across the United States convened in "think-tank" fashion to consider ways to avoid "raiding the cookie jar" when museums face (sometimes inevitable) financial crises. Though thoughtful and productive, by design the discussions centered only on early intervention measures aimed at preventing museums from deaccessioning objects to cushion their bottom line.

Important preventative strategies surfaced, but the discussion groups did not examine museums already in crisis or scrutinize the current policy and ethical standards that govern museums. These preemptive tactics can be found on the AAM website, but for museums in dire circumstances, it may be too late to employ them. Organized in partnership with the Association of Art Museum Directors (AAMD), the American Association for State and Local History (AASLH), the Association for Academic Museums and Galleries (AAMG), and the New England Museum Association (NEMA), the session and the discussions it sparked merely scratched the surface of the problem at hand: how exactly do we save both the art *and* the museum?

Deliberation over the ethics of deaccessioning in museums has flooded news sources since the 1970s, over nearly a fifty-year period. It would be difficult to find another topic that has been as heavily considered throughout a half century. Should artifacts only be sold to ensure direct care of collections? Can proceeds be used for non-direct-care plights such as operating costs, expansions, or shoring up endowments? Is it better for a museum to close, rather than risk having its treasures sold and placed in the private domain? Which action best serves the museum's community? Clearly the debate spurs more questions than answers but through it all, one thing remains consistent: we take our art seriously.

Tracing the exact beginnings of deaccessioning would be a challenge, since the procedure has been used as a collection management strategy for decades. Museums deaccession for a host of reasons, including the desire to refine the collection by "trading up"; to accommodate a shift in the focus of the collection; to finance collections care upgrades; and the most controversial one, to mitigate a financial crisis by cashing in their assets. When a museum sells art to increase acquisition funds to enable the purchase of artworks in better condition or of greater caliber than those they hold, it is considered admirable. When museums deaccession to accommodate a change in the focus of their collection or fund collections facility upgrades, it is palatable. But when a museum deaccessions art for the purpose of strengthening the institution, rather than its collection, the full weight of the professional dissonance can be felt. This is not without reason; it is, in fact, a key industry standard and one of the only ways to protect the cultural treasures that museums hold. The AAM's guidelines for collections care, last updated in 1993, provide a tool kit for museums grappling with the complex ethical issue of deaccessioning and the use of its proceeds for the "direct care of collections." However, the interpretation of that phrase remained problematic.

For that reason, in 2015, the AAM appointed a Direct Care Task Force, charged with drafting a white paper to assist museums in determining the appropriate use of the proceeds obtained from deaccessioning. The resulting white paper and its accompanying matrix (which suggests criteria for the use of proceeds and "direct care" so that museums can self-regulate) developed by the Task Force describes the history behind the AAM Code of Ethics (1993) and presents a thoughtful rationale for adhering to its principles. It also reviews ethical principles of collections stewardship, provides guidelines for "direct care," and recommends strengthening collections policies with regard to deaccessioning.[1] Without these standards, museums would be left on their own to navigate ethical questions when they arise. The white paper defines collections stewardship, cultural assets, and the responsibilities associated with caring for them in this paragraph:

> Collectively, museums share a responsibility for collections stewardship that "entails the highest public trust and carries with it the presumption of rightful ownership, permanence, care, documentation, accessibility and responsible

disposal." Museums acquire items of cultural or scientific value for their collections through donation, purchase, rescue or field research and hold these items for the benefit of present and future generations. Although these items may have a monetary value, once they become part of a museum's permanent collection, that value becomes secondary to their importance as a means to enhance understanding of our world and ourselves. Consequently, museum collections are considered cultural—not financial—assets, to be held for the public benefit.[2]

The rationale for adhering to guidelines set forth by the AAM is compelling:

By adhering to these ethical principles, museums demonstrate that they uphold the highest professional standards regarding the care of their collections. They also demonstrate that they maintain their holdings for the benefit of present and future generations, thereby encouraging public confidence and respect.[3]

Viewing a collection as a financial asset is a slippery slope, but almost everyone outside the profession embraces that practice. Admirably, most museum professionals put ethics before everything else, but what happens when an institution's survival is at stake? Recent cases and their outcomes have shown that there may be opportunities to implement creative solutions on the horizon.

Before the 1970s, deaccessioning went mostly unseen by communities outside the museum sector, but in September 1970, all that changed. That fall, the Metropolitan Museum of Art purchased Diego Velazquez's portrait of *Juan de Pareja* (c. 1650), which was up for auction. The painting, one of Velazquez's masterpieces, was purchased by the Met for $5.5 million, then a record price for a single work of art.[4] A *New York Times* editorial stated that despite the price tag, the Met's acquisition of a "superb painting enhanced the quality of its collection and enriched the life of the city."[5]

The deal was considered a great conquest until 1972, when the *New York Times* reported that the Met secretly sold works from the modern art collection bequeathed by Adelaide de Groot, to help finance the iconic Velazquez purchase.[6] The revelation led to a seven-month investigation by the state Attorney General's Office (AGO) and resulted in the museum having to notify the AGO of any deaccessions of artwork valued at more than $5,000.[7] The Met's calamity brought deaccessioning of art into the public consciousness, and since then, museums and their boards have been heavily scrutinized whenever significantly valued art is deaccessioned from the collection.[8]

Deaccessioning is a complex issue, there's no doubt. There's been some excellent discourse written on the topic citing evolving trends and opinions in the art and museum world. Even with all the discussion, still no "one-size-fits-all" solution has emerged. Perhaps because each institution and situation is so unique, they warrant customized remedies.

In addition to the aforementioned symposium at Harvard, professional museum organizations AAM, NEMA, ASLH, and AAMG, along with other regional groups, have hosted round-table discussions in recent months, intended as "think tanks" to generate proactive steps for museums in trouble, grappling with all aspects of the deaccessioning dilemma. Although many creative and practical ideas emerged from the sessions, none really provided an answer to the difficult question of whether it is better for a museum to close its doors or use collections assets to stay afloat.

The most recent case in the limelight, the Berkshire Museum, ignited a frenzy of international publicity when the museum attempted to sell artwork to finance a plan to reinvent itself and avoid closure. The museum proposed to deaccession and sell forty works of art, including *Shuffleton's Barbershop* by artist Norman Rockwell, as a result of a change in mission. The case has sparked much debate, as auction sales often result in purchases by private collectors, stirring the souls of impassioned museum professionals, attorneys, art lovers, and museumgoers alike, on both sides of the issue. In a surprise turn, and after much consideration and consultation from the Massachusetts AGO, the Berkshire Museum was permitted to sell just enough of its art to resolve the financial crisis and set the museum on the path to success. This was a groundbreaking compromise, and one that other troubled museums may opt to exercise in the future.

Although the timing of the resurrected deaccession debate, the influx of cases, and the dispute around the use of the proceeds are largely driven by museums still suffering the effects of financial challenges brought on by the Great Recession of 2008, it is always hanging in the balance. The pointed questions that have surfaced as museums search for answers are abundant: Can the monies be applied toward museums' operating costs? Can they be put toward budget deficits for museums facing financial ruin? Should public trust be reevaluated? Does the Financial Accounting Standard Board (FASB) rule for nonprofits need to be updated? What other avenues can museums explore to remain viable in the future? How can museums be accountable to both masters: the industry's professional standards for collections care and the need to stay afloat? Creative solutions are essential at this juncture, which might include implementing preventative measures before a financial crisis; reevaluating the industry standards, the FASB rule, and the circumstances that warrant its application; and redefining the role museums should play in their communities. These measures could prevent troubled museums from closing their doors or cutting already-sparse staff, hours, or programs, thus compromising their future, and ultimately help to support museums in realizing their commitment to the immediate community.

The deep effect the Great Recession had on museums forced them to make extensive cutbacks—or permanently close in some cases—and deaccession portions of the collections at the risk of lawsuits and condemnation. According to Sue Chen, who wrote "Art Deaccessions and the Limits of Fiduciary Duty" for *Art Antiquity and Law*, the financial crisis that caused museum endowments to shrink by approximately 24 percent quickly turned deaccessioning from a tool used to improve collections to a tool inevitably used to save collections.[9] Chen stated that "museums should not have to choose between saving itself and caring for its collections."[10] While legal guidelines are cloudy, museums are guided by these professional ethical codes disseminated by the American Alliance of Museums (AAM) and the American Association of Museum Directors (AAMD). Though not legally enforceable, these codes are firmly prescribed in the museum community to avoid association sanctions. Neither association has amended its deaccessioning policy since the 2008 financial crisis.[11]

This book, *Is It Okay to Sell the Monet? The Age of Deaccessioning in Museums*, represents only a small sampling of the expertise in the field. It presents current arguments, proposed solutions, and case studies that contribute to the deaccession patchwork. During its development, it quickly became clear that it was also an illustration of the passion and commitment with which thoughtful, intelligent museum professionals, attorneys, museum board members, and professional museum/art organizations and arts communities work to resolve the serious ethical quandary that museums face in the twenty-first century.

Jennifer L. White's article, which inspired the title for this book, appeared in the *Michigan Law Review* (1996): "When It's OK to Sell the Monet: A Trustee-Fiduciary Duty Framework for Analyzing the Deaccessioning of Art to Meet Museum Operating Expenses." In it, White states that "art museums present the paradox of being simultaneously very rich, because of the value of the assets they hold, and very poor, due to the illiquidity of those assets and high operation costs."[12] This irony holds true twenty years later and is likely to remain unchanged in the future.

White states:

Although drastic, museums must be able to consider the possibility of selling some of their assets in order to remain solvent. A lack of museums would make real the belief that art is only for the wealthy. Surely the public cannot be served best by a policy in which one interest—the art itself—is allowed to prevail absolutely over the very important interest of providing public access to the art through the maintenance of museums as healthy institutions. The only way museums can serve the interests of the public is if they are given the means to survive, which may require periodically allowing them to deaccession works from their collections. It is unrealistic to demand that museums hold on to works that do not serve their mission or those for which they cannot care properly, while forsaking the benefits of selling these works to others who might put them to better use.[13]

White uses the example of the New-York Historical Society, forced to close after 188 years in operation (February 1993) due to their financial crisis. She commented that "[m]useums will continue to desire new art for their collections, but in cases like the Historical Society, their most pressing concern is survival."[14] The organization reopened in 1995, when the court allowed them to deaccession and sell sixteen million dollars' worth of old master paintings and apply the funds toward operating expenses.[15] The director summarized the controversy with the following: "[To] consider deaccessioning only to buy more art when the Historical Society has been closed for over two years due to lack of working capital just doesn't make any sense at this point."[16] History does repeat itself, and the lessons learned can hopefully pave the way to practical solutions that museums can add to their toolbox.

These are exciting times for those with a passion for or against deaccessioning, though this author isn't advocating for or against the procedure, and the perspectives in the chapters that follow will hopefully challenge the field to reframe deaccessioning crises as opportunities to fashion new and better solutions that can be implemented without condemnation. The first section frames the "Context of the Debate" (part 1) and provides an examination of the ethical dilemma by Bernard Fishman, a seasoned museum director, who offers experience and a selection of case studies demonstrating the impact deaccessioning had and creative solutions that resulted. Fishman asserts that although adhering to the "ethical mandates of deaccessioning made sense for museums past, this directive should be examined and debated in the light of modern conditions and needs, and potentially altered in the face of achieving greater public benefit."[17] Michael O'Hare's article, "Museums Can Change—Will They?" follows and challenges museums and their administrators to think outside the box to envision solutions while using their latent wealth to create more engaging visitor experiences.

"The Mechanics of Disposal" (part 2) is an overview of the logistics that museums encounter when the opportunity to deaccession arises. Stefanie Jandl and attorney Mark Gold explore how museums grapple with the tension between keeping deaccessioned objects in the public domain or releasing them into private hands through auction sale in "Keeping Deaccessioned Objects in the Public Domain." Darlene A. Bialowski, independent registrar, offers expertise on due diligence and deaccessioning by illustrating conundrums that collections staff may encounter. Christopher J. Robinson, attorney and former art dealer, investigates deaccession blunders that have occurred throughout history of this controversial museum practice.

The third section of the book (part 3) examines the "Use of Proceeds: Ethics and the Role of Professional Associations." Sally Yerkovich, the Director of the Institute for Museum Ethics, summarizes the ethics surrounding the use of proceeds from deaccessioned objects in her essay, "Use of Funds from the Sale of Deaccessioned Objects: It's a Matter of Ethics." Yerkovich outlines the history behind and implementation of professional codes of ethics for museums and follows the changes to these codes through the years. In 2015, an initiative to define *direct care* resulted in a Task Force assembled from a variety of institutions that led to the Direct Care White Paper: *Direct Care: Ethics, Guidelines, and Recommendations*, published in 2016. This essay is followed by an informative article exploring the Financial Accounting Standard Board (FASB) that created the debacle for museums implementing deaccession policies by Lori Breslauer and Sarah Ebel from the Field Museum, "Making the Case: FASB's Accounting Standards Should Be Realigned with AAM's Long-Standing Guidance on the Use of Sale Proceeds." Next, attorney Mark Gold examines monetizing museum collections with an array of case studies, and Ashley Downing, Curator for the Dupage County Historical Museum, writes on the gray area around the use of proceeds and direct care for museums in "Flying under the Radar: What Does Direct Care of the Collection Really Mean?"

Finally, part 4 includes deaccessioning case studies that have impacted several museums. The variety of outcomes, unique circumstances, and special collections provide insight into potential solutions that might be considered by other museums. The Wheaton College collection's Newell Bequest illustrated by Leah Niederstadt resulted in wonderful new acquisitions for the College that enhanced academic programs. Katherine E. Lewis presents digital deaccessioning, a relatively new procedure that museums face in the twenty-first century with the age of technology. The case study on the Higgins Armory Museum and the Worcester Art Museum by James C. Donnelly Jr. and Catherine M. Colinvaux depicts an elegant example of combining collections in a unique manner, assuring their care and preservation. Two essays on Randolph College scrutinize the governance of the institution and controversies that developed with regard to its collection in "Randolph College: A Study in Governance" by Peter Dean and John E. Klein and "Randolph College: A Sequel, A New Relationship, and More Controversy" by Peter Dean and Bradley W. Bateman. Finally, the Berkshire Museum case study that unfolded in 2017–18, by Julia Courtney, represents the most recent debacle of deaccessioning in the museum world.

It is my hope that the insightful essays offered in this volume will help museums better shape their collections plan and deaccession policies in a manner that integrates ethical standards, best practices in collections management, and the practical need for financial soundness. With the applied collective intellect of museum professionals, attorneys, art lovers, and museum supporters, there's no doubt that solutions are within our grasp. Hopefully, the truths and opinions expressed here will provide insight and prove to be an effective tool for museums as they continue to navigate the ethical and financial challenges of the twenty-first century.

I

THE CONTEXT OF THE DEBATE

1

Two Cheers for Deaccessioning

Bernard Fishman

To seek permanence in this world is ultimately a fool's errand; though, as the old song goes, "sheer persistence can be noble stuff." Museums and their ancestral manifestations were originally experienced primarily as places of inspiration, often-religious inspiration in the earlier examples. Combined with aesthetic and didactic impulses, this emotional directive continues to guide institutional collecting today. The freewheeling and fluid collecting activities of the past, which have in many cases given us the extraordinary accumulations we prize today, sometimes through collection methods we officially deplore, have in recent generations been admirably contained and regulated by our self-appointed national and international museum institutional guardians. Yet in bringing orderliness, decorum, rules, and categorizations, the museum profession has also sometimes chilled the possibilities for institutional adaptability that are essential for continuing vitality and strength in a world that is always shifting and changing. This is particularly evident in matters of deaccessioning.

The human instinct to preserve the past for inspirational purposes is certainly very ancient. It may have helped stimulate the invention of writing, which in Egypt occurred in part to enable society to record personal names and historical events for both religious and political purposes. Egyptian, Mesopotamian, and Classical temples and sanctuaries were the first proto-museums, intentionally preserving statuary dedications, monumental inscriptions, artifacts from military victories, and sumptuous works of mainly religious art for public admiration and emotional resonance. In some fashion they might also preserve the dedications of the more humble, as we learn from the poetry of Sappho and other sources. In Egypt an early sense of historic appreciation resulted in frequent visits by literate people to historic sites of past renown and the leaving at these places of respectful graffiti recording the visits and the admiration that aroused them. Rulers in the ancient Mediterranean world often took pride in restoring or repairing the monuments or buildings of selected ancestors or heroic figures, frequently mentioning the original builders as well as their own restorative activities in self-regarding texts.

We know little about how such ancient temple collections or historic sites were managed. Presumably priestly guardians or temple authorities made most of these decisions, taking into account the desires or commands of the gods, as those were interpreted, of rulers, military strongmen, or the politically powerful, subject to their own inclinations as resources or allegiances allowed. The natural effect was, over time, to clutter these sanctuaries with many kinds of dedications, all given originally to be "permanent" gifts to the gods. The first deaccessioning decisions probably presented themselves not long after accessioning began. At Egypt's great temple complex of Karnak, there is early evidence for a very dramatic kind of "deaccessioning" procedure. The discovery of carefully arranged caches of buried statues within the sacred temple precinct suggests that the temple precincts were over time becoming unacceptably crowded with statuary dedications, and so ways of clearing the grounds had to be devised. As the "audience" for ancient proto-museums included supernatural beings as well as fleshly devotees, tourists, and temple staff, the continuing interests of the gods and departed kings could not safely be ignored. Since the gods would presumably still recognize the devotional validity of dedications even when such offerings were buried in the ground, it would be permissible to remove the statues from public sight, as long as they were safely and respectfully buried within the sacred circuit. Similar caches have been discovered at other ancient sites. These hidden collections imply that "resource impact" was a factor in the management and disposal of ancient collections as well as modern ones.

Presumably the Egyptians, being bureaucratically minded, had lists of the inhumed sculpture. Certainly, in the Hellenistic period, the great Library at Alexandria had extensive catalogue lists of its books. It would be instructive to know what collection catalogues or finding aids were in place for ancient municipal or state archival collections, which doubtless would have included many artifacts as well as documents. Since Roman historians like Suetonius and Tacitus were able to gain access to and use ancient documents such as personal letters from past emperors, some kind of preservation and retrieval system had to have been in place for certain collections. Perhaps the municipal archives of Herculaneum, where carbonized organic materials sometimes survived the pyroclastic flows that destroyed the town, will one day be uncovered and will reveal examples of how such materials were managed.

That there existed some ancient organizational process directed toward long-term preservation of important records is indicated in Egypt by a number of extraordinary historical and legal documents, on fragile papyrus, which have survived from the late second millennium BCE and which evidently derived from the area of the Theban necropolis, to be discovered under unknown circumstances in the nineteenth century. They may have been part of the library of Medinet Habu, a pharaonic funerary temple that for centuries served as the administrative headquarters for the area. There was certainly something amazingly effective, or very lucky, about that collection's arrangement or placement that allowed portions of it to survive in good condition for some three thousand years, a record of preservation that seems outlandish to compare to the couple of centuries even our oldest modern museums have been in operation.

It is likely that systematic organization was available only to the most important collections, whether of objects or archives, and to those supported by strong institutional resources. As with many small historical or municipal collections of our own day, the less magisterial assemblages probably used what I might call the "genizah" system, after the Cairo synagogue documents rediscovered in the nineteenth century. That is, the items were only minimally "catalogued," if at all, and were kept in more or less disorganized and relatively undocumented gatherings to be periodically swept out when their contents seemed too arcane or obsolete to be of further use. Sometimes obsolete material survived because it was stashed out of sight and its guardians could forget about it, as with most of the Cairo genizah examples. More often it was just disposed of. Such ancient trash has very occasionally turned into modern treasure by its unexpected persistence, as with the now invaluable written refuse from the Oxyrhynchus town dumps, where excavations uncovered thousands of personal and official documents millennia after they had been thrown away, unexpectedly preserved by Egypt's dry climate.

The chief point of recounting the above is to stress that deaccessioning has been a necessary part of the collection preservation process since the earliest times. Our questions about deaccessioning today fall into a pattern reaching back to the first periods of civilized societies and touch on many of the same concerns, especially space availability, public access, resource restrictions, and "contemporary" relevance. And we should not assume that the valuable strictures promulgated by the American Alliance of Museums are necessarily more compelling to us than the need to maintain Hera's temple in good and accessible condition, while averting the goddess's potential wrath, was to her devotees. Another point of value here is to cultivate a degree of modesty about our current museum and archival institutions, and the human condition in general. We have certainly learned a great deal about the techniques of collection sustainability and public access, and rightly glory in the beneficial institutions of preservation and learning that we have created and spread all over the world. However, we should still be awed by the vastness of time and the uncertainty of human affairs.

The keepers of Amun-Ra's Karnak Temple and of the Alexandrian library or the libraries of Trajan in Rome probably thought of their institutions as eternal and would have been unlikely to imagine them as the abandoned or even invisible ruins they are now. Their priests and scholars and administrators would of course have acted as though their institutions were immortal and their contents destined for "permanent" preservation. They could not easily have foreseen the arrival of earthquakes or fires or Assyrians or Vandals. We are not far removed from such horrors ourselves. Many museums and historic sites were damaged or destroyed in World War II and even within the last few years we have seen the venerable French Institute in Cairo sacked by a mob, with its stately building burnt out and its precious books and papers swirling into the street. Rioters entered the Cairo Museum and wantonly damaged objects, including items from Tutankhamun's tomb. Imagine that for a moment: relics preserved in the Valley of the Kings for almost 3,400 years, only to be shattered less than a century after the tomb's modern discovery. How easily can we imagine a frenzied crowd wrecking the Metropolitan Museum of Art while smoke drifts over Central Park, or a suicide bomber in the midst of the Louvre? Let us call for permanent preservation a little less shrilly, and with a glance over our shoulders at the specters of human savagery and nature's fury. Let us be a little more humble about our ability to defeat eternity and a little more forgiving of the imperfect attempts of our institutions to sustain themselves and yet serve the public through more immediate preservation of themselves and their holdings. We can only shape our own times, and even that very imperfectly. We can project legacies and shadows for a short distance, but decades are cloudy and centuries invisible. Neither ourselves nor our works were made to last. That we can extend our lives and theirs is one of the glorious setbacks we have delivered to nature, but that victory is inevitably temporary and wasting. Permanence is not possible.

Over nearly thirty-five years I have directed five museums in five different states. I was the founding director of one of them. All could be described as history museums, though several included archives or research libraries as well. All had small art collections, and one had a large natural history collection. Most managed historic buildings, eleven in one case and two National Historic Landmark properties in another. Two were less than thirty years old when I arrived, and two were fairly close to two centuries old. Their annual budgets ranged from $60,000 to $2.5 million. Two of them achieved national accreditation during my term and one other was involved in the reaccreditation process. Staff size, facilities, endowments, attendance, all varied enormously from one organization to another. I have also assessed some twenty museums as a Museum Assessment Program reviewer or through private consultancies. I have led or studied more museums, and museums of widely differing capacities, than is typical for an individual director. I've seen and organized many stages of accomplishment among these places. And as you might have guessed, I had another, earlier, career, as an Egyptologist based in Egypt. I found that to work as an archaeologist and epigrapher was an excellent teacher about the nature of human and cultural continuity and mutability, the inevitability of organic decay, and the general futility of "forever." Deaccessioning, or something like it, was a constant feature of each of these engagements.

Most modern museums or museum-like organizations began in a small way, with energetic volunteers coalescing around some conjunction of perceived public good and personal interest. Exceptions, which usually differ only in degree, involve mainly private collections, which tend to combine public service with the founder's desire to negotiate the terms of mortality, governmental enterprises, and museums within educational institutions.

Especially where history is concerned, an important impulse seems to be to preserve something being lost or perceived as being in danger: a way of life, an ethnic drama made murky by current developments, an institution changed beyond recall, human epics eroded by time. The thought of oblivion is terrifying to most people and museums are among the antidotes to that hobgoblin. It is not accidental that the first museum-like assemblages were so often connected with religious establishments, where memory, cultural survival, social linkage among believers, relations with controlling deities, and the perpetuation of one's identity after death were paramount concerns.

Widespread support for professional museum practices and public accountability have over the past couple of generations seeped into the consciousness of even embryonic museums. The staff members or volunteers of almost every community historical society or historic house museum know nowadays that climate control for collections is important, even if not regularly achieved, and know that good collection documentation is highly desirable, even when that goal remains elusive. They know these things about collections and often come closer to realizing them than, for example, knowing about or accomplishing good disaster planning. The pattern in museum development is that as professional practices gain adherence and standards improve, many of the old "sins" of early development are allowed to remain without much, or adequate, change, and are merely laid over, like a stratigraphic bed, by newer and better methods. Down at the bottom the "Burgess Shale" of museum origins retains the numerous traces of uncertain and jelly-like practices, while at higher levels more rigid and recognizable structures proliferate.

In addition, and this is an essential thing, museums normally become more knowledgeable and more focused in collecting as they evolve. They may at one point collect almost everything that pertains to their ostensible mission, regardless of condition, rarity, display or research potential, or other qualities. Long-term resource support may not be a significant concern at first because initial needs are imagined to be modest, and because establishing a recognized and durable institutional presence is more essential than learning and practicing the arcana of collection management. If museums survive, however, they mature. Purposes and possibilities come into better focus, as does a more capable and realistic sense of the costs required to achieve more developed and ambitious goals. Museums as institutions recapitulate some of the stages that dedicated private collectors also frequently reach, where collections are regularly pruned and upgraded, with the old and discarded acquisitions sold or traded to finance the new, with a growing premium on acquiring rarities in excellent condition. This presumably was the kind of model in the minds of the (mainly art) museum directors who first considered the rules of good museum practice and determined that deaccessions were only to be permitted if proceeds realized from them went to acquire other works for the "permanent" collection.

Museum collections differ from private collections in many ways. One is the sheer bulk of the respective holdings. The collector has hundreds, or perhaps thousands, of items, while the mature museum might have tens or hundreds of thousands, even millions. Museum collections are now almost universally recognized to require thorough documentation, public educational or interpretive programs, conservation, purpose-built or purpose-adapted facilities, and transparent governance through plans, policies, boards, professional staff, etc., all of which are optional or even burdensome to the private collector. Compared with a private collection, the modern public museum bears a noble load that, like icebergs or armies, requires a vast, largely unseen support system to keep the thin wedge of visible enterprise in respectable operational condition.

Of primary value is the public mission of a museum. To have such a mission is a chief difference from the personal collection built for solitary or familial pleasure or for gaining status among friends, rivals, or subordinates. Ambitious private collectors not infrequently seek to transform their private hobby into a public good, especially in later life, in one of the often late-developing traits that suggest age does sometimes bring understanding and a kind of wisdom. To maintain a public museum mission is an expensive proposition, involving as it does staff, technology, visitor or research services, marketing, facilities, and supplies. Moreover, that educational mission is often dependent on collections, used for hands-on learning, exhibits, publications, study, visualizations of various kinds, audience presentations, and a host of related programs.

It might not be easy to credit, but some Catonians, antiquarians of the spirit, still question whether education should necessarily be among a museum's primary goals. While in the midst of a major controversy over the potential sale of a key museum object, summarized below, more than one critic of the sale, which was intended to create endowments for collections management and education, cited the owning organization's nineteenth-century founding charter as a reason to oppose the proposal. That document, written when public museum "education" was not yet recognized as an actual category of museum activity, of course made no mention of what would be considered educational programming. That omission, apart from any perceived violation of professional ethics, was in some quarters considered sufficient to dismiss any actions that used support for education as a justification.

A similar kind of need has engaged numerous public libraries, some of which have long recognized the value of expanding programming, beyond just lending books and videos and providing access to research resources. Most libraries today seek to offer robust educational and other public activities. Good public libraries are now expected to offer a host of public engagements, with the delightful result that they have in some measure been turned into bustling social centers and makers' marts ringing with the voices of children and their families. In Rhode Island, the Providence Athenaeum, an old-style semiprivate subscription library moving increasingly into a public role, was in 2003–5 obliged to expensively defend in court its right to sell a valuable original set of James Audubon's *The Birds of America* in order to create a permanent endowment for the institution. In the interest of bringing its activities closer to what contemporary audiences required, to better serve its own community, and to help maintain an antique building with severe structural repair needs, an institution founded in 1836 sold a famous but widely disseminated and reproduced set of antique books and so was helped to both survive and sustain its relevance. The endowment thus created was not brought into existence wantonly and was to be carefully managed and its funds husbanded with diligence; in fact the sale spurred an examination and tightening of the library's rules governing the use of endowment funds. The sale became a source of creation, not loss. Few miss the largely unused Audubons—another original example of the set was in fact, at another library only a few blocks away—but many now enjoy what they support. The expectations and outcome of that episode constitute an important story of an amply justifiable deaccession.

This touches on the essential point of the deaccession matter: to what extent can a deaccession enhance the public good in some ongoing way, beyond providing temporary financial assistance to the institution involved? The present public benefit is the paramount thing, and to give the enterprise some real value, a distinct degree of sustainability should be involved as well. Certainly assembling a collection is a serious enterprise with weighty responsibilities and should not be treated lightly, but the public good underlies the whole affair, and surely is the highest value. Most of the time collections serve the public in a light and somewhat passive way, waiting in a kind of institutional "green room" to be called upon occasionally for exhibition or active examination, but mainly just waiting, enjoying the benefit of gentle conditions intended to enhance the preservation of the items involved, with the help of trained specialists on call like nurses in a healthcare facility. Nowadays digitization has made the public less aware of the strictly preservation-related need to maintain and organize collections because images of and information about objects are more and more frequently available electronically, supposedly reducing the need to seek out the originals and enhancing preservation outcomes through reduced handling and exposure. It is becoming more and more possible to imagine museums as preponderantly institutions of digital access, with reduced emphases on permanent and temporary exhibits and vast collections of authentic items preserved at considerable expense in accordance with ever-rising standards, but rarely visited.

Thus, it becomes even more obvious that the only justification for maintaining a motionless menagerie of art objects and artifacts is the ultimate public good intended to result, and it is not at all clear that this good is met in its most ethical form by removing some objects forever through approved deaccession only to be obliged to replace them with others that inevitably reflect the particular tastes, politics, resources, or opportunities of the moment. The public good is the institution itself, the guardian of these works, as long as it can meet or decently strive to meet the generally accepted but always evolving standards of collection care and educational use. It was not promulgated on Mount Sinai that deaccessions should be ethically permissible only if they result from a limited set of largely material conditions and are followed by strict replacement with other acquisitions. To embrace that directive has been a voluntary professional choice that arguably helped buttress museum professionalism at a certain stage in its development, but that should be examined and debated in the light of modern conditions and needs, and potentially altered in the face of achieving greater public benefit.

Deaccessioning is a constant, ongoing factor in all museum work, and in archaeology too: does it really make sense to permanently warehouse hundreds of thousands of excavated potsherds or tons of lithic debris that will almost never be looked at again? In most cases, reburial should be among the acceptable options. But the most trying encounter with deaccessioning occurred when the author became director of a historical museum that had for years had been courting financial trouble and that had compounded that weakness through misdirected strategic directions.

This institution had already consumed half of its endowment, once $9 million, to cover ongoing deficits. At the time of the author's appearance it had a budget in the $2 million range, but its expected annual deficit had grown to about $600,000. Its board, newly constituted for the most part, was struggling with this recent revelation. Internal imbalances and miscalculations had been many, including the creation of a satellite museum that had been presented to the board of the moment as a money-making proposition but that in fact had actually burdened the organization with another $100,000 to add to the annual deficit. The most damaging decision, however, had been to embed the museum's future within the creation of a museum consortium project attempting to unify in one massive building and programmatic enterprise, more than fifteen separate museum-type organizations of vastly different sizes and capacities. The consortium project already represented years of planning and fundraising, and its building turned out to be a poisoned chalice, requiring renovation sums far beyond the project's budgetary assumptions or potential to raise funds. No business plan realistically met the challenges posed by the large operating costs the facility would have required once built, or how the programmatic visions of such a flock of diverse institutional participants would be accommodated or supervised within a single operational establishment.

A previous director of the organization had conceived and initiated the consortium project, and eventually left the museum to direct it. Under a successor the organization continued to be the project's leading and largest participant, and had for years incubated the effort and continued to support it with substantial staff time and money, to its own strategic detriment and institutional exhaustion. It had been largely unable to initiate necessary improvements in collections management and communications, while allowing its staff to shrink, its public functions to dwindle, and its facilities to deteriorate.

The author's initial years at the organization were largely occupied with a dramatic and difficult program of institutional restructuring, shrinking, and reorganizing the staff, reorienting priorities, and following a comprehensive new strategic plan. After unsuccessfully urging the consortium project to do the same, the museum withdrew from it: the consortium project, undermined by its weak finances and unresolved operational contradictions, ended its existence some years later. With solid and nearly unanimous resolve, the museum's new board faced and authorized these daunting new directions. The museum righted itself and balanced its budget, but only at a cost of reducing its operations by more than a quarter. It had achieved solvency and some stability, but had lost too much in the previous years to be able to undertake the vast work of reconstruction it now recognized it needed. A careful analysis determined that, to properly upgrade its collections management, hire essential staff, establish solid public programming, and repair its facilities, it would require an endowment of some $20 million, almost five times what then remained. The organization was in the condition of a crippled vessel that had with difficulty survived a severe storm but was too depleted to restore itself further.

It was in those circumstances that the possibility of selling, at public auction, its most valuable collection object occurred. The author/director's idea was to use the proceeds to create a permanent endowment to support collections management and public education, and not at all to employ any of the principal for operational expenses. The possibility of such a sale had been briefly considered before his arrival, under an interim director, but was rejected as a dangerous distraction when the museum was in such a state of flux and uncertainty, with a new board hardly in place and a new director on the way. But perhaps inevitably the size of the needed rehabilitation, now well understood and quantified, brought the consideration to the surface again.

The object in question was considered the finest of its type in the world, and had been donated to the museum some sixty years before. Based on the sale of a similar but slightly less elaborate piece owned by another institution a generation before, it was expected to realize enough to bring the museum's endowment to the figure identified. The earlier sale of the similar item had been undertaken to finance the rescue and complete restoration of one of our country's great historic buildings. That structure, though owned by a nonmuseum private entity, is frequently accessible to the public and in its restored state is one of the glories of its city. In that case, as with others, an object of interest mainly to specialists, and that would never have appeared in a "greatest objects" compendium, served what is arguably a higher public purpose.

The museum spent an additional year to carefully consider the true need and possible outcomes of this potential sale. The new strategic plan included a process to determine what possibilities existed for raising substantial funds through a capital and endowment campaign, which was carefully explored. One generous and far-sighted local foundation made a significant gift, the first of several over subsequent years, to advance the restoration of the museum's most endangered building. But in spite of these efforts, no combination could produce more than a fraction of what the sale of the object would deliver. After considerable discussion and debate the museum board voted, by an overwhelming majority, to sell the object, in order to raise a permanent endowment. The museum agreed that it would announce the proposed sale in advance, in order to inform the public and allow for the remote possibility that the publicity would bring forth new opportunities that could change the equation.

The four board members who did not vote to sell the object all resigned, and two of these engaged in something like a campaign to raise public opposition against the sale. Antagonism as well as support was expressed in the press, and fifty regional museum professionals signed a petition against the sale. Most of the comments that reached me were positive, but very significant opposition was expressed by a number of important figures in the cultural life of the area, as well as by some descendants of those involved in the original gift of the object to the museum. Conspicuously lacking in the criticism was any real examination or recognition of the dimension of the museum's need or assessment of the cumulative value of the museum's public work over many generations. Many recognized that the museum was seeking a way of restoring and sustaining professional competence and a high level of public service, but others felt that such an action could not justify this breach of accepted professional principles.

The author had to cultivate a dollop of stamina to endure the slights that came with supporting the proposed sale and board vote: it is a matter of public record that the director of the Providence Athenaeum resigned when the pressure from the proposed sale of the Audubon volumes grew too great. He was also saddened to recognize that to many the future of a valuable and venerable institution seemed to matter less than the disposition of a single celebrity object. That only a few really cared about the object itself was demonstrated when the museum put it on special display for those wanting to see it before it might leave the state; we even arranged for a special security presence to protect it from any threats or disruptions. Over several days only about two hundred people came to see it, and we were soon able to dispense with the guard. The opposition seemed more concerned with presenting an admirable display of high-minded group solidarity than of directly mourning the departing object or exploring the real difficulties the museum was trying to address, let alone questioning how the museum had managed to wedge itself into such a tight and unforgiving spot. Not a single critic offered any actual or tangible support for the society should the object *not* be sold. The nearest to such an act of generosity was the comment "I'll lend you my Rolodex" from one of the community's more admirable cultural leaders.

It seemed immediately obvious that the institution was more important than a single possession, a belief that helped sustain my involvement and resolve. Recognizing, as I have expressed above, that no human product can last forever and that beneficial work for the living public is the most important value any of us can reasonably aspire to, I thought selling the object to achieve a greater good was a cause worth defending. I anticipated with both dread and resolve the coming day, approaching fast, when we would sign an agreement with an auction house and the sale process would move inexorably forward.

Then something like a real miracle happened, the greatest in my career. A nonlocal philanthropic enterprise, not previously connected with the museum, revealed itself and, over a number of cautiously negotiated episodes, offered the museum significant help in support of a carefully calibrated reconstruction plan. This plan would require the museum, over a sustained period of time, to strengthen its professional standards, elevate its public presence, and greatly add to its public financial support. To gain further levels of assistance the museum would need to meet progressively and quantifiably more demanding goals of accomplishment.

Ultimately, the hope was that the museum would in time meet the goals and build an endowment not far short of what selling the object would have produced, in the process making the organization stronger in many ways, and not only financially. And this, dear reader, we achieved. Over the next six years much of my work, with the help of a couple of dedicated board members, was directed toward reaching those goals and building a new institution, one better equipped to serve and better able to survive. The way was not smooth or straight, but winding, and much changed over its course, but at the end of my time as director the museum's endowment, in cash and pending bequests, very nearly matched what the object would have added. What seemed almost impossible to achieve, as seen from the depths of the museum's worst crisis, came to pass.

In all that anxious time of rebuilding there was no actual requirement that the museum renounce selling the object. Of course the museum did not sell it, even though many people, for years afterward, assumed that we did, and would sometimes ask me how much we got for it. I was also occasionally asked how the museum consortium project was coming along, years after the museum had withdrawn from it and the project itself had expired: a reminder that people often pay less attention to things than some of us might wish, and that our bubbles may magnify things much more for us looking out than for those peering in. A good plan, a reliable and very generous primary partner, the further generosity of other supporters who came to believe in the truth of our reconstruction and the value of our ongoing mission, and of course sustained effort, not least by several key staff members, eventually ended the society's financial emergency. There was no longer any need for arguably desperate acts.

In time, we wrote into the museum's governing documents that the object could not be sold. It was our pledge of faith that never again would the museum face such a dilemma as had nearly wrecked it. But as they used to say, life is short and art long. The best defense against the need for such measures as deaccessioning and selling key museum objects is to have a healthy, well-run organization with clear plans and needs, and that will never have to consider such actions except in an untroubled atmosphere of calm deliberation. But very few organizations can achieve those high performance standards continuously for decades together, let alone generations or centuries, without accidents or even disasters. The museum's near-death experience will doubtless be a constant reminder of the dangers of fiscal riskiness and strategic drift, and can probably be counted on to reinforce exemplary management and performance for many years. If it were a stock, that museum would now be a very profitable, stable, and dependable investment. But victory is a wasting asset. Memories eventually fade or get turned into comforting and not deeply regarded myths; healthful restrictions become perceived as limiting and burdensome; directors tend to want bold newness and become less and less restrained by ancient cautions. There is some fundamental childishness in human nature that drives us to boredom when things go quietly well for too long. So it is always unwise to assume that one can coach the future for an extended time, let alone forever.

To my mind these are all arguments for allowing deaccessioning to become a more normal and less confining museum activity. Museums, like other institutions and like people themselves, grow and change and need flexibility in their development. Museums are hardly immune from financial difficulties: indeed it might be said that to be in charge of a museum, especially one not substantially supported by governmental or university resources, is like having an intimate relationship with fiscal uncertainty and financial repair that must become second nature and a source of endless attention. I believe that regulated deaccessioning and sale ought to be an ethically acceptable way for museums to build permanent endowments that support legitimate museum purposes, primarily the care of collections, though in my personal view not expenses that could be considered general operating support. With less grant money available than was the case thirty years ago, endless political attempts to restrict governmental aid to museums, and so many diverse and worthy projects to attract the attention of philanthropists, museums should make forceful and continuing efforts to build long-term endowments, to add stability in somewhat unstable times. Of course, deaccessioning for this purpose should be carefully approached and should require safeguards against irresponsibility or personal enrichment; of course endowments created this way should be thoughtfully structured to ensure that fund principal is protected and that income is used only for professionally defensible purposes. It would be out of place to discuss such protections in any detail here. My main point is to argue for acceptance and flexibility, and make a case for allowing museums to use this process judiciously to achieve the highest good of institutional stability, general public benefit, and ongoing public education.

I urge museum professionals to step away from the rigid limitations and professional ostracism that have in the past made deaccessioning, except to acquire new collection objects, a subject of almost sinful regard. I urge our profession, as the librettist writes in a different context, "to not punish evil too much" and indeed to transform a former "evil" into a source of assistance and support, albeit within limitations. For fifty years and more, museums have had to define themselves professionally and establish mutually recognized written standards for ethics, operations, and procedures. This has now been largely accomplished, thanks to the American Alliance of Museums, the American Association for State and Local History, and other professional associations. As a sodality of like-minded guardians of significant aesthetic, historical, and scientific legacies we should feel collectively confident to be able to examine some of the assumptions of the past with open minds, and make adjustments as might benefit the present and future. We should work to help ensure in this way that we have the variety of reasonably stable and useful museums that we all would wish to see perpetuated into a future perhaps more in need of the civilizing value of museums than ever.

2

Museums Can Change—Will They?

Michael O'Hare

> *Our great art institutions are cheating us of our artistic patrimony every day, and if they wanted to, they could stop.*

I tell my students, and only somewhat flippantly, that arts policy is the most important policy arena. Seriously? Well, most people think health policy is right up there—but why live longer if life isn't worth living? And if you don't think government has a lot to do with whether and how you can engage with art, you just don't understand the situation.

Think about a world in which our great paintings and sculpture are mostly on view instead of where they actually are, which is mostly locked up in the basements and warehouses of a handful of our largest museums. In which you didn't have to go to one of a half-dozen big cities to see them, and didn't rush through an enormous museum for a whole day because you paid so much to get in. In which you weren't constantly afraid that you aren't entitled to what you see, or competent to engage with it. That world is actually within reach, and the main reason we don't have it is that the people to whom we have entrusted our visual arts patrimony have nailed each other's feet to the floor so they can't move toward it, and done so with the tacit approval and even collaboration of government.

Big museums have long refused to recognize their unexhibited collections of duplicates and minor works as a financial resource. As a consequence, they are wasting value by keeping these works hidden. If they were redistributed to smaller institutions, and even to private collectors and businesses, they would fund an explosion of the value for which we have museums in the first place: people looking at art and getting more out of it when they do.

The story will wind its way through accounting rules, professional ethics, and tax policy, but we can start right in a museum. This is such a conventional ritual that it requires conscious effort to realize how many things about it could be different, and maybe should be. Let's do a field trip and look around!

A MUSEUM FIELD TRIP

We arrive during regular business hours or on a weekend, as the museum is open evenings only once a week. The building looks a lot like a temple, and is probably situated like one, in a park or up on a hill. We walk in past a wall of names that no one is looking at. Famous artists? No—donors. Every name on this wall records a financial transaction—but what exactly was sold in those deals? Strangely, though anywhere from a third to 90 percent of the millions of dollars acknowledged here is actually tax money, not private funds, the government and the taxpayers aren't listed.

Usually there's no less museum for anyone else if we go in, but this visit is going to cost some serious coin (though we didn't pay anything when we visited the National Gallery of Art in Washington). The posted tariff offers the same thing at different prices to different people, as well as quantity-discounted admission with a newsletter subscription. This is called a "membership," though it doesn't entitle us to vote on anything.

We take a floor plan and perhaps an audio guide, and plunge into a maze of galleries without windows or clocks, an environment as disorienting as a Las Vegas casino. Of course, the galleries are full of art. . . . Well, not actually full, as the paintings are spaced across the walls rather loosely. Through the rooms people (mostly women) come and go, talking occasionally in hushed tones of Michelangelo, and texting. Visitors look at each work for about six seconds, bobbing in and out to read tiny labels with an almost random selection of information. Some galleries have explanatory panels introducing the ensemble on view, with text that may be historical or biographical, may be in art-criticalese jargon or at the most elementary, introductory level, but always laudatory and enthusiastic about the work on view: everything here is absolutely superb.

The art is sorted by place, medium, and date of origin. At about 1900, we experience either relief or anxiety on realizing that decoding symbols (is St. Jerome the one with the lion, or the arrows?) is no longer useful, and we start to see things and images that don't seem to be about—or of—anything, and that we would never realize are art if they weren't in a museum. We might chat among ourselves about the art, but our engagement is quite one-way. At a concert we can at least applaud; at a restaurant we actually eat the food; at a gallery the art is for sale; and at the science museum we can touch and pick things up.

We've been on our feet for three hours now, though we did occasionally find a bench. Let's go sit down and have lunch! The restaurant menu radiates educated upper-middle class: We can get a latte, but not a hot dog. What's that—you're tired and maxed out? We could leave and come back tomorrow, but then we'd have to pay another admission charge. So we keep going and try to see it all.

On the way out is a store selling an immense variety of things, of which not one would qualify for display in the museum, though all have something to do with art. Lots of books, and lots of tchotchkes. Art supplies, with which we could make something ourselves, are always in the children's section.

Not everything of interest is obvious here, especially what we can't see. We didn't see art being made, or learn anything about how that happens. (What's *silverpoint*, again? *Giclée*?) We didn't see the wheels of the art world turning (dealers, auctions, collectors, artists, and critics); indeed, one would infer from a museum that what we are looking at has nothing to do with either the business of art or the process of making it. For every object on view, another twenty are in storage; almost none will ever be displayed. And, perhaps most important, we didn't see the 80 percent of the population who didn't go to an art museum at all in the last year.

WHAT ARE MUSEUMS FOR?

An art museum is a business, often a big one, but a special kind. In the United States, almost all of them are tax-exempt, educational nonprofits, with unique privileges given in return for certain kinds of social value; in other countries, they are typically government agencies, though this difference in legal form has minimal effect on their behavior. In both cases, they get to spend tax money. Either public money is appropriated directly or, in the American system, contributions to museums are tax-deductible, and each gift carries a public subsidy. Furthermore, museums are typically exempt from state and local taxes, even though they receive the usual services of the fire and police departments, sidewalks, and the like.

They are also charged to care for the physical art objects that embody civilization and culture. Of course, science, literature, political institutions, religions, and performing arts are cultural storehouses too, but the plastic arts are unique in being at risk of loss by physical destruction. Losing the autograph score of Bach's Mass in B minor would be a pity, but there are lots of copies adequate to perform it from; the loss of the *Athena Parthenos* was forever.

To think about how art museums could do their job better, we need a better idea of what that job is beyond just "owning art and showing some of it." In his 1979 book, *The Art Museum: Power, Money, Ethics*, journalist Karl Meyer could write, "Since the turn of the century, museum professionals themselves have been trying to define the nature of the art museum," and things have not been much clarified since. Museum mission statements are all over the map. The most common words (after *art*) in a 2011 survey of mission statements were *collect, museum, program, exhibit, cultural, educate, public, artist*, and (oddly) *words*. The verbs here are behaviors of the museum, not the visitors (*educate/exhibit*, but not *learn/see*). With very few interesting exceptions—of which my favorite is the Detroit Institute of Arts' deliciously terse "Creating experiences that help each visitor find personal meaning in art"—these statements describe what museums undertake to do, but say almost nothing about what they expect to accomplish for their audiences. There is a lot of attention to making art accessible but little about art actually being accessed, or what happens to visitors who seize those opportunities.

What about *visual* cues? Well, reviewing the home and "about" pages of major American museums, I found only three showing anything other than art from the collection or the building from the outside. Detroit's "about" illustration is distinctive and notable: it has young people looking at one of the Rivera murals (which we see only in a sidelong, partial view), guided by a docent who is not just talking but using her whole body. It is a picture of engagement with art, not just having art. In contrast are the Met's aerial view of people milling about in an enormous lobby that could have been taken in Grand Central Station, and Chicago's picture of staff and the back of a large canvas.

I think the extremely abstract and passive presence of the museum's public in these statements is an important and symptomatic failing, and I propose a different assignment: the purpose of an art museum is *more, better engagement with art*. Anything a museum does that can't be connected back to this goal is peripheral and incidental.

Of course, this short version hides multiple dimensions of performance. "More" can entail more people looking at the art, looking at it for longer times, and looking at more, as well as more kinds of, art. Recently, museums have realized that "more" should also mean more kinds of people, especially across ethnic and social class categories. Half of people with graduate degrees went to art museums last year, but only 10 percent of high school graduates; 24 percent of whites went, but only 12 percent of blacks. And museums properly think about people in a very long future, most not yet born, and almost neurotically protect their collections for those future viewers from fire, flood, umbrellas, humidity changes, and finger oil.

"Better" is the more interesting part of my recipe. Perception, science has shown, is an active process. The only art engagement that matters is created inside the head of a viewer who combines a visual (in this case) stimulus from an artist's work with a whole library of prior experiences and knowledge, ideas (not always art ideas) that "come to mind" (not always the conscious mind) when she confronts something presented as art. Better engagement results from presentation and installation, including mundane matters like lighting, air conditioning, and whether you can actually get to the work through a crowd. It also results from managing the library of experience that you open up and "see" the work with, including how today's engagement with a painting (and its explanatory label, and its neighbors on the wall) enriches your engagement with an upcoming lifetime of art experiences.

Better engagement is what justifies the research function as well. People have a different experience of a work when they know who made it, whom he or she studied with, who commissioned and owned it, and how an engraving gets on paper. Better engagement puts the museum in the business of making a more competent and more demanding arts public. Because this process is lifelong, it can't merely be delegated to the schools, though the current savaging of arts education in K-12 schools is a tragedy, and a blunder, that we have to leave for another discussion.

My simple goal statement already entails a variety of ways to make a better museum, and forces attention to ruthless trade-offs. For example, it may be easier to get a lot of people to come to the museum to see work that professional judgment thinks ephemeral or even schlocky, or for a bunch of wrong reasons (pornographic edginess, or high auction prices), but they can't have a better experience if they don't come at all. Works on paper have a finite lifetime of exposure to light, so every minute they are displayed is a minute they are denied to future generations. No simple formula can be confidently applied to optimize a museum's discharge of its responsibilities, but steering by the "more, better engagement" star is useful.

Museums may have economic development benefits, attracting Richard Florida's "creative class," and they have served economic elites as indicators of status and distinction for generations. They are certainly good for curators' children's orthodontia, and a museum retrospective directs a Niagara of money into the pockets of an artist and her dealer. But all these are incidental and, as we will see, sometimes at odds with the point of a museum. The ball to keep our eye on, again, is arts engagement.

WHAT SHOULD WE WANT MORE OF?

How could museums do more and better? Well, for "more," they could show more of the art they have. Any top-rank museum exhibits no more than a twentieth of its collection, often much less. There is some rotation in and out of storage but, as a rule of thumb, consider the least distinguished object in a gallery, and you can be sure that there are one or two just a teeny bit inferior, and a dozen nearly as good, in a warehouse or the basement. The Met, for example, shows twenty-seven of its forty-one Monets, but only three out of its thirteen Eugène Boudins. When it comes to engravings and drawings, the ratios fall dramatically: for example, none of the Met's 134 etchings, and only two of its twenty-three drawings, by Fragonard are on display. If it really damages the experience of a painting to see it any closer to its neighbor (recent museum practice has been to greatly increase the spacing between works, and never "sky" them one above the other), more art for the public would mean building more galleries and expanding museum buildings.

Second, for "better" engagement, museums could have educational programs that, as a nurse grad student of mine once said, "start where the patient is" and begin before the visitor leaves home. Enjoy history? Here's how this painting explains it, and why it happened when and where it did. Basement woodworker? Here's how they made the inlays in this chest. Religious? This painting is a theological tract, and here's how it works. Political lefty? Let me introduce you to George Grosz. Think you might want to own original art? Here's how to start.

Unfortunately, most museums are in very straitened financial circumstances, and all this costs a lot of money. The recession hit them hard, with charitable giving and government support cut way back and operating expenses hard to reduce. Ideas like these are pipe dreams, right?

Well, no. To understand why, we need to look at some museum financials, almost all of which are online as part of their annual reports. Take a look at the typical museum's balance sheet asset column. There's the building itself—worth millions, but it's pointless to talk about selling that. Furniture and equipment? Not much there, and we're using it. Endowment? Only a few dozen millions, and the whole point of an endowment is to grow it, earn some income, and hold it for safety, not to cash it in. Tractor to mow the lawn? Now we're scraping the bottom of the barrel.

But wait a minute. Where's the art? Incredibly, it's not there. No museum known to me recognizes its art collection on its balance sheet. When it buys a painting, there's an expense, and then it just disappears, as though they bought lunch for everyone and ate it. This might not matter if the amounts were small, but they are actually quite breathtaking. I have estimated the value of the collection of the Art Institute of Chicago (AIC) by triangulating in various ways from a couple of the rare cases in which museum collections were actually appraised (Detroit and the Berkeley Art Museum). The 280,000 objects in its collection turn out to be worth between $26 billion and $43 billion.

This finding has dilated the pupils of everyone I have ever shared it with. "*How much*??! Wow, what would the Met's number be? The Louvre's?" A common management assessment of a firm is "return on equity" (ROE). This is roughly the net value the firm creates each year, divided by the net assets it holds, comparable conceptually to the interest on a loan or the gain from an investment. We can make a coarse calculation of this kind for a museum by valuing the visitor hours and research it provides in a year (with caution; these cost-benefit-analysis valuation techniques are always approximations). In the case of the AIC, the ROE is less than 1 percent. As the AIC is a wonderful museum in many ways (go there!), this is in no way a worst or even a bad case—but no established private firm would be allowed to stay in business, or keep its management, if that's all it could earn with the resources investors (that's us, citizens) entrusted to it. Private firms, when they get up and running, have to promise ROE numbers in the 5 percent range to get people to give them control of resources, and a big museum is not a startup deliberately running a high burn rate to set up big profits in the future. Of course, this kind of talk feels like rough and untrained hands being laid on the precious beating heart of immortal and ineffable art, so let's leave it at this: *knowing the monetary value of a large museum's collection raises very salient questions about how that resource is actually being used, and whether that use is the best it can do.*

Accordingly, the most important policy reform museums need is for the Financial Accounting Standards Board (FASB), a private organization that establishes the rules accountants have to use, to require them to value their collections and report them as assets. And if the FASB doesn't do this (an attempt to do so a couple of decades ago failed), state attorneys general, who oversee nonprofits, should do it, not to mention museum trustees, who cannot responsibly oversee their institutions without this information. The excuses for this omission are that it would be a big bother to appraise a large collection, and as the museum never intends to use the art as a financial resource by selling any or borrowing against it, there's no point. But simply asserting that those 134 Fragonard etchings have no monetary value doesn't make it true: if you call a dog's front legs arms, it still has four legs, and the Detroit Institute of Arts' collection was absolutely on the table as a financial asset in the city's bankruptcy. What if the refusal to value collections were relaxed? How could placing a valuation on those enormous collections create more, better engagement with art?

Given that so little of it is ever exhibited or ever will be, maybe we could start at the bottom and sell some stuff out of storage that has no real prospect of being shown. What would that buy? Selling just 1 percent of the collection by value—much more than 1 percent by object count—would enable the

AIC to endow free admission *forever*. You read that right: free admission forever, on the sale of just 1 percent—with a nice *lagniappe* of reduced storage expenses, to boot. *Free* is the right price for a nonrival good (you're not displacing anyone else) like attending a museum that isn't congested, and makes it much easier for people to engage with art in a sane way, a couple of hours at a time (better engagement!). As it happens, the AIC triggered a big debate recently when it raised prices to pay for its new building (adult general admission is now $23). When the British national museums went to free admission in 2001, attendance more than doubled—more engagement!

How much should museums charge for admission? As I suggested, the main reason the price should usually be zero rests on the most fundamental normative principle of economics: everything should be sold at *marginal cost.* If a museum isn't congested, the marginal cost of one more visit is a little wear on the floor and a few cents' worth of air conditioning; unlike a seat in a concert hall, it doesn't deprive anyone else of his visit. Note that this principle is technical, and neither a moralistic assertion that art is priceless or besmirched by money, nor a political judgment: if you wake up a Chicago economist and a lefty progressive in the middle of the night, they both say "marginal cost pricing"!

Farebox revenue is hard to give up, but to make it easier for a low-income public to attend, some museums have adopted a "pay what you wish" approach (with very heavy-handed suggestions as to amount). Is it psychologically easier to attend if you're made to feel like a charity case? And why ask people to estimate the value of the experience before they have it? It would be relatively easy to do experiments to let visitors decide how much to pay as they leave and see what happens. I did that once, many years ago, for a special exhibition with an extra charge, and revenues were substantially higher than when visitors were charged going in.

If the museum is so crowded that your visit interferes with someone else's—and a few like MoMA, the Louvre, and the Uffizi are in that state— it's appropriate to charge admission that will ration access by price (and to subsidize attendance for those who can't afford the fee). But it would be much better to expand the museum! When a lot of families move to town, we don't start auctioning seats in class, we build more public schools. Going back to our AIC example, selling another percent of its collection would pay for 30 percent more exhibition space (either where it is now, or in a big satellite somewhere), to actually show us more art.

Let's go crazy and sell *another* percent—that would endow $17 million a year of operating budget, a fifth of the institute's current "instructional and academic" staff costs, which would enable it hire to something on the order of 200 more full-time researchers, educators, designers, and people studying the audience to understand what really goes on when people get up close to art. All this, and the AIC would still be sitting on 97 percent of the value of its current stockpile, but showing a third more of it, and better.

In business language, we could say that the AIC has drastically misallocated its capital resources between the assets of "building" and "art," and also misallocated resources between production (the staff) and capital. Idling capital is a waste, just like idling labor, and if done in secret as it is here, may even justify associated charges of fraud and abuse.

If you open this discussion with museum people, as I have done, you find out very quickly that you have walked into a hornet's nest called the "deaccessioning debate." Deaccessioning is fancy art language for selling, and the first thing the director you have provoked will tell you about is the museum directors' code of ethics, which forbids him to ever sell art except to buy more art. If he did, he could never lend anything to other museums or borrow any art from them. He probably couldn't have coffee with his pals at the next convention either: outer darkness, and how appropriate for unethical behavior.

Of course, this code was not brought down a mountain by Moses; the directors themselves made it up. A code of ethics is a good thing, but it isn't a law of God or nature. Once upon a time, the lawyers' code of ethics forbade them to advertise. Now it doesn't; the republic and the bar endure. The museum directors' code says "Gifts and bequests should be unrestricted whenever possible," in part because a donor's restrictions on how a work is shown, or whether future judgment finds it deserving of display at all, lets donors short-circuit professional expertise forever. But important museums like the Met and the Stanford University collection have violated this rule spectacularly and haven't been excommunicated, so maybe these ethical principles are not quite the moral absolutes they claim to be.

A piece-by-piece appraisal of a large collection is an enormous undertaking (though it was somehow accomplished fairly quickly for the Detroit museum), and the cost of such an exercise might justify omitting it from financial reporting. But it isn't necessary to do this to get a useful estimate of the total value, say plus-or-minus 10 percent. Things like art values have an exponential distribution, with a large percentage of the value in relatively few items. Museums know what their masterpieces are, and these few thousand items would have to be appraised individually. But the rest can be sampled by drawing randomly from accession numbers (every object has one) and actually appraising as little as 5 percent of the other work. This process is never perfect, but completely doable: museums appraise individual objects when they insure them for loan exhibitions and (obviously) when they are offered art for purchase. Large companies value unique assets with thin markets, like buildings and patents, well enough to inform regulators and managers.

What the no-sale provision is good for is to protect the big old museums, which have collections far larger than they can ever show, from even thinking about having to share, or about operational changes like the ones described above. It's about managerial comfort and institutional prestige, and has nothing to do with the public interest.

My colleague Eugene Smolensky asked rhetorically on reading an early draft of this essay, "If we could reallocate all the art across museums optimally, how much of it would wind up where it is now?" Museums like those in San Francisco, which were late to start seriously collecting while those in Eastern cities already had a half-century head start, can never catch up under current rules, while lots of art that smaller markets would kill for is locked up in the vaults of the Met and the AIC and their ilk. The existing allocation is interesting; here, for example, is the distribution of some Monet paintings in US museums:

Distribution of paintings by Monet in the United States

Metropolitan statistical area	Number of Monet paintings (not displayed)	Population (in millions)	Persons per Monet
Washington, DC	27 (10)	5.6	207,000
Chicago	33 (6)	9.5	288,000
New York	49 (13)	19.6	400,000
San Francisco	4 (1)	4.3	1,075,000
Los Angeles	11	12.8	1,170,000
Florida (state)	2	18.8	9,400,000

Is this patrimony distributed so as to create the most art engagement value possible? Is it fair? The small Harn Museum of Art in the college town of Gainesville, Florida, is so proud of its single Monet that it issued a reassuring press release when it was lent for four months to a temporary exhibition across the state in Naples; the AIC, on the other hand, sees fit to keep almost a fifth of its Monets in storage.

DEACCESSIONING AND ITS DISCONTENTS

The debate about selling from collections has been characterized by an unusual combination of naïveté, careless and tendentious language, and posturing. Without rehashing it all, let us note here, first, that works sold from the unexhibited collection of a museum are not "lost," especially if they are sold to another museum. Indeed, even if they go to a collector's private home, they will be seen by more people than when they were in the vaults; the same is true if they are bought by businesses for their offices—and these sales could reserve a right to borrow the works back now and then. (People don't buy original art and lose or mistreat it or hide it—they almost always show it and care for it.) But garage sales by our overstocked, big-city major museums would mainly put important art on the walls (not in the basements) of museums in places where art is scarce. The reason I'm so interested in simply changing the accounting rules, so we can see these assets as we see the endowment, is that I expect sunshine to provoke a conversation in which simply asserting selling to be evil will have less force, and options like the ones I floated above will be in play.

If we establish that sold art doesn't leave the planet or go into a landfill, defenders of the dog-in-the-manger approach will claim, "These paintings were given to us with the understanding that we would never sell them! And if we sell even unrestricted items, no one would ever give us anything again!" To which we may ask, "What will they do with it instead?" (And "How much *more* art that you have no space to show do you really want?") Art usually goes to museums when collectors' heirs don't want it. Here is where the tax code becomes important, along with the sociology of the big-time art world. A lot of paintings in museums were received as tax-deductible gifts, and the donor's deduction is based on the full market value of the painting, even though no tax was paid on its appreciation in his hands. So giving a painting bought for $10,000 that could now be sold for $110,000, minus the $28,000 capital gains tax a wealthy donor would pay, costs the donor $82,000 (and thank you, certainly)—but earns him back a tax break of 39.6 percent (his marginal tax rate) of $110,000, or $43,560. The gift actually only costs him $38,440; taxpayers pony up the rest. (Calculations for bequests under the estate tax are different; in general, that tax subsidy now only benefits the wealthiest collectors with multimillion-dollar estates.)

This whole arrangement may or may not be good public policy; in my book written with Alan L. Feld and J. Mark Schuster, *Patrons Despite Themselves*, we examine this question extensively and of course conclude, "It's complicated!" But the charitable-contribution deduction is certainly not necessary to have museums, as it was nonexistent or *de minimis* when the great US museums were being established and unimportant outside the United States, where there are lots of nice museums full of art. The part of the scheme that's important here is that the donor gets the same deduction regardless of whether the work is given with a restriction on sale. This makes no economic or moral sense: a painting the museum is stuck with storing and protecting forever is simply worth less than a painting that may be sold, just as unrestricted money gifts are more valuable than gifts with strings attached. A nice amendment to the tax code would require the IRS to reduce the appraised value of donated art to reflect any restrictions, including restrictions on sale. This would at least make collectors think twice about demanding them.

It would not control winks and nods, however: a collector might well shop his painting around to find a museum willing to make an unofficial agreement. We have to think about the sociological context of this deal-making, not just explicit rules, because donors gain social status by being able to say that they collected work fine enough to be accepted into "the collection of" the most prestigious museum that will take it. If museums established an ethical obligation to never assure retention, and made it clear that while gifts are welcome, restrictions really are against the rules, collectors would find it harder to play them against each other this way.

A bigger question is, why do large museums that can only show a fraction of what they already have (or even of the really good stuff), and that are increasingly besieged by visitors whose numbers in the space available seriously damage the art-engagement experience, continue to fight for acquisitions that would create much more value if dispersed to smaller "markets"? Why don't they more effectively steer donors to give money for programs that put more people, more effectively, in front of more art? Eli and Edythe Broad, the 800-pound gorillas of the Los Angeles art scene, have a refreshingly different take here, explaining to the *Los Angeles Times* in 2008 why they gave the Los Angeles County Museum of Art dibs on borrowing (and ponied up for an enormous building expansion) but would not donate works:

> our job is to have our collection be seen by the broadest possible public. And with all due respect to the museums, they will only lend to their peers. LACMA will lend to the Met. They will lend to the Modern, to the Louvre, to the National Gallery. But they will not particularly make a point of lending to Knoxville, Portland, where they can't get anything in return.
>
> So we thought a lot about this and we said we're gonna make this a public collection, and we're going to favor LACMA. Whatever LACMA wants to have on their walls they can have on their walls for as long as they want to have it on their walls. But if they want to put it in the basement, we want to be able to have it shown elsewhere.

GOVERNANCE AND POLICY

A century ago, art museums changed society's relationship to art by spearheading the transition from private collecting by and for the rich and powerful into the modern public museum. Today, they can change that relationship again. The symphony and the opera don't have the resources for such an enterprise, but museums do; what sort of innovations should we be demanding?

The most important opportunity is the explosive availability of art as very high-quality digital content, the revolution that has upended the worlds of music, drama, and text. Of course, original artworks will always trade in a separate market from reproductions, and seeing the "real thing" close-up is not the same as having a perfect image projected on your retina from a screen. But the second is not inferior to the first, just different and complementary, especially when it's available on demand from a "custom-made" museum you can organize for yourself with a few clicks, out of works thousands of miles apart. The Google Cultural Institute serves up virtual walking tours of almost five hundred museums around the world, with thousands of works available in very high resolution, actually higher than you can usually get standing in front of the real painting.

What hasn't happened, but is under way, is the release of painting, print, and drawing collections from their storage vaults into the digitized cloud (sculpture is a different story). When it happens, it will be less of a problem that big museums show so little of their collections "live," and the opportunities for creative and enriched modes of engagement will have expanded enormously. But crucially, it will be less important for a museum to actually possess (for possible research study) works it doesn't show.

Merely invoking technology or shoveling out more information can easily miss the mark; success is also a matter of attitude and empathy. When I worked in a museum, I had some troubling epiphanies, like the time the curator of a quarter-mile of decorative arts galleries, full of chairs with ropes across them *and nowhere for a visitor to sit*, interrupted my staff meeting presentation about seating to say, "Mike, I don't know why we're spending time on this; if I want to sit down, I can go to my office. I don't need chairs in the galleries!"

I still remember being infuriated by the label on a pair of metal devices in a vitrine, etched in my memory as "Pair of objects for striking fire, with three lines of Qu'ranic script. They are beautifully made and invite our touch." OK, I'm an engineer and a shade-tree mechanic. You have my interest: *How* do you strike fire with them—hit them together? Rub? Did they hold flints? Do you use them together, or one at a time? What is "Qu'ranic script"—a calligraphic style, like Kufic? Is it a pedantic way to write what *hoi polloi* call "lines from the Koran"? And I understand why they're under glass, but why, Mr. Curator, are you rubbing it in that you can touch them and I can't? "Education" like this may be well-meaning, but it is inept.

I also had some eye-opening times, such as when a curator would walk me through his galleries and just talk to me about the art. It's really breathtaking how interesting these folks can make their stuff, and no, you don't get it by reading their published work, or from the labels they write, or the audio guide; it only happens when they aren't looking over their shoulders at their peers and showing off how erudite they are. Everyone can't have that kind of personal engagement, of course, but could we give every visitor something like it? I don't want someone talking in my ear when I'm watching a play or listening to a string quartet, but this can happen right in front of a painting; what an opportunity!

As a visitor, I keep encountering missed opportunities and misfires, usually resulting from an insouciant unconcern for what would really enrich the experience for a typical visitor—that is, a visitor a museum should want to make repeated visits. The de Young's big David Hockney exhibition in 2013 was full of the artist's experiments with synchronized videos, iPad drawing, and the like, mostly well-documented and explained. But it also included Hockney's thirty riffs on Lorrain's *Sermon on the Mount*, with no image of the Lorrain anywhere to be seen. Not educated enough to bring it up in memory, I had to find it on the web on my phone. No, the original of 1656 is not copyrighted. The unspoken message here is, if you don't have the Lorrain original in your head, you're not really qualified to be here.

A few months later I ran into the original at the Frick, where it would have benefited greatly from association with a couple of Hockney's covers (as reduced-size reproductions, of course). Of course, while Hockney hasn't slowed down for a minute at seventy-six, the Frick has long been frozen in aspic. Here's a wasted opportunity to put an important work into a context of artistic borrowing and exchange, and make a four-century-old painting speak to a modern art lover.

Audio guides and smartphone apps, more and more common, are the beginning of an exciting new way to engage with art. "Beginning," because there's plenty of headroom for improvement. A stellar Kandinsky exhibition at the Neue Galerie had an audio guide, but I had to start up Spotify on my phone with earphones to associate his theater set designs for a *Pictures at an Exhibition* ballet with the respective parts of the music, which could perfectly well have been available on a headset on the wall next to each piece, or on the audio tour device. I know the music pretty well, but not well enough to be sure I wasn't remembering "The Great Gate of Kiev" when I was looking at the old castle set. Much too often, the audio commentary itself is delivered in an off-putting academic style with a stuffy accent, a lecture from someone who would rather be somewhere else. Why can't it be conversational and share real enthusiasm and curiosity?

Getting with the tech revolution is not the only opportunity museums could seize by starting to use their enormous idle wealth responsibly. Real research about the visitor experience, which flowered briefly (mostly in science museums) between the 1930s and '80s and then withered, could inform presentation so it actually works better, instead of just looking good to other curators and designers. At present, museums know very little about their audience and even less about the people who don't attend. (Where, for example, did we get the bizarre idea that six seconds is the right amount of time to spend with a painting worth looking at—and isn't it the responsibility of art museums to fix that?)

Building more space (and endowing its maintenance and operation) is an obvious path toward "more engagement," at least for the people who attend now. What about those who don't? Again, we need more research, but many of my students at a big public university simply don't feel entitled, by background or competence, to art in a museum. When I take them on a field trip, I can sense a strong defensive and insecure reaction: "If I don't see what's so great about this, I must be not good enough for it." Art-historical expertise and connoisseurship are not chopped liver. But they are not everything, not even everything about art. How is it that one can go in and out of every great museum and have no idea that there is a large body of research in cognitive psychology and the brain science of perception that (as the eminent art historian E. H. Gombrich was not too blinkered to see) makes art more important, more interesting, and more relevant? Ms. Curator, you may be way up there in the art world pecking order, but you are no Gombrich: learn from him! There is simply no reason a visitor to the de Young Museum in San Francisco should need his kids to take him across town to the Exploratorium to learn about this.

Would it hurt society's relationship to art if the institutions that display it had a less religious and awestruck affective orientation to the work? A less one-dimensional scale of value—that doesn't sort objects out on a "masterpiece" index and induce visitors to scoot past wonders in search of the most famous few pieces—would help. Indeed, why don't museums show us some fashionable bad art and explain why it is such, and authorize us to believe that if we think this or that piece is silly or a con, we might be right? Certified excellence isn't the only way to be interesting and considerable. Why aren't they more willing to entertain the idea that a lot of stuff selling for big money is faddish, schlocky, or silly (but may still be interesting), rather than torturing themselves into making excuses for an embalmed shark or one more metal balloon animal? *Why can't we see the experts disagree and argue with each other?*

Management failures usually start with governance failures, and museum boards are way too heavy on wealthy collectors and too light on psychologists, artists, educators, and science-museum curators. Board selection is a hermetic, self-replicating process focused on wealth and social status to the exclusion of expertise, judgment, and wisdom; Met director Thomas Hoving memorably captured this willful blindness with his immortal, "Any trustee should be able to write a check for at least $3 million and not even feel it." Why don't members elect a trustee or two to provide real guidance? Even members of a bowling league, not to mention citizens of a state, have governing responsibility and authority.

The director of a top-rank museum like the Met or Chicago—certainly two or three of them together—could put paid to the code-of-ethics deaccessioning roadblock as quickly as Saudi Arabia could dismantle OPEC. However, real progress in more effective and creative use of collections will most likely begin with minor or specialized museums and those constrained by smaller collections, like the San Francisco Museum of Modern Art. Unfortunately, the prestige pecking order of museums, to the extent that we assess them by size and fame of collections, makes it extremely difficult for the dinosaurs to learn from these improvisational, adaptive little creatures, and they need help from larger institutions.

One of these, of course, is government, including (in the United States) grant-giving and subsidizing agencies like the National Endowments for the Arts and Humanities and the National Science Foundation's social science programs, and overseers like state attorneys general. Museums that have not estimated their collection value and reported it should not be eligible for NEA grants. The distinctive US system delegates government-like powers to tax-exempt nonprofits, including museums and the FASB, so discussion of "arts policy" has to attend also to the governance and practices of the institutions themselves. The first task for all these parties should be accountability, both financial (valuing their collections, at the least) and operational. The second should be pressure to use museums' enormous latent wealth to create, well, *more, better engagement with art* in all the dimensions of the phrase.

Museum culture is deep and ingrained. Realizing the latent value in our patrimony will, finally, require a public that asks our institutions, graciously but insistently, whether they are using the priceless resources they have been given to serve the public interest as well as possible.

II

THE MECHANICS OF DISPOSAL

3

Keeping Deaccessioned Objects
in the Public Domain

Legal and Practical Issues

Stefanie S. Jandl and Mark S. Gold

INTRODUCTION

When the hammer fell on Lot #363 of the Sotheby's auction in New York City on January 29, 1995, the last of 863 objects from the collection of the New-York Historical Society had been offered for sale over a three-day period. Unlike other auctions at Sotheby's, however, these sales were not final. For a period of forty-five days museums, libraries, and archives chartered in the state of New York were given a rare opportunity: they had the right to preempt any sale and, in some cases, at a price less than the hammer price.

New York City was the site of another unique disposition of art objects in 2009 when the Brooklyn Museum's legendary costume collection was moved across the East River to the Metropolitan Museum of Art. The collection-sharing agreement between the two museums provided for the transfer from one museum to another—a gift, not a purchase—of the best objects from the Brooklyn costume collection and the sale by public auction of the remaining objects.

These two cases were in part shaped by an ongoing, and perhaps increasing, public and professional discourse around keeping deaccessioned art objects in the public domain. These cases undoubtedly contributed to the conversation. For their efforts, the disposing museums in each instance received less in proceeds than the objects would have realized from a customary commercial sale. In each situation, the goal was to keep as many deaccessioned objects as possible in the public domain—an ideal shared by many museum professionals and museum audiences. In some cases, it is a goal embraced by the museum itself. In other cases, it may be a goal imposed upon the museum by others.

In all circumstances, though, the goal would seem to be contrary to the obligation of museum boards of trustees to realize the highest possible sale price for the benefit of their institution. What are the implications of the tension between the desire to keep deaccessioned objects in the public domain and the fiduciary—and perhaps legal—duty to ignore that desire and achieve the best result for the selling museum? How have museums resolved that tension? What are the legal and practical considerations, and costs, for disposal in the public domain?

ETHICAL ENVIRONMENT

While the law informs museums about what they can and cannot do, ethical standards (established by the profession) guide museums as to what they should and should not do. Standards of conduct for the art museum community in the United States are articulated by two professional organizations, the American Alliance of Museums (AAM) and the Association of Art Museum Directors (AAMD).

Within its Code of Ethics for Museums, AAM states that a member museum will ensure that "acquisition, disposal, and loan activities conform to its mission and public trust responsibilities"[1]—hardly a roadmap of ethical conduct, but a succinct reference to its legal responsibilities. In a 2008 position paper on cutbacks and retrenchment, AAM advises that if a museum determines it is unable to appropriately care for some objects in its collections it should "carefully consider whether it is appropriate for the material to remain in the public domain at another nonprofit institution."[2] AAM, therefore, offers no truly helpful ethical guidance on the disposal of objects removed from a museum collection.

AAM launched a Collections Exchange Center in 2003 to facilitate the purchase, sale, or transfer of deaccessioned objects between member institutions, but the program never received great usage and was terminated. At present the American art museum community has no practical support from national professional organizations for the retention of deaccessioned art objects in the public domain.

AAMD includes "sale or transfer to, or exchange with another public institution" among the preferred methods of disposal, but does not seem to endorse the concept enthusiastically, noting that "While it is understood that museums must fulfill their fiduciary responsibilities and act in the museum's best interests, museums may give consideration to keeping a deaccessioned work in the public domain."[3] One could infer that while AAMD intended to make it ethical to keep objects in the public domain (presumably at some cost to the transferor museum), it was also ethical not to. And they expressed no preference.

As professional codes of conduct neither the AAM nor the AAMD positions are legally binding. They barely articulate what is undoubtedly a universal wish that objects remain in the public domain, but have little, if any, impact on the discourse.

LEGAL ISSUES

The legal environment in which museums operate in the United States is a product of state law and enforced at the state level. (The exception being restrictions imposed by virtue of federal tax-exempt status, which are not relevant here.) While the statutes and judicial decisions may vary somewhat from state to state, there are some generally accepted principles that relate to the disposition of deaccessioned objects by museums.

Any decision to dispose of objects in a manner that results in the museum realizing less than full market value will be made by the board of trustees (sometimes designated as the board of directors) of the museum. The board is bound by law to adhere to fiduciary duties and obligations to the institution, and particularly the duty of due care and loyalty. Almost every articulation of that duty shares common language requiring a trustee/director to perform his or her duties in good faith, in a manner he or she reasonably believes to be in the best interests of the institution, and with such care as an ordinarily prudent person in a like position would use under similar circumstances.[4]

The issue is immediately raised, therefore, as to how the board of any museum might determine that the disposition of objects for no payment or at a price less than could have been received in an arm's length transaction would be in the best interest of the museum.

Indeed, many states have statutory or case law that prohibits public charities such as museums from disposing of any assets for less than fair market. Often the judiciary makes that determination, with consideration given to the charitable purpose of the transferor and transferee.[5]

In the United States, the office of the Attorney General of each state is responsible for oversight of public charities within the state. With very limited exceptions (such as the disposition of certain restricted assets), only the Attorney General can challenge museums on their disposition decisions, and his or her review is limited to ensuring that the governing body has complied with its legal and fiduciary duties to the institution. The Attorney General will usually not substitute his or her judgment for that of the board in the good faith exercise of its decision-making power.

The Attorney General can take a more proactive stance if the survival of a nonprofit entity is at stake (and thereby the preservation of its assets), as it did with the New-York Historical Society to be discussed below.

The laws applicable to museums require that the board make decisions based upon the best interest of the museum. The board's obligation to do so would seemingly preclude the museum giving away, or selling for less than fair market value, objects that could be monetized for the benefit of the museum. This should be so regardless of whether the board feels a desire or an obligation to take a broader view and look at the benefit to be derived by the public at large rather than just their own institution. Indeed, it would seemingly be the duty of the Attorney General to insist that only the disposal of assets at fair market value would be in the best interest of the museum for which they are responsible.

With rare exception, museums do just that. They sell their deaccessioned objects for the highest price possible, either through public auction or private sale. And yet there are still instances of museums opting instead—or being forced to opt instead—to realize less in proceeds in order to keep the objects in the public domain. How are the principles of law described above applied to permit or accomplish that outcome?

The answer to that question lies in the concept and definition of mission, coupled with the fact that the perspective and interest of an Attorney General are very much limited to the state he or she serves.

Every museum has a mission—its charitable purpose. The mission is normally set forth in its organizational documents and can evolve, and even change materially, over time. Both AAM and AAMD require member museums to have a clearly articulated mission statement. A museum's mission is generally included in documents filed with the state or maintained internally, and it can be inferred from the organization's conduct.

The significance of mission is that it can be used to justify expanding the boundaries of "best interest of the institution" to encompass decisions and acts that are seemingly not. The expansion is most often of a geographic nature that would define the museum's constituency beyond those people who pass through its doors, take advantage of its collections and services, or live in the same community.

For example, if a museum's mission were articulated to be the education of the people of a rural county in Massachusetts by exposing them to objects from other cultures, its board could argue successfully that they have adhered to their mission by giving an object to another museum in the same county. If, however, the object was to be given for no consideration or at a discounted price to a museum in Bentonville, Arkansas, it could be anticipated that the Massachusetts Attorney General would intercede to prevent the transaction as a breach of the board's duty to its institution and its mission.

Indeed, there seems to be a willingness—perhaps a propensity—on the part of Attorneys General to be guided by geography. In the case of the New-York Historical Society, geography trumped the financial need of the institution. In the case of the Brooklyn Museum, also discussed below, a sense of geography apparently kept the Attorney General from any concern about the transfer of a large collection of objects for no consideration—essentially for free.

It would not be unexpected that the way in which an Attorney General would interpret the mission of a particular museum could be informed in part by the outcome desired by an Attorney General—either for philosophical or political reasons.

One need only explore the pages of auction house catalogues to appreciate the paucity of efforts being made by museums to keep objects in the public domain by offering other museums a discount on pricing or other beneficial terms. Anecdotally, there are few cases in which museums turn over their objects to other museums for no payment unless the transfer is in the context of the closing of a museum without creditors seeking repayment.

In fact, the boards of most museums consider their museum and its viability to be their mission and the focus of their responsibility. This is a position supported by law. It is intriguing, then, to look at cases in which museums have taken steps—developed by them or imposed upon them, but always at a financial cost to themselves—to keep objects in the public domain.

NEW-YORK HISTORICAL SOCIETY

A low-water mark in the 200-year troubled history of the New-York Historical Society was realized in early 1995, when it deaccessioned 863 objects and sold them at auction through Sotheby's.[6] The deaccessioning and sale were part of a multifaceted plan to stabilize the museum for the future. It was crafted with the office of the Attorney General for the State of New York and encompassed governance issues as well. The high-profile auction represented the first time that an effort was made to give an advantage to institutions willing to keep the objects in the public domain.

The rules of the auction were the direct result of the involvement of the Attorney General's office, acting pursuant to its power of oversight of charitable institutions in the state. Those rules provided that "Qualifying Institutions" would have the right to make a preemptive bid following the auction and purchase the object at a discount from the highest bid. The amount of the discount was 10 percent if the successful bid was $25,000 or less, 5 percent if the successful bid was more than $25,000, but less than or equal to $100,000, and 3 percent if the successful bid was greater than $100,000 and more than the high presale estimate by Sotheby's, exclusive of the buyer's premium that had to be paid on the successful bid without discount.

"Qualifying Institutions" were defined as nonprofit museums, libraries, and archives formed or chartered pursuant to New York law that exhibited their collections or otherwise made them available to the public on a consistent basis. Each Qualifying Institution was required to agree to retain the purchased object in its collection for at least ten years. As an additional incentive, financing was made available by the museum to Qualifying Institutions.[7]

The intention implicit in this plan was to give Qualifying Institutions a financial advantage to acquire these objects and keep them in the public domain. The auction represents the singular model of this magnitude to make that effort. There is no doubt that it was imposed upon the museum by the Attorney General and was not born of a desire on the part of the board to keep these objects in the public domain. The board was most assuredly focused on the survival of the museum, but dependent on the approbation of the Attorney General to a long-term survival plan.

At auction, more than $12.2 million was realized from the sale of 183 old master paintings on January 12, 1995; $1.5 million was realized from the sale of paperweights on January 18, 1995; and $3.9 million was realized from the sale of Americana and decorative arts on January 29, 1995. Those numbers included the buyer's premium, with a net to the New-York Historical Society of $16 million.[8]

On January 19, 1995, the Metropolitan Museum of Art announced that it had exercised its option to purchase Lo Scheggia's *Triumph of Fame*, a 1449 birth plate of Lorenzo de' Medici, which had been on view at the museum on a long-term loan from the New-York Historical Society, for $2.2 million. Because the highest bid was below the high estimate given by Sotheby's, the museum received no discount on its purchase, nor did it take advantage of the financing offered to Qualifying Institutions, so the New-York Historical Society lost no money on that preemption.[9]

The Loeb Art Center at Vassar College exercised its preemption rights to purchase a fifteenth-century painting from the Brussels school for $179,000, and the Brooklyn Museum, after the auction, purchased a fourteenth-century Florentine altarpiece by Nardo di Cione for $354,000.[10] Of the 863 lots in the auction, forty-three (less than 5 percent) of them were purchased by thirteen Qualifying Institutions.[11]

Beverly Schreiber Jacoby, cochair of the Community Advisory Board of the New-York Historical Society, offered a thoughtful analysis of the process shortly thereafter. Based on the number of objects preempted by Qualifying Institutions, she concludes that the preemption model did not achieve the desired result of keeping as much of the collection as possible in the public domain.[12] Although the loss to the New-York Historical Society by virtue of the preemption discount was minimal, it is notable that the institutions that took advantage of the discount were in a much more stable financial condition than the New-York Historical Society, resulting in the troubled museum essentially underwriting the purchase of its objects by more well-off institutions.

In addition, Jacoby concludes that the availability of preemption actually discouraged potential bidders from bidding on the more expensive pieces. There was no incentive for the Qualifying Institutions that may have engaged in the bidding to do so since they could purchase the object afterward; consequently, their absence depressed the final price and the money ultimately realized by the New-York Historical Society. Jacoby speculates that loss to be in the range of $1,500,000 to $2,650,000.[13]

The preemption model, which has not been replicated on this scale, appeared to seek a balance between the competing goals of maximizing the monies realized by a museum in distress with the possibility of its disposed assets to remain in the public domain. Its effectiveness at achieving those goals is not widely accepted. The preemption plan is also notable for its geographic bias. This plan was not about keeping objects in the public domain. It was about keeping objects in the public domain in New York.

BROOKLYN MUSEUM

New York City, the fashion capital of the United States, was the site of the largest, and probably the most ambitious, collection transfer between museums in recent American history. In January 2009 the Brooklyn Museum transferred ownership of its renowned collection of American and European costumes, comprised of 23,500 objects, to the Costume Institute at the Metropolitan Museum of Art.[14] The most important objects were accessioned into the holdings of the Metropolitan Museum, where the collection retains its own identity as the Brooklyn Museum Costume Collection at The Metropolitan Museum of Art, while other objects have been sold at auction over a several-year period with proceeds benefiting the Brooklyn Museum. The combined holdings of the two museums have formed the preeminent collection of costumes in the world and are an unsurpassed resource for scholars, designers, and the public. The *New Yorker* magazine referred to this landmark collection transfer as "an unusually collegial open adoption."[15]

The Brooklyn Museum's costume collection was established in the first years of the twentieth century to serve the emerging American design community.[16] It features a depth of holdings from legendary American and European fashion designers, which together offer the most comprehensive narrative of any collection of fashion history from the late nineteenth century to the mid-twentieth century. Despite this wealth of holdings the Brooklyn Museum began questioning its ability to appropriately steward the collection in the early 1990s. Costume collections pose particular challenges with the fragility of the objects and the expense, staffing, and space needed to properly maintain them. The financially strained Brooklyn Museum had been criticized for neglecting and failing to exhibit the collection, which no longer had its own curator since a 1990 budget crisis.[17] As best-practice standards evolved, the Brooklyn Museum realized that it was increasingly unable to care for the deteriorating collection.

By 2004, the board of the Brooklyn Museum was actively considering its options, which included transferring the costume collection to another museum within New York City. A core issue, however, was the fact that the collection was not fully inventoried and catalogued—a prerequisite for deaccessioning in compliance of AAM guidelines—and the museum had no resources to undertake such a project. When the Program Officer for Museums and Conservation at the Andrew W. Mellon Foundation learned of the Brooklyn Museum's predicament she invited the museum to apply for a grant to catalogue the collection. After several months of work in which the Mellon Foundation helped shape the final proposal, the Brooklyn Museum was awarded $3,925,000 to inventory, catalogue, digitally photograph, and assess the Western costume collection.[18] The grant included making high-resolution images of the top 4,000 objects available to an international audience via the nonprofit digital image library, ArtStor.

Implementation of the Mellon grant commenced in 2005 and took a team of twelve to fifteen people over three years to complete.[19] At the end of the project the collection was fully inventoried and catalogued, and its condition and storage needs were assessed. This collection review enabled the Brooklyn Museum to affirm that it was not in a financial position to be an effective steward of the collection, supporting a decision to deaccession.

In looking at its options, the board believed it had what its chairman characterized as an "enormous responsibility" to keep the core of the collection intact and in New York City.[20] The museum then invited acquisition proposals from two city institutions and selected the Metropolitan Museum of Art as the collection partner because it presented the strongest proposal and because its mission was most closely in alignment with that of the Brooklyn Museum.[21] Although the board recognized the sale of the collection as an alternative, at no time was it considered seriously.[22]

In January of 2009, the Brooklyn collection was deaccessioned and physically moved to the Metropolitan Museum. In accordance with its agreement, the Metropolitan accessioned the best four thousand objects, made arrangements to auction off a group of mutually agreed upon non-museum-quality objects, and work is ongoing in the process of examining the remainder of the collection to make determinations for accession or auction based on quality and overlap with the Metropolitan's collection.[23] (Both museums must agree on each object selected for auction.) The Brooklyn Museum continues to have access to the collection for its own exhibitions.[24]

In accordance with their extensive acquisition proposal, the Metropolitan Museum organized an exhibition[25] of the Brooklyn collection that complemented a simultaneous exhibition held at the Brooklyn Museum.[26] A catalogue of the Brooklyn collection was published,[27] a two-day symposium was held that explored details and issues of the collection cataloguing and transfer,[28] and the Brooklyn collection was the focus of the Metropolitan Museum's 2010 Costume Institute Gala Benefit. Finally, the museum dedicated a curator and a fellowship to the Brooklyn collection for five years.[29]

A number of factors gave shape to this historic collection transfer and enabled the collection to remain in the public domain. The Brooklyn Museum, albeit challenged, was not in dire financial condition, but the costs of storing and conserving the collection were considerable. The Metropolitan Museum was in stable financial condition and able to assume the costs associated with the transfer and with the stewardship of the core of the collection. The proximity of the two museums meant that the collection would be located just across the river from its original home. The geography of this deal met the needs and desires of all stakeholders—including the Attorney General of the State of New York, who seemingly had no interest in questioning or disrupting the transaction.

The costume collection transfer, which the two museums refer to as a "partnership,"[30] offered an innovative and expanded notion of what ownership means, one that was consistent with the Brooklyn Museum's mission statement—to "act as a bridge"[31] between the visitor and the collections.[32] Because the costume collection was rarely exhibited at Brooklyn, placing it at the Metropolitan Museum meant that the works could be properly cared for and exhibited, thus giving the public increased access to the collection. With two costume exhibitions and the publication of the collection catalogue, the Metropolitan immediately increased the visibility of the Brooklyn collection, which was elegantly consistent with the mission of the Brooklyn Museum.

Financial and practical considerations were also involved in the success of this collection transfer. The project could not have gone forward without the extensive financial commitment from two well-funded organizations, the Mellon Foundation and the Metropolitan Museum. At nearly $4 million, the Mellon Foundation grant offered a rare opportunity to address a collections need on a scale difficult for most museums to secure. As the receiving institution, the Metropolitan Museum of Art had an unparalleled ability to allocate staffing, expertise, and funding (which included securing corporate sponsorships) to receive, care for, and exhibit the collection.

As exemplary as this collection transfer was, it also demonstrates the inestimable value—and infrequent confluence—of third-party financial resources (Mellon), a willing and financially stable partner, the lack of financial urgency on the part of the transferor museum, and a broad view of mission on the part of its board to make a result like this possible. As with the New-York Historical Society, this plan was also not so much about keeping objects in the public domain. It was about keeping objects in the public domain in New York City.

OTHER EXAMPLES

In April of 2005 the New York Public Library announced that Sotheby's, as its agent, was accepting sealed bids for the purchase of Asher B. Durand's *Kindred Spirits*. A prominent work of the Hudson River School that had been donated to the library one hundred years earlier, the painting depicts the artist Thomas Cole and the poet William Cullen Bryant standing on an overlook in the Catskill Mountains of New York. The terms of the sale included a provision for a one-year deferral of payment for any New York institution. The Metropolitan Museum of Art was seen as a likely purchaser.[33]

The high bidder, however, turned out to be Alice L. Walton, for Crystal Bridges Museum of American Art, a museum then being built by her family's foundation in Bentonville, Arkansas. Purchased for a sum reportedly in excess of $35 million, the bid eclipsed the joint bid submitted by the Metropolitan Museum of Art and the National Gallery of Art.[34]

The departure of the painting from the state of New York was met with public criticism. However, since the library was not in fiscal or administrative crisis and the transaction was arm's length and for fair market value, there was no role for the New York Attorney General. The president of the library did acknowledge his delight (and undoubtedly some relief) that the work was remaining in the public domain—and in the United States, if not New York.[35] Criticism would no doubt have been much more vocal and sustained had the work vanished into a private collection.

On November 11, 2006, the Board of Trustees of the Thomas Jefferson University in Philadelphia, Pennsylvania, announced the planned sale to the National Gallery of Art and the Crystal Bridges Museum of American Art (an interesting partnership in light of the results of the sale of *Kindred Spirits*) of Thomas Eakins's *The Gross Clinic* for $68 million in a private sale arranged by Christie's.[36] The artist, the painting, and the subject matter—a legendary medical school teacher performing surgery—were deeply connected to the city of Philadelphia, and the prospect of the painting's departure provoked local outrage.[37]

Since the sale presumably was an arm's length transaction for fair market value, there was no role to be played by the Attorney General for the Commonwealth of Pennsylvania. Nevertheless, and reportedly having learned from the criticism leveled at the New York Public Library for the sale of *Kindred Spirits*, the university included in the terms of sale a provision that local art museums and governmental institutions had an opportunity to match the offer with a preemptive bid. With loans and the support of hundreds of donors anxious to keep this iconic work in Philadelphia, the painting was ultimately purchased jointly by the Philadelphia Museum of Art and the Pennsylvania Academy of the Fine Arts.[38]

The university lost no money by virtue of the preemption, but the sale does reflect a heightened sensitivity to the geographic affinity of some objects and the desire to avoid controversy. As seen before, this was not about keeping an object in the public domain. It was about keeping an object in Philadelphia.

The 2013 transfer of the core collection of arms and armor from the Higgins Armory Museum in Worcester, Massachusetts, to its neighbor, the Worcester Art Museum, although not technically a deaccessioning, presents an elegantly designed model of efforts to keep objects in the public domain—in this case, in the context of a museum destined for closure. A case study of this transaction appears elsewhere in this volume, but there are several aspects of the transaction that help inform our discussion here.

The Higgins Museum had assets (a physical facility, the collection, and investments) that far exceeded its liabilities. It also had a governing body that appreciated that the condition of the physical facilities and the cost to repair or replace them, in the context of museum visitation and revenue, rendered the museum not sustainable for the long term. Higgins had the benefit of assets, engaged and thoughtful trustees, and time.

After years of considering all strategies for keeping the museum open, the trustees focused on trying to establish a strategic alliance that would perpetuate the mission of the museum. In pursuing alternatives, the trustees established the following four priorities:

(a) ensuring the Higgins core collection continues to exist intact as the highest priority;
(b) preserving the collection in the City of Worcester if reasonably possible;
(c) seeking a transfer of assets and Higgins institutional culture, including the spirit of its very successful programs and educational activities; and
(d) seeking an economically sustainable and transformative combination with the receiving institution.[39]

In articulating these priorities, the trustees highlighted principles similar to those that drive the efforts to keep deaccessioned objects in the public domain.

Strategic alliances were explored with several other institutions, including museums in Philadelphia, New York City, and Boston. Though just forty miles away and within the Commonwealth of Massachusetts, Boston was seen as an even farther distance in terms of demographics, access by public transportation, and in the context of the great pride and affection that the people of Worcester had in the Higgins Museum.[40]

Ultimately, a comprehensive document titled "Covenants for the Transfer of Assets" was crafted with, and executed by, the Worcester Art Museum that preserved the core Higgins collection, kept it within the city of Worcester, and outlined the structure to preserve the collection and continue and enhance already robust programming. It also allowed for the deaccessioning and sale of objects outside of the core collection to support those activities in the collection's new home.[41]

It is reasonable to speculate that the Attorney General of Massachusetts would not have happily embraced a transfer of the core collection to Pennsylvania or New York. But the confluence of geography, financial sustainability, and loyalty to mission made it easy for her to consent to the transfer. Court approval (required because the transfer was for less than fair market value) followed quickly.[42]

On March 28, 2014, just three months after the closing of the Higgins Armory Museum, the Worcester Art Museum opened *Knights!*, a critically acclaimed exhibition and the first step toward the meaningful integration of the two collections. Arms and armor from the Higgins collection were exhibited alongside Worcester artworks—including classical sculpture and renaissance paintings—to illuminate the historical context in which the armor was made and used. Enhancing the exhibition's reach was ambitious programming that engaged numerous schoolchildren, families, and community members in the exhibition and its ideas. Though situated in a new home, the Higgins collection, its core intact, is still cared for, exhibited, interpreted, and enlivened by the same mission-driven values as before, and it is still very much at the heart of the Worcester community.

In the summer of 2017, the Berkshire Museum in Pittsfield, Massachusetts, with a statutory purpose and mission of promoting for the people of Berkshire County and the general public the study of art, history and science, announced a plan to deaccession and sell at auction forty works from its collection. The goal was to raise $40 million to establish an endowment to address the average structural deficit over the past decade (approximately $1.15 million) with another $20 million to support its "New Vision," a New Vision to allow it to address community needs, which were identified after a two-year engagement with the community.[43]

Among the forty works, and accounting for more than half the total estimated value, was Norman Rockwell's *Shuffleton's Barbershop*, donated by
the artist to the museum and considered one of his artistic masterpieces.[44]

The reaction among some quarters of the local (and national) arts community, as well as the national museum associations, was negative and strident.
The conflict was played out in the courts and in the press. The Attorney
General launched a review that lasted for several months. Of particular focus
was *Shuffleton's Barbershop*, as to which some felt that there was an implied
restriction of it remaining in Berkshire County, although there was no direct
evidence, relying upon the close relationship between the artist and the museum and its executive director to establish a restriction.

Despite the museum and the Office of the Attorney General disagreeing on
the existence of restrictions, a settlement was made, resulting in the filing of
a Petition in the Supreme Judicial Court seeking permission, with the support
of the Attorney General,[45] to the following:

- The private sale of *Shuffleton's Barbershop* to a nonprofit museum in the
  United States, subject to its loan to the Normal Rockwell Museum (also
  in Berkshire County) for eighteen to twenty-four months; and
- The sale of as much of the remaining thirty-nine works as necessary for
  the museum to realize an aggregate of $55 million from the sales.

Berkshire Museum essentially received the permission it needed from the
Attorney General to achieve the New Vision and its financial sustainability.
But it came at a cost of receiving less revenue from the sale of *Shuffleton's
Barbershop* than it could have presumably received at a public auction without restriction, and having to sell more objects than it otherwise would have
sold to reach its goal. But the desire to have this important and painting remain in the public domain was at the core of the settlement.

CONCLUSION

One goal of this essay was to explore how museums resolve the tension between the desire to keep deaccessioned objects in the public domain and the
desire (and perhaps duty) to achieve the best financial result for the disposing
museum. The reality is that any tension is almost always resolved by selling
deaccessioned objects in a manner designed to maximize the proceeds to the
selling museum without regard to whether or not the objects remain in the
public domain as a result.

The New-York Historical Society and the Brooklyn Museum represent
deviations from that normal practice of such magnitude as to make them

watershed moments. Even as deviations, however, they provide lessons of greater applicability. This is so even though the effort to keep objects in the public domain was imposed upon the New-York Historical Society by the Attorney General of the State of New York and its own board drove the effort by the Brooklyn Museum.

One of the lessons learned is that geography matters. It mattered to the New York Attorney General that the collections of the New-York Historical Society remain in the state of New York. It mattered to the board of the Brooklyn Museum that the costume collection remain in the city of New York. Even the modest incentives offered by Thomas Jefferson University and the New York Public Library demonstrated at least sensitivity to local concern and the potential for local criticism. And, clearly, the experience of the Higgins Armory Museum demonstrates the high priority given to—and facility of transaction provided by—geography.

In thinking about geography, it is probably more accurate to refer to political boundaries, rather than proximity. In four of the five instances cited, the neighboring state of New Jersey was equally convenient for public access, but likely a world away in terms of an acceptable outcome.

The outlier in these examples is the Berkshire Museum. When the terms of the settlement agreed to by the Massachusetts Attorney General are played out over geography, it would seem like that office has a less parochial view of public domain. *Shuffleton's Barbershop*, after a short local loan, will be leaving the state. Since the museum will presumably receive less money for it than it would have received in a public auction without restriction, it will need to sell *more* works (but less "important" works) that are unlikely to remain in the state after the sale, but appear to be a sacrifice worth making to keep *Shuffleton's Barbershop* in the public domain.

Additionally, the Attorney General agreed that it would be consistent with the fiduciary duty of the Board of Trustees to sell other works for lesser sums to keep them in the public domain, without limiting it to remaining in the state. What remains to be seen is whether the expansive view of fiduciary duty, combined with an abandonment of the parochial perspective of similar officers across the country in emphasizing in-state public domain priorities, will serve as a model to other Attorneys General as they look at similar situations. In doing so, and if its statements are applied to other museums, the Massachusetts Attorney General has given more latitude to the boards of museums to take a broader view of the mission of their museums and, at the same time, open the market of potential buyers beyond state borders to keep works in the public domain.

The position taken by the Massachusetts Attorney General is in contrast to the near contemporaneous position taken by the New York Attorney General in the case of the James Prendergast Library in Jamestown, New York, which planned to sell nearly its entire art collection, which some considered of great significance to the town, to support the library's financial sustainability. Two individuals offered to purchase forty works for $1.2 million with the intent of having them remain in the city. The New York Attorney General objected to the sale without knowing whether they might bring in more in a private auction.[46]

Mission is important as well. A board's sense of its mission informs its willingness to sacrifice proceeds for public access. There was clear and strong consensus on the part of the board of the Brooklyn Museum that its costume collection was of such significance—and so integral to—the city of New York as a capital of fashion that it was unthinkable that the highest quality and most important objects from the collection would be dissipated among smaller museums and private collections.

Similarly, the fact that the Higgins collection had its genesis in the obsessive collection of a local steel manufacturer whose business included the production of "doughboy helmets" during World War I, embedded the museum and its collection in the history of the city. To have it moved even down the Turnpike to Boston would have been a blow to the city that had been its home since it opened to the public in 1931.

Likewise, protecting the core of the collection was perceived to be at the heart of the museum's mission for both the Brooklyn Museum and the Higgins Armory—of higher priority than the incremental monetary benefit of selling it to the highest bidder.

Mission is also what informs an Attorney General of his or her role in the transaction. It can be used to justify support for or opposition to a particular plan, even if the position taken is based on political or other considerations.

One would be hard-pressed to find support in the museum community or within the general public that deaccessioned objects depart the public domain and end up in private collections. Yet the legal and ethical duties of board members, in almost all instances, require them to subordinate their personal preferences in that regard to the best interest of their museum. In fact, it is near imperative that they do so in an institution under financial siege unless museum closure is certain.

In other instances, however, the financial sacrifice can be ethically and legally made, but only when the board concludes that the public domain alternative is clearly within the mission of the museum and the Attorney General agrees. It is a rare museum that is blessed with the confluence of sufficient finances, a broad enough mission, and the agreement of both the board and the Attorney General that the gift or incentive crafted to keep the object in the public domain is in the best interest of the museum and serves its mission.

The original version of this essay first appeared in *Museums and the Disposals Debate*, edited by Peter Davies (MuseumsEtc., 2011): www.MuseumsEtc.com.

4

When Out of the Book Won't Do

Next Steps in Resolving Deaccession Conundrums

Darlene A. Bialowski

Museum professionals and the museums they serve are bound by ethics, standards, and best practices whether those guidelines are imposed by a professional affinity organization a museum belongs to or whether they are adhered to as a matter of best practice. When situations arise that reach beyond established guidelines, or a standard is too general to cover the situation, where can museums find help? When is it appropriate to think outside the box to seek resolution?

Rather than examine the history, the ethics, or the repercussions of deaccessioning, this essay will help identify conundrums that fall beyond the usual handling of a deaccession, and provide guidance on how to expand procedural options when challenged with the question "now what?" An understanding of the definition of "deaccession" is paramount before attempting any related procedure. This understanding will also inform whether or not an object can be deaccessioned in the given situation.

It is easy enough for any American Alliance of Museums (AAM), Association of Art Museum Directors (AAMD), or American Association for State and Local History (AASLH) member to research the respective definition of the term "deaccession" set forth by these organizations. However, individuals outside these associations may not be as familiar. Simply, the term deaccession is defined as the legal/procedural removal of an *accessioned* object from a collection. If the object has never been accessioned (i.e., formally registered into the collection through institutional protocol), it cannot be removed by *deaccessioning*. Furthermore, an accessioned object cannot be deaccessioned if the institution does not hold title to the object.

THE BEGINNING OF THE DEACCESSIONING PROCESS

Typically the process begins at the board or museum committee level. An institution's collections management policy (CMP) should regulate which governing body is responsible for collections decisions, and the final decision should be confirmed by vote. Once the decision has been made to remove the object from the collection, an explanation should be provided to members of the board/committee so that they can make an informed decision. If an institution does not already have a CMP in place in which procedures and best practices are outlined, creating one is an important next step in the spirit of best practices.

There are a variety of reasons for removing an object from a collection: the object no longer fits the museum's mission; it is a duplicate of another in the collection (object in better condition would typically be kept); no information about the object exists; the object requires significant conservation not currently in the budget and resources are inadequate for its care; the object has been determined a fake or forgery or its authenticity questioned; the object has been identified as stolen or looted.

One of the first steps is to locate all available information on the object. This could include anything from a basic description (in decades prior, inadequate descriptions were typical) to a fully described object with a complete database record; a file; an accession sheet (often listing all pertinent information along with a thumbnail-size image); a Deed of Gift or Transfer; and hopefully, acknowledgment of any restrictions. If one is fortunate, copies of invoices, ownership documentation, and conservation reports might be included in the cache. More often it is basic information, an image of sorts, and paperwork supporting the object's registration.

EXAMINATION OF THE RECORDS

The entire body of information related to a particular object should be examined before the object is considered for deaccession. This is where due diligence at the point the object was accepted would be helpful. However, there are lots of reasons why these steps are not fully performed: lack of time, lack of staff, misidentification of the object, scant documentation, etc. The professionalization of collections management is still relatively new, so most museums have a backlog of poorly documented objects. Whatever the case may be, research is the essential next step to determining rightful ownership.

It may be helpful to develop a checklist of missing information and conduct research accordingly. This documentation will prove to be useful to future staff. In caring for an object for the future, you are also caring for the object's records. Common first steps include:

1. Review the file, catalogue information, and database.

   - Does the description in the record match the actual object?
   - Is the description complete enough to identify the object if no image(s) are available? What if there were multiples?
   - Has the medium/material been correctly identified? This might require outside expertise.
   - Has the Getty Object ID checklist been consulted to capture or verify information?

2. Measure the objects.

   Measure the object from as many angles as appropriate, taking care to correctly measure its form.

   - For paintings: note if the measurement is the front of the framed work (including the part of the work visible within the inside border of the frame) or the stretcher on the back. Note if the measurements are as to the framed work or just the image or paper/canvas.
   - For sculpture: note if the measurement includes the base or any accoutrements not part of the sculpture. Note the points on the object from which dimensions are captured, including a sketch if possible.
   - For all objects: identify the orientation being measured; don't assume that the orientation is a given. Typically the sequence is height by width by depth. Include measurement of the depth of a frame, the diameter of a bowl, etc.

3. Examine the object's condition thoroughly.

   - Identify and note any condition issues, as well as the location of the issue on the object.
   - When photographing the object, both overall and detailed images are important. Details should have a context, so an overall image of the entire object is especially important for condition issues.

4. Photograph the object.

   - Take photographs from as many angles as possible while the object is still in your possession.
   - The written description of the object should be as complete and accurate as possible in order to help identify the object if it is separated from its identifying tag/number and no photograph is available.
   - Misidentification of a stolen object might hinder the object's recovery if there's little information and only a poor description or image accompanies it.
   - In-house digital photography allows numerous images to be taken and edited later, with no associated cost.

5. Research provenance.

- Background research should be thorough, documenting steps taken as well as the information gathered.
- If the object warrants complicated provenance research, beyond the experience or capacity of the museum, hiring a contract provenance researcher or historian is advisable.
- If due diligence wasn't performed when the object was accessioned, that can be rectified during the deaccession process.

DISPOSAL AND RECORD KEEPING

Once the due diligence has been performed and the object has been prepared for its final removal from the premises and is ready to send off to the next destination (e.g., private sale, auction house, or to another institution for transfer), clear shipping records should be generated. This should include location of the transfer and manner of shipping, and it should be fully recorded in the museum's object files.

Once the object is considered deaccessioned, all records should note the new designation. Most contemporary databases make it easy to change an object's status. In addition the hard copy of each object file should be notated. There's no standard for file management for deaccessioned objects, so it's advisable to either keep the file with the permanent collection records but identify it as deaccessioned, or create a separate location for deaccessioned file storage. All records need to be updated accordingly, including card files, ledgers, and the database. If the object remains on the museum premises, be sure that it is isolated and its eventual shipment/movement is identified. Too often this is where many found-in-collections challenges are born.

Museums are starting to include information about deaccessioned objects on their website, disclosing the what, when, and why of objects in question, often with images. This effort should be applauded. The information is important for research and documentation and is an opportunity for the institution to highlight its responsibility to the public through transparency.

IDENTIFICATION MARKS

Understanding deaccessioning procedures and the rationale for them helps staff when it comes to implementing these procedures. Hopefully, all cultural institutions will someday be more transparent than they are currently. Until organizations such as AAM, AAMD, or AASLH require a higher level of transparency, institutions won't likely change their practices. So much of the responsibility falls on individual professionals, specifically those in collections management and registrational roles.

As previously mentioned, one area of practice that is not referenced in publications in the field is what to do with the institutional markings that identify the object (part of the accession process). The systematic removal or retention of identifiable marks on an object as it is prepared for deaccessioning seems to be up to the museum that holds the object. The former AAM website provided guidelines for deaccessioning and related procedures. Portions of the document have been integrated with the information provided in this essay.

For example, the information in the AAM Communications Plan included the following:

> "Identifiability," will the staff remove catalogue and identifying markings or not? If the object is to remain in the public domain, these markings are part of its provenance and removal of the markings can interfere with future scholarship. On the other hand, if the material enters the public domain, the museum may not want to be identified with it.

It is important to leave the object's physical provenance intact. But no matter if it remains in the public domain or is transferred into the private sector, it is the author's opinion that this information should *never* be removed from an object.

Protocol encourages that transparency markings from an institution should be left in place to indicate the object's former ownership. If there is no transparency, the chain of custody is essentially broken, reducing the available information for future scholarship.

When the sale of an object deaccessioned from a collection is publicized, many in the field consider that publicity to be taboo, and it's considered a "dirty little secret." But deaccessioning is accepted and widely practiced in museums for a variety of previously discussed reasons. So where the deaccessioned object is being auctioned, auction houses should recommend that the institution identify itself as the seller to encourage revelation of the object's past.

In talking about this issue over the years with colleagues, questions about the lack of transparency have elicited a range of responses, including:

- "I don't know."
- "I'm not in agreement with the decision, but [my boss], [the director], [the Board] gives no flexibility in their decision."
- "The Director doesn't want anyone to know we owned it."
- "It's not stated in our CMP, so we don't need to."
- "We never have so we probably never will."

- "We/I don't trust the new owner to not lose the records/documents; therefore, the institution should retain everything."
- "It's none of their [the new owner's] business."

This surprising range of comments ultimately begs the questions: Why would an institution that is caring for the objects for future generations not have proof of the identity of all past owners? Why wouldn't all of the object's documentation be part of that care when the object is deaccessioned? This related issue is also not clearly addressed within typical deaccession procedures.

Allowing original documentation to be attached to the associated object and passed to the new owner keeps the provenance chain intact. Anyone who performs and/or understands provenance research realizes that thorough documentation is the primary and most effective resource beyond the object itself. Historical documents, along with all physical evidence of an object's history (identifying marks) left intact on the object, can resolve questions of title, building a complete sequence of title.

Valid reasons for leaving physical evidence intact and approving the reallocation of original documents to the new owner include

- retaining the ownership trail of the object;
- assisting with future provenance research;
- providing answers to questions of authenticity with a forgery or fake; and/or
- aiding in the research of related objects or the artist's career/life/process.

The reason why this practice is not implemented seems to vary by institution. Many professionals believe that the institution deaccessioning the object should implement standards and best practices for retaining original documentation.

In addition to the explanations listed, other reasons for not sharing this information ranged from the fear that new owners will lose the documentation, to the concern that the object may be going into private hands, so the original documents should at least stay with the last public cultural organizational, to "we never did it before," all of which generally lack substance and supporting facts.

Once the decision to deaccession is made, under the premise that the object is no longer appropriate for a collection, why would retaining original documents be a necessity? Wouldn't photocopies suffice for any future need?

If an institution purchased an object at auction, from a dealer, or was gifted an object from a donor or sister institution, and only photocopies of the documentation were exchanged, would there not be an inquiry as to why the originals were not passed with the title? The new owner should have rights to all original documents relevant to an object's history, and separating the documents from the object is counter productive.

Leaving identifying marks intact (e.g., the accession number) and leaving *all* labels and tags on the object is ideal, as this documentation is an integral part of the object's history. Research can be vastly facilitated when the information remains with the object. For example, a label on a painting has been known to resolve questions of the chain of ownership decades later.

WHEN THE GUIDELINES DON'T FIT

Even in the best of museums, there will be instances when deaccessioning an object won't fit the typical plan, and corresponding uncertainty about how to proceed creates a challenge. Again, there are few resources delineating best practices in these instances.

Some examples of questions that might arise include:

- Is the object an intended fake or forgery?
- Is the object an undocumented antiquity?
- Is the documentation legitimate?
- Is the object authentic?
- Is the object similar to a stolen object, or perhaps the actual stolen object?
- Does the museum even own the object?
- Is it ivory or inlaid/decorated with material that falls under the Endangered Species Act?
- Can the object be sold?

With these questions in the forefront, where can museums find answers? This depends on the specific object and nature of the issue at hand. There is no general checklist, and how to proceed is determined on an object-by-object basis, dependent on the nature of the object.

The suggestions that follow offer resolution options or will, at the least, point you in the right direction/network.

FAKES, FORGERIES, AND AUTHENTICITY

Topics in this category include, but are not limited to, works of art (such as paintings, works on paper, sculptures, prints, and photographs); decorative arts (including ceramics and glass); and antiquities. All of these objects can be created with the intent to deceive. Keep in mind that forgers will try anything if there's a profit to be made.

Due diligence is essential when reviewing objects for acceptance. Questions should include: Where did the object come from? How did the dealer or donor obtain it? What's the story behind it, and is it credible? Are there conservation records? Has the signature been matched against authentic examples that exist? Any questions that piqued your uncertainty should be explored.

Physical examination with raking light and a black light can be very telling. It's an important tool as it reveals so much more than the naked eye can see. A black light can expose the restoration of a painting or perhaps an under painting, show pencil marks or signatures of furniture makers, reveal evidence of an alteration on an antiquity, or show removal of identification marks. The investigation may lead to more questions and require further research.

Turning to colleagues at local institutions who work with similar objects, works by the same artist, or similar collections can be a logical next step. Curators, area scholars, or experts may be able to provide leads or authenticate an object. A conservator may also be a valuable resource. Utilizing colleagues will either lead you to more questions or to resolving the problem. Specialists from reputable auction houses can often provide consultation and, with more than one expert on staff, multiple opinions can be obtained, which is advisable.

To determine authenticity, consider the option of laboratory testing. This might require travel and a financial investment not appropriate for every object, but it is a viable option in some cases. The museum would be confident that it has truly done due diligence. Selling an object that isn't authentic perpetuates deceit in the public domain.

Research, and questioning experts, is the only way to find answers. Even if answers are not conclusive, the documented process and due diligence are valuable and show the effort and intent.

UNDOCUMENTED AND INSUFFICIENTLY DOCUMENTED ANTIQUITIES

This is a special area of concern. Basic familiarity with purchase and customs forms and country codes can help answer whether documentation is legitimate or not. Examination of the description of goods presented on the forms is necessary. If the dealer from whom the object was purchased is identified, that person could be contacted for further information. Any gift or purchase would typically be researched in this way. Keep in mind, the more time that passes, the more difficult it may be to conduct the research.

In addition to examining purchase or customs forms, find out if the type of object, from wherever it originated and dates, matches known areas of looting in war-torn countries in the last century. For example, a critical time period for Nazi-era provenance research is 1932–46, allowing for activity prior to and just after World War II. Transfers of property happened shortly after the war, and a lot came through New York galleries. If documentation shows evidence of this, or there are gaps in the timeline or records, it is best practice to prioritize the research on that particular object.

If documentation or initial research suggests an object is from a more recent time period and is, for example, from Syria, it is best to search the Red Lists of objects at cultural risk published by the International Council of Museums (ICOM). Keep in mind, these are *not* lists of stolen objects, but a visual representation of objects in cultural institutions in countries where there is conflict and are the type of objects most vulnerable to illicit trafficking.

STOLEN PROPERTY

Discovery of stolen property is another issue that might arise when researching an object's history in preparation for deaccessioning. The object could be stolen from an institution or a private individual. Unfortunately, the available databases are not all fully accessible to non-law-enforcement individuals or are not complete records of all stolen objects—just those that have been reported. But checking these databases periodically is advisable. A few include the Art Loss Register, Interpol, the FBI Stolen Art Database, and Artive (formerly Art Recovery International). There are also specialized databases for Holocaust-era issues. If access is free to the database, there might be a fee for in-depth information or limited access to certain records if you are not a law enforcement agent. In addition, there are companies that will conduct research for a fee.

If an object is believed to have been stolen, gather all documentation, anticipate questions you may be expected to answer and prepare answers, then seek legal counsel. An attorney familiar with art law can suggest options and/ or can assist in transferring the object to its rightful owners.

If your institution does not have in-house legal counsel or access to an attorney, ask local, state, or regional colleagues for referrals.

One important point to remember is that if the object is covered under a fine art insurance policy and if the government seizes the object while it is in your institution's possession, there is no insurance coverage.

If a looted antiquity or undocumented antiquity finds its way into a museum's collection, the best tactic is to return the work with the advice of legal counsel. Sometimes it may be as simple as shipping a returning object or hand delivering it to the country of origin's embassy within the United States.

If an object falls into one of the above examples, the object can't ethically be owned by an institution, as there is no clear title. But if it is an instance in which you lack the documentation of a transfer of ownership, be clear in documenting research made in the process. Was the object received at a time when little paperwork was generated for gifts? Is the object mentioned in minutes from board or committee meetings? Are there any notes in files, on catalogue cards, in ledgers with references? Are there related objects for which files might hold some link or piece of information? Is there still a staff member available with institutional knowledge?

Clarifying ownership can be tricky and may not lead to a resolution. If there is no clear answer after rigorous research has been performed, reasonable effort has been expended. The object may be sold with the realization that an answer may later arise or never be determined. At that point, the situation is considered resolved to the best of your ability.

SPECIMENS UNDER REGULATIONS

Objects made from ivory (and identified as genuine) or objects with embellishments from endangered species fall under rules and regulations of the US Fish and Wildlife Service and the Endangered Species Act.

Legislation can and will change; readers should research the most current information for governance of the sale of such objects. With technology as it is, the most updated research can be realized quickly than ever before. Build a network of officials and contacts through colleagues and professional development opportunities. These individuals are often happy to assist, as dealing with questionable objects appropriately is essential for their work. Whichever option you choose for your research, always be sure to examine the most current materials.

As is evident, there are object challenges with no black-and-white answer and few guidelines to follow that require creative thinking and research skills. But that does not mean that the resolution for these scenarios should not be sought and the same level of due diligence performed, as is completed for any other object considered for deaccessioning. Solving the issue will make the process easier down the line.

CONCLUSION

In summary, there will always be questions for which there are no answers; in these situations, common sense is the best resource. Developing relationships with insurance representatives, legal counsel, customs agents, curators, and conservators at other institutions can prove invaluable. Be honest about the situation and contacts will reciprocate, leading to a more productive outcome. Remember that some of the best advice will come from colleagues who have already experienced similar situations or know experts who can offer assistance.

The bottom line is, if due diligence is rigorously and thoroughly performed and all avenues are explored while fully documenting results of the research in preparing objects for deaccessioning, the best outcomes will result. Ask questions, seek answers, and get results. Even if the process is challenging, and determining the right way to proceed can be difficult, doing what is right is rewarding and assures objects and their records will be cared for in perpetuity.

5

Are You Sure That Was a Copy?

Deaccessioning Mistakes

Christopher J. Robinson

Mistakes happen. But when it comes to museums and deaccessioning, there are degrees of mistake, and recognizing how vulnerable museums can be to disposing of valuable works in error, the parties involved may not always agree or be forthcoming about mistakes when they happen. This article is not intended to enter the heated debate on the ethics of deaccessioning, the protocol that should govern it, or the use of funds from deaccessioning. It is clearly a challenge to find the balance between providing neutral guidelines (clear enough to discourage abuse) and sufficient flexibility to accommodate emergencies or special circumstances.

Deaccessioning may come with regrets or remorse over financial crises not predicted or avoided, or the disposal of fine art deliberately let go under the pressure of changing trends or the rebranding of a museum's mission. Regrets can be particularly tragic when an institution sells a misidentified work of art because it was not recognized for what it actually was: a painting by the artist, not a copy or studio work, or a painting in need of conservation that is, in fact, in better condition than suspected under layers of varnish. Whether the work is sold at auction for a fraction of its value or exceeds all expectations, deaccessioning by mistake can reflect poorly on the institution and its staff.

How often do collecting institutions let a high-quality work go because it has been misidentified as a copy, determined to be a studio work, created by a follower, or is in poor condition? It may not be in the interest of the museum or the purchaser to publicize this embarrassment to the institution or the windfall to the painting's new owner. Art dealers who routinely rely on their expertise and take risks on misattributed or overpainted paintings say it happens more often than we realize. Given the increased reliance on public auction to sell deaccessioned artwork, these errors can be difficult to conceal.

This article will focus on three examples where it is likely that the deaccessioning museum, if it had known the true nature or condition of the work it was selling, may well have decided that deaccessioning was not appropriate. In the first example, exactly what was sold is not known. It may turn out that the substantial contribution to the museum's acquisition fund was worth the bad press. With the other two examples, there is little doubt that something went seriously wrong.

PORTRAIT OF A YOUNG GIRL, PETER PAUL RUBENS

On January 31, 2013, Sotheby's hosted an Old Master Paintings auction in New York. During the sale, several bidders vied for a small portrait (oil on panel) of a young girl (14 x 10¼ inches), whose creator was purported to be a follower of Peter Paul Rubens.[1] The terminology set forth in the Sotheby's catalogue stated that they were only comfortable guaranteeing that the work was, in their opinion, "a work by a painter working in the artist's style, contemporary or nearly contemporary, but not necessarily his pupil."[2] The painting's presale estimate, set at $20,000 to $30,000, reflected that caution, with the acknowledgment that the work was of high quality, at least in certain areas. When the bidding was over, the painting was purchased for $626,500 (including buyer's premium), and it was clear that something extraordinary had occurred.

The work had been consigned, along with a group of other paintings, by the Metropolitan Museum of Art (Met) in New York to benefit the museum's acquisitions fund. Had the museum made a terrible mistake? After all, the painting was accepted by scholars as a work by Rubens up until 1959 when Rubens scholar Julius Held rejected it.[3] Although other scholars had since concurred with Held's opinion, some did so with reservation and others remained convinced of its authenticity. In 2015, three years after the auction, the new owner lent the newly conserved painting to the Rubenshuis Museum in Antwerp for an exhibition. At this time, the museum's director, Ben van Beneden, was of the opinion that the painting was in fact by Rubens himself.[4] Katelijne Van der Stighelen, author of the work's catalogue entry in the forthcoming catalogue raisonné of Rubens portraits, shared this endorsement.[5] As Bendor Grosvenor asked in his blog, "Is this the greatest deaccessioning blunder of recent times?"[6]

The Met remained, at least publicly, unrepentant. And indeed, a review of the painting's attribution history illustrates the extreme difficulties in making definitive judgments about many works with uncertain attributions in museum collections.

The painting appears to have been universally accepted as a Rubens, beginning with the first time the attribution was published, in 1936, by German scholar W. R. Valentiner. It held this status until challenged by the American Rubens scholar Julius Held in 1947 and then more conclusively in 1959.[7] Held considered the work to be a copy after a lost portrait of Rubens's daughter, Clara Serena. The painting appeared to be based on a drawing of Clara Serena that Rubens created in the Albertina, Vienna.[8] Art historians had already noted the familial likeness between the sitter in the Vienna drawing, the Met painting, and another oil painting in the collections of the Prince of Liechtenstein in Vaduz.[9] However, these same historians differed in their explanation of the relationship between the works, a relationship complicated by the fact that the supposed sitter had died in 1623, at the tender age of twelve.

Held was a professor at Barnard College, part of Columbia University, for thirty-three years until his retirement in 1970. He continued to study and publish until shortly before his death at the age of ninety-seven, in 2002. Held had a profound influence on Dutch and Flemish art historical studies, especially in the United States, and his work on the thorny area of Rubens oil sketches was particularly valued. It is not surprising that, after the work entered the Met's collection as a gift of the New York collector Josephine Bay Paul in 1960 (one year after Held published that the work was a copy), Held's doubts were echoed by other scholars, both in verbal and written comments, as noted by the paintings department of the museum.[10] At last, one expert who had accepted the painting as genuine in 1953 had changed his mind by 1975.[11] So inconsistent was the handling of the paint that some scholars doubted that it was a seventeenth-century painting at all. The museum, hedging its bets, catalogued it as "*Portrait of a Young Girl* in the style of Rubens, XVIII/XIX century."[12] Walter Liedtke, Curator of Dutch and Flemish Paintings at the Met until his tragic death in 2015, summarized the state of confused scholarship on the work in his first volume of the Met's Flemish Paintings catalogue, describing it as a "copy after Peter Paul Rubens, probably XVII century, possibly depicting Clara Serena Rubens."[13]

Scholars continued to be highly skeptical about the attribution. In the catalogue of a major 1985 exhibition of the Liechtenstein Princely Collections (Vaduz) at the Met, Director of Collections Reinhold Baumstark noted in his entry on the Rubens portrait of Clara Serena that "two oil sketches in the MET and the Musee Diocesien, Liege, are portrayals of Clara Serena . . . but they are too weak to be accepted as works by Rubens and should be attributed to his followers."[14] Similarly, Anne-Marie Logan, in an exhibition of Rubens drawings at the Met in 2005, said that the Met's Vienna drawing was a portrait "from the Rubens school of very much the same young girl though in a simple dress; it was probably done after a lost Rubens work in oil."[15]

Figure 5.1. Peter Paul Rubens: *Portrait of Clara Serena,* oil on panel (after cleaning).

When the Rubens painting was consigned to Sotheby's for auction in 2013, it sparked much interest. Not only was the subject charming, but its quality was evident, despite some minor, curious weaknesses. Reports indicate that five or six bidders vied for the painting until it was sold to a London dealer on behalf of a collector.[16] Immediately, the press speculated as to whether the Met had made a mistake in selling it. Others cautioned that even if the work was thought to be a Rubens, it would be challenging to prove given the fragmented state of Rubens scholarship.[17] Evidently, many scholars stood by their opinion that the work was not by the artist's hand.[18]

Two years later, in March 2015, news circulated that the work was to be included in an exhibition of Rubens's family portraits at the Rubenshuis in Antwerp and that the organizers believed the work was authentic.[19] It was on long-term loan from the collection of the Prince of Liechtenstein, a curious development given that the former director of the same collection had confidently rejected the Rubens attribution when the work was at the Met. Cleaning the painting resolved some of the picture's uneven impression. Moreover, it was suggested that the frail appearance of the sitter in comparison to the earlier Liechtenstein oil sketch and the awkward relationship between the head and the rest of the picture may have to do with the fact that the work was datable to the early 1620s, just prior to—or even after—Clara Serena died at the age of twelve from an unidentified illness.[20]

The painting's charm, coupled with its tragic story, its probable genesis, and recent dramatic sale, made the portrait of Clara Serena a visitor favorite at the exhibition. When the exhibition closed, its owner agreed to leave it on loan at the museum.[21] It remains to be seen whether art historians will reach a consensus that favors the Rubens authorship. Questions about the wisdom of the painting's deaccession from the Met and the internal processes that underlay the decision are to be expected, given the work's popularity and its potential significance to art history.

ANTHONY VAN DYCK, *PORTRAIT STUDY OF A MAN*

Modern collectors admire oil sketches that provide insight into the artist's mind, but that wasn't always the case. Many fragmented sketches have been tidied up, squared off, cut down, or enlarged to create a more polished-looking work to suit the market, leaving the original hidden beneath the reworked paint. This was the case with the oil sketch created by artist Anthony Van Dyck that was deaccessioned by the Saint Louis Museum of Art (SLMA) in 2010.

Among the large-scale compositions that Van Dyck is known to have painted, which are now lost, are two multifigure portraits of members of the city council in the Brussels Town Hall, the first painted in 1628, the second in 1634.[22] Destroyed in a French bombardment in 1695, the large works were greatly admired for the artist's ability to capture the likeness of the individual counselors on a grand scale. Given the importance of the two commissioned portraits and the number of sitters (one included twenty-three life-size portraits), it is curious that no sketches or artist preparations survived. An oil sketch of the composition, now in the Ecole des Beaux-Arts in Paris, was identified in the mid nineteenth century, but little else exists.[23] There are very few known preparatory oil sketches attributed to Van Dyck. In the 2004 catalogue raisonné, only 25 preparatory oil studies have been identified and documented for 744 finished works by the artist.[24] Perhaps creating sketches was not part of the artist's practice, or perhaps they had simply been misidentified.

Another example included an oil study in the collection of the Saint Louis Art Museum (SLAM), accessioned in 1952 as a gift from local collector Sydney M. Schoenberg Sr.[25] Published as a work by the Van Dyck scholar Gustav Gluck in 1931, and bearing an old inscription on the back, "Vandyke. Ipse pinx. / Collection de Tallard," it had surfaced on the art market a few years earlier.[26] Soon after its arrival at the SLAM, Van Dyck expert Horst Vey rejected the attribution, as he considered it a copy after a lost work.[27] The handling of the paint appeared leaden, and it lacked Van Dyck's famous energetic brushstroke. But Vey did note that the sitter resembled the figure seated second from the left, in the lost 1634 Brussels painting. Perhaps the painting was somehow related to the two smaller head studies in the Ashmolean Museum, Oxford, that were accepted as signature works by Van Dyck. Identified as early as 1916, the paintings depicted two more of the sitters from the lost 1634 composition.[28]

The Oxford paintings were quick oil sketches of the sitter's head and shoulders summarily but deftly sketched on a neutral gray-over-red ground and were likely created from life. The Saint Louis painting continued to be a puzzle. Published in the 2004 Van Dyck catalogue raisonné (of which Vey was an author) as a copy, authors speculated that the painting might be from the nineteenth century.[29] Others disagreed. Erik Larsen published it as a Van Dyck work in his 1988 catalogue on the artist, and eminent scholar Michael Jaffe concurred with this opinion.[30] Nonetheless, when it came time for the museum to assemble a group of works for deaccession, this copy after Van Dyck was considered a good candidate, and the decision was made to sell the work through Christie's Auctions in New York in 2010.

Described by Christie's as by a "Follower of Van Dyck," the work surpassed its $7,000 to $10,000 estimate, selling to London dealer Fergus Hall for $35,000.[31] As is so often the case, close examination and cleaning of the painting revealed an underpainting, and the work's true relationship to the Oxford oil studies became evident. The finished quality of the painting disappeared once the overpainting was removed, exposing the same deft brush handling of the head, ruff, and shoulders as is visible in the Oxford studies. Once cleaned, the painting was universally accepted as created by Van Dyck. Vey passed away in 2010, but Susan Barnes, coauthor of the 2004 catalogue raisonné, accepts the painting as genuine, as do scholars Christopher Brown (formerly at the Ashmolean Museum) and Malcolm Rogers.[32]

Ironically, soon after the work was deaccessioned, other related head studies by Van Dyck created for the 1634 commission came to light, the first in dramatic fashion. It was spotted by a priest in 2013 during the taping of the British *Antiques Roadshow*. The priest claimed to have purchased it for 400 pounds in 1992 at a Cheshire antiques shop.[33] Disfiguring overpaint was removed to

**Figure 5.2. Anthony Van Dyck: *Portrait Study of a Man*,
oil on canvas (after cleaning).**

Portrait of a gentleman, bust-length (oil on canvas with paper exten-
sions), Dyck, Anthony van (1599–1641) (follower of) / Private Collection / Photo © Christie's Images / Bridgeman Images

reveal a study similar in size and on the same gray ground as the Saint Louis
painting, likely of one of the figures in the 1634 group portrait. With some lingering condition issues and a high estimate of 300,000 to 500,000 pounds, the
study failed to sell when offered at Christie's in 2014.[34] A year later, a fifth oil
study of a head from the same project was discovered in a European collection
and sold at Christie's in December 2014 for 494,500 pounds.[35]

When shown together in 2016, in a major exhibition of Van Dyck's portraiture at the Frick Collection, New York, the compositional study, the former Saint Louis oil, and the work from the *Antiques Roadshow* made a big
impression. One commentator remarked that the "three works elicited a near
religious experience."[36] Any lingering doubts of the authenticity of the oil
head studies in this series were dissolved by their obvious connection and the
brilliant observational powers demonstrated by Van Dyck.

Though the timing of the deaccession seems unfortunate, it is possible that the two works in the series that came to light in 2013 and 2014 were recognized for what they were—original works by Van Dyck—because of the publicity surrounding the 2010 sale and reattribution of the Saint Louis picture. If the painting had remained at the museum, the additional works that surfaced may have led to a reevaluation of the Saint Louis painting and, after conservation, an understanding of its beauty and art-historical importance. Even before the emergence of the additional paintings in the series, an exploratory cleaning of the sketch at the Saint Louis Museum (given the known connection to the Ashmolean oils and the lost multifigure composition) would have been a wise, relatively inexpensive investment. In retrospect, the $35,000 boost to the museum's acquisition fund must seem deeply disappointing in exchange for the rare oil sketch from the hand of Van Dyck. At least the Met Rubens and the Saint Louis Van Dyck were oil sketches, and not important finished compositions. But that is not true for the third and most disheartening example.

FRANCOIS BOUCHER, *LEDA AND THE SWAN*

A recent gift by Linda and Stewart Resnick to the Los Angeles County Museum of Art (LACMA) in celebration of the museum's fiftieth anniversary brought closure to the curious saga of a beautiful work by the eighteenth-century French painter Francois Boucher.[37] Exhibited at the Paris Salon in 1742 as a pendant to the equally stunning *Diana Bathing*, *Leda and the Swan* is one of Boucher's most sensuous compositions. The painting's more recent provenance reveals that the Boucher was given to the Art Institute of Chicago as part of the eclectic collection of a Chicago businessman. It was later deaccessioned by the Art Institute, purchased by a dealer, and sold to the Resnicks, who gifted it to LACMA. This path illustrates the risks of deaccessioning old master paintings.

For many years, one of the strangest museums in the Chicago area was the George F. Harding Museum. Harding, a wealthy and influential politician and businessman, had amassed an extraordinarily diverse collection before his death in 1939. Best known for its arms and armor, the collection also included medieval and renaissance furniture and decorative arts, musical instruments, Frederic Remington sculptures, an wildly diverse group of two hundred paintings, and oddities such as the sleigh in which Napoleon retreated from Moscow and a sofa once owned by Abraham Lincoln.[38] The museum was housed in Harding's gothic-inspired castle on Chicago's South Side, but over time its audience dwindled. After the house was condemned in 1962, the collection was crated and moved into storage, where it languished for over a decade.[39] A not-for-profit corporation from 1930, the museum was controlled by a Chicago banker, Herman Silverstein, who sold works from the collection to pay for office repairs and for the salaries of its four directors, and allegedly diverted funds for his own use.[40] Having quietly sold a number of items, including a Delacroix and several important musical instruments, Silverstein consigned a group of paintings to Sotheby Parke-Bernet in New York for auction in 1976; among them were Rubens's *Saint Francis* and Boucher's *Leda and the Swan*.[41]

Soon after Sotheby's distributed its small catalogue to select dealers, the Illinois Attorney General, alerted to the discrete sales, obtained an injunction.[42] A lengthy lawsuit against the museum trustees over the mismanagement of the collection ensued. The case alleged that museum administrators and trustees acted in self-interest and cited their lack of oversight. This instance continues to be cited in legal treatises as a prime example of nonprofit mismanagement.[43] In 1982, the case was settled and the collection was transferred en masse to the Art Institute of Chicago and distributed to its appropriate departments.[44]

The Boucher painting had been offered in 1976 as an authentic work by the artist with the estimate of $40,000 to $60,000, although some thought bids would go as high as $75,000.[45] There were concerns that one of the leading authorities on the Boucher, Alexandre Ananoff, doubted the work's authenticity. In the first volume of his catalogue raisonné on Boucher, published that same year, the Paris-based Ananoff described the work as "a studio copy after the original version in the National Museum, Stockholm."[46] The Stockholm work had a splendid provenance, purchased from Boucher in Paris by the great Count Tessin. It was shipped to Sweden the same year it was displayed at the Paris Salon.[47] When the Art Institute of Chicago needed to raise acquisition funds in 1985, they decided to sell a group of unwanted works from the Harding Collection including the Boucher, only three years after acquiring it for the Institute's collection.

It was curious that even with a scholarly consensus, the painting was consigned to Sotheby's in 1985 as "from the Studio of Francois Boucher" and would sell for ten times the $15,000 to $20,000 estimate.[48] The dealer, Guy Sainty, who bought the work was impressed by its quality, and by its signature that looked authentic.[49] Having purchased it, he was proven to be right. An early print depicting the Salon painting included a dedication to the original eighteenth-century owner of the Chicago painting.[50] X-rays indicated changes of placement of some of the picture elements, indicative of an original work, not a copy.[51] X-rays also revealed that beneath the composition laid another, more conventionally composed version of the same subject. This was a known print after a lost preparatory drawing by Boucher, though no finished painting of the composition had survived.[52] Critical research revealed that the painting in Stockholm had been purchased and shipped by Tessin to Sweden several weeks *before* the Paris Salon of 1742, in which Boucher exhibited his original work.[53] Evidently, Tessin had seen and admired the painting in Boucher's studio and asked the artist to have a copy made, the copy now in Stockholm. The painting formerly in the collection of the Art Institute, which was deaccessioned, was in fact the original from the Salon.

In the weeks after the sale the Institute defended its decision to deaccession what was now recognized as one of Boucher's most beautiful salon pictures residing in the United States. Richard Bretell, the chief curator of paintings and sculpture at the Art Institute (a nineteenth-century paintings expert), stated that it was consigned to auction "because we believed fundamentally it is a copy of the best version of the painting, which is in Stockholm."[54] No one from the Art Institute appeared to have shown Ananoff the painting before the museum decided to sell it. A week after the sale Ananoff told Rita Reif of the *New York Times* that he "had never seen the Art Institute version and that while he had indeed published the Stockholm version as original, he had never commented on the artistic merits of the Chicago painting."[55]

Deeper research or additional due diligence might have created a different outcome. The observation that the Stockholm painting could not have been the work exhibited at the 1742 Salon because it was shipped to Sweden before the exhibition opened had already been published in 1984, the year *before* the work was deaccessioned by the Art Institute, in the catalogue of an exhibition at the City Art Museum in Manchester, England, titled *Francois Boucher: Paintings, Drawings and Prints from the Nationalmuseum, Stockholm*.[56] The declaration in that catalogue that the Salon version of *Leda and the Swan* had "disappeared" should presumably have given the Art Institute pause.[57] More significantly, in 1986, the year after the sale at Sotheby's, the Stockholm version was included in the monumental exhibition of works by Boucher held at the Met, organized in collaboration with the Detroit Institute of Arts and the Reunion des Musees Nationaux in Paris.[58] A show of this size is typically the result of many years of research and preparation, and indeed Boucher scholar Alastair Laing, who organized the exhibition and contributed to its scholarship, had come to the conclusion that the Harding painting was in fact the original Salon version.[59] It seems inconceivable that the Art Institute would not have known of the forthcoming exhibition and Laing's opinion prior to deaccessioning the painting. The exhibition catalogue entry on the Stockholm *Leda and the Swan* includes a full discussion of the (by then deaccessioned) Art Institute version and a detailed provenance; although it lists the Harding Collection and the work's sale at Sotheby's in 1985, it curiously (and perhaps tactfully) omits any reference to the absorp-

Figure 5.3. Francois Boucher: *Leda and the Swan,* oil on canvas (after cleaning).
Promised gift of Lynda and Stewart Resnick in honor of the museum's fiftieth anniversary. Photo Credit: photo © Museum Associates/LACMA

tion of the Harding Collection into the Art Institute or indeed any mention of the Art Institute at all.[60]

If the museum had done forensic testing on this picture, examined Ananoff's research, or explored the latest scholarly opinion on what was the prime version of its painting in Stockholm, as it does not appear to have done, the museum might have suspected that it had a significant painting in its hands. If the painting's quality was evident to the dealers who viewed it at the auction, why had the museum's professional staff not come to the same conclusion? Certainly, the sale of the work, three years after it entered the museum and after decades of relative obscurity, may have been too hasty to formulate the type of art historical consensus that often comes from prolonged exposure in a world-class public institution. And the suspicion remains that its inclusion in the Harding collection, amid so many paintings of uneven or merely decorative quality and where the focus was solidly on the arms and armor,[61] may have prejudiced those at the Institute and led them to assume the worst.

Now the painting has come full circle. From Boucher to follower to Boucher again. From private collection to a museum, attempted deaccession, transfer to another museum, deaccession, a private collection, and back to public view in a museum. A more telling example of the perils of museum deaccessioning to the point of farce would be hard to find.

On July 5, 2018, the portrait of Clara formerly in the Metropolitan Museum of Art was offered for sale at Christie's London as an autograph work by Rubens with an estimate of $4 million–$6.8 million. It did not sell.

III

THE USE OF PROCEEDS: ETHICS AND THE ROLE OF PROFESSIONAL ASSOCIATIONS

6

Use of Funds from the Sale of Deaccessioned Objects

It's a Matter of Ethics

Sally Yerkovich

When the American Alliance of Museums (AAM) drew up its *Code of Ethics for Museums* in the late 1980s, one of the areas of contention was a museum's use of funds realized from the sale of deaccessioned objects. According to Robert R. Macdonald, then President of AAM, "there are [sic] ardently held positions on both sides of the issue."[1] Some felt that museums should be able to use the proceeds from the disposal[2] of objects from collections for whatever financial need the museum might have.

Others believed that a museum holds its collections to benefit the public and funds from the disposal process should only be used to purchase additional collections items. To complicate the matter further at about the same time, debates about whether museum collections should be viewed as convertible assets and capitalized were occurring because of proposed changes in accounting standards. In the end, the Ethics Committee that formulated the code chose to follow the International Council of Museums' (ICOM) example and restrict museums to using funds realized from the sale of deaccessioned objects to the purchase of new collections items.

The creation of the 1991 *Code of Ethics for Museums* was inspired by the publication in 1986 of the *ICOM Code of Ethics for Museums*. It built upon two earlier documents: the AAM 1925 *Code of Ethics for Museum Workers* (AAM's first code) and *Museum Ethics*, a report issued in 1978 by AAM that expands upon ethical issues then deemed critical to the profession. The 1991 Code emerged from a three-year process involving extensive research and debate among Committee members that was informed by discussion among professional groups as well as commentary from the field. In the spring of

1991, the Council (now board of directors) of AAM passed the new *Code of Ethics for Museums*.

Edward H. Able, the Executive Director of AAM, introduced the 1991 Code and hailed it in *Museum News* as the "strongest step the museum community has ever taken to guarantee to the public . . . that the ethic of public service is the bedrock of museum operations."[3] Yet only six months after approving this much-heralded document, the AAM Council voted to suspend the code because of the controversy it had provoked.

Museums immediately took issue with several elements of the 1991 Code, but the disagreement over the ethical principle related to the use of funds realized from the disposal of deaccessioned objects was the most divisive. The provision in the 1991 Code read:

> disposal of collections through sale, trade, or research activities is solely for the advancement of the museum's mission, and use of proceeds from the sale of collection materials is restricted to the acquisition of collections.[4]

AAM heard from close to three-quarters of its member museums, all objecting strongly to this statement. Opinions about its appropriateness differed from institution to institution depending upon the museum's discipline. History museums, for example, argued that their responsibility to maintain and conserve their collections is of equal if not, in some cases, greater importance than their duty to develop their collections. Natural history museums agreed. Historic sites did as well, noting that the preservation of historic buildings and landscapes is often part of their collection stewardship responsibilities. Science museums also chimed in. These institutions were shifting focus from creating exhibitions based on their permanent collections to developing displays with pedagogical objects and evolving modes of technology. If they were required to keep and then maintain all of these purpose-built items, representatives of science museums maintained that their ability to fulfill their missions would be hampered.[5]

AAM's Ethics Commission, a group created by a recommendation in the 1991 Code, was given the task of resolving the issues raised by the 1991 Code. After two years, this group proposed a greatly revised code that was no more successful than the 1991 Code.

Ultimately, the AAM Board adopted the 1991 Code with revisions. Specifically, the statement concerning the use of funds from deaccessioned objects was changed to read:

> disposal of collections through sale, trade, or research activities is solely for the advancement of the museum's mission. Proceeds from the sale of nonliving collections are to be used consistent with the established standards of the museum's discipline, but in no event shall they be used for anything other than acquisition or direct care of collections.[6]

The phrase *direct care of collections* was added to the ethical principle about disposal in an attempt to accommodate the needs of the museum field's diverse disciplines. The phrase was not defined, but it was expected that its meaning would be clarified over time as individual museums described it in collections management policies. Discussions at the time as well as a brief AAM Ethics Committee study in 1996 reveal that most felt *direct care* referred to conservation and that under no circumstances would it be permissible to use funds from the sale of deaccessioned objects for operating costs or as a stopgap when a museum faced a financial crisis.[7] Over time, however, the phrase was not codified.

Twenty years later, after the 2008 recession left many museums struggling to regain their foothold, deaccessioning and the process of disposition were again in the news. When the AAM Board asked the Accreditation Commission to identify the ten most critical issues facing museums, the Commission identified the lack of clear standards for the appropriate use of funds from deaccessioning as the most important. They focused specifically upon the definition of *direct care* of collections and cited recent controversies: the Detroit Institute of Arts, Delaware Art Museum, Field Museum, Morris-Jumel Mansion, Fort Ticonderoga, Maier Museum of Art, Rose Art Museum, and National Academy Museum, where the use of funds from the disposal of objects was in question.

The Commission identified one of the sources of the problem in the different practices stipulated by professional organizations serving the field. The Association of Art Museum Directors (AAMD) mandates that funds realized from deaccessioning be used only for acquisitions to a museum's collections. The ICOM Code of Ethics for Museums states that "Money or compensation received from the deaccessioning and disposal of objects and specimens from a museum collection should be used solely for the benefit of the collection and usually for acquisitions to that collection."[8] The American Association of State and Local History (AASLH) Statement on Standards and Ethics called for funds from the disposal of objects to be used for acquisition as well as the preservation of the existing collections, and AAM's Code of Ethics focused upon acquisition and direct care.

The Accreditation Commission noted that these inconsistencies weaken the standards, create image problems for the field, and reduce museums' credibility. Burt Logan, Accreditation Commission Chair, stated, "Even people unfamiliar with museum standards intuitively understand that museums hold collections in the public trust and that collections are not financial assets to be used to make up for financial shortfalls."[9] At the May 2014 meeting of the AAM Board, Logan urged the Board to take action: "museums need guidance, reporters need answers, the public needs education, [and] the field needs a unified message about the use of proceeds."[10]

The Accreditation Commission called for the creation of a cross-disciplinary task force that would conduct an eighteen-month field-wide initiative to define *direct care.* The AAM Board concurred and later that year created a task force charged with providing "clarity on the standard and guidance on the acceptable practices in its application."[11]

Designed to represent the breadth of the museum field, the Direct Care White Paper Task Force included representatives of art, natural history, children's, and historic house museums as well as historical organizations, science centers, botanical gardens, and zoos. A representative of the National Trust for Historic Preservation joined the group as did an attorney specializing in art, museum, and cultural heritage law.

The Task Force began its work in early 2015 by surveying the field to discover if there might be a consistency in the way that museum professionals define *direct care.* The survey listed fifty items that might be considered direct care of collections and nineteen that might be considered part of acquisition costs, and it asked respondents to identify the uses of funds from the sale of deaccessioned objects that were acceptable and which were not.[12] The Task Force used the survey results to determine how it would proceed in drafting the white paper and providing guidance to the field.

The Task Force made its recommendations at the end of 2015, and in April 2016 AAM issued *Direct Care: Ethics, Guidelines and Recommendations,* the Direct Care White Paper. After a brief history of the term *direct care* and an overview of the Direct Care Task Force's work, the White Paper identifies the ethical principles that underlie professional practices concerning the disposition of museum collections. The following principles are critical to the work of museums today and must be respected and upheld in order to ensure that museums will continue to benefit the public well into the future:

- Museum collections are considered cultural, not financial, assets, to be held for the public benefit.
- [A museum's] governing body must make decisions that are consistent with its mission and its obligations to the public with regard to collections stewardship.
- [The governing body] should ensure that funds realized from the sale of deaccessioned objects are never used as a substitute for fiscal responsibility.[13]

The document goes on to provide a definition of *direct care,* which relates directly to the ethical principles:

Direct care is an investment that enhances the life, usefulness or quality of a museum's collection.[14]

Acknowledging the differences in practice among the various museum disciplines, the white paper includes seven sidebars, summarizing disciplinary

Direct Care of Collections Matrix

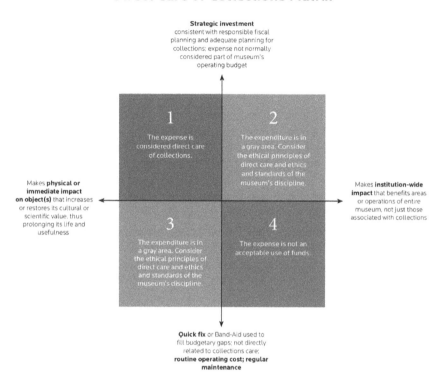

Strategic investment consistent with responsible fiscal planning and adequate planning for collections; expense not normally considered part of museum's operating budget

1 The expense is considered direct care of collections.

2 The expenditure is in a gray area. Consider the ethical principles of direct care and ethics and standards of the museum's discipline.

Makes **physical or immediate impact on object(s)** that increases or restores its cultural or scientific value, thus prolonging its life and usefulness

3 The expenditure is in a gray area. Consider the ethical principles of direct care and ethics and standards of the museum's discipline.

4 The expense is not an acceptable use of funds.

Makes **institution-wide impact** that benefits areas or operations of entire museum, not just those associated with collections

Quick fix or Band-Aid used to fill budgetary gaps; not directly related to collections care; **routine operating cost; regular maintenance**

collections (e.g., salaries; preservation/restoration of historic structures or landscapes that are not interpreted to the public and are not treated as part of the collection)

On the vertical axis, indicate where the expenditure falls between the following criteria:

- a strategic investment consistent with responsible fiscal planning and adequate planning for collections; an expense not normally considered part of the museum's operating budget

- a quick fix or Band-Aid used to fill budgetary gaps; not directly related to collections care; routine operating cost; regular maintenance

The quadrant in which the two points intersect indicates whether the expenditure is appropriate.

Figure 6.1.   Direct Care of Collections Matrix, American Alliance of Museums.

Reprinted from American Alliance of Museums, Direct Care of Collections: Ethics, Guidelines and Recommendations, April 2016, Washington, DC: American Alliance of Museums, p. 10.

standards for arboreta, botanical gardens, and public gardens; art museums; children's museums; history museums and historic sites; natural history museums; science/technology museums/centers; and zoos and aquariums. It also provides two decision-making tools—a matrix and guiding questions—to assist museum staff and their institution's governing authority to determine if its use of funds for direct care is appropriate, given the museum's particular circumstances.

Finally, the white paper includes AAM's recommendations for the application of the *direct care* definition by individual museums. First and foremost, a museum's Collections Management Policy and its Code of Ethics should include a statement limiting the use of funds realized from the sale of deaccessioned objects to the acquisition of collections and/or the direct care of collections. If a museum allows proceeds to be used for direct care, its Collections Management Policy should articulate the scope of the definition of direct care of collections it will apply. Just as the deaccessioning and disposition processes are separated to ensure that museums deaccession for the right reasons, having a collections policy that stipulates how the museum defines *direct care* can help ensure that the museum's definition has come from a thoughtful process exempt from the pressures that can sometimes surround financial decision-making.

Secondly, a museum's Collections Management Policy should define the process the museum will follow in determining how funds will be used and identify the key members of the professional staff (collections, curatorial, management, and leadership) and governing authority who will be involved. This should ensure that a museum's professional staff is always involved in the decision-making process about the disposition of objects from a museum's collection.

Lastly, AAM recommends that both Collections Management and financial policies stipulate that funds realized from the sale of deaccessioned objects be put in a segregated account. Further, AAM urges that earnings from that account be used consistently with the museum's policies regarding the use of those funds (i.e., either for acquisition or direct care).

One year after the report's publication, response from the field is positive. Its guidance and recommendations are helping collections managers, curators, directors, and board members in their decision-making. Deaccessioning continues to grab headlines and social media attention, but the options may be clearer and more accurately reported. As more time passes and all museum collections age, stewardship of museum holdings will become more and more critical and along with that an understanding of *direct care*. Practices concerning accessioning as well as the role of collections in a museum may change as the world becomes more virtual. Nonetheless, responsible collections management will remain central to a museum's responsibilities, and the disposal of items in a museum's collection will continue to garner attention both within the field and among the public that benefits from our holdings.

7

Making the Case

FASB's Accounting Standards Should Be Realigned with AAM's Long-Standing Guidance on the Use of Sale Proceeds

Lori Breslauer and Sarah Ebel

SUMMARY

For more than twenty years, the accrediting body for US museums, the American Alliance of Museums (AAM),[1] has allowed proceeds from the sale of nonliving collections to be used for both acquisition and direct care,[2] and the collections policies of many museums have adhered to these AAM standards. However, questions have arisen concerning the possible misalignment of AAM's long-standing position on the use of such proceeds with the accounting standards promulgated by the Financial Accounting Standards Board ("FASB" or the "Board") originally in FASB *Statement 116*[3] ("FASB 116") and currently found in Topic 958 "Not-for-Profit Entities" in the FASB Accounting Standard Codification (ASC), specifically section 958-360-25, and the ASC definition of "Collections" (the "Definition") (collectively "ASC 958" or "the Standard"), which provides conditions for determining when a museum need not capitalize its collections for accounting purposes.[4] On its face, the Standard appears to suggest that if a museum does not capitalize its collections, then it may use proceeds from the sale of collection items only for new acquisitions and not for direct care. At least three museum experts have agreed with this surface reading.[5]

However, a holistic reading of the Standard and consideration of its history and overall purposes suggest, instead, the following:

1. FASB 116's drafters intentionally aligned the Standard with AAM's contemporary standards and best practices, as embodied in AAM's then-current *Code of Ethics*, but subsequent policy revisions by AAM have resulted in a misalignment between FASB and the museum field which bears correcting; and

2. Direct care is consistent with a holistic reading of the Definition and the Standard's overall purpose to provide conditions that demonstrate museum collections can and will be maintained and are held in further-ance of public service rather than financial gain.

Therefore, the Definition should be revised to bring its language back into alignment with AAM's standards—allowing use of proceeds from the sale of collections to be used for both acquisition and direct care—as this is consis-tent with its drafters' intent, the Standard's purpose, and the museum field's ethics, best practices, and expectations.

DISCUSSION

In his 2006 book on collections management policies, *Things Great and Small*, John E. Simmons writes:

> The museum's use of funds gained from deaccessioning will determine whether it must capitalize its collections (i.e., assign a monetary value to all the collec-tions and report that value as capital assets on the institution's financial docu-ments). Statement 116 of the Financial Accounting Standards Board (FASB) specifies that if deaccession proceeds are used for anything *except* the acquisi-tion of new collections, the museum is required to capitalize its collections or risk a qualified audit.[6,7]

Similarly, in 2007, Julie Hart, then AAM's Assistant Director of Accredi-tation, wrote in handouts for the one-day seminar "Legal, Ethical and Profes-sional Guidelines for Collections Stewardship" that, for museums that choose not to capitalize their collections, FASB 116 requires that proceeds from sales of collection items must be subject to an organizational policy requiring pro-ceeds be used *only* to acquire other collection items.[8] Hart went on to explain, "In other words, if you do not capitalize, your collections management policy cannot say proceeds can be used for direct care or maintenance or preserva-tion, etc.—only acquisitions."[9]

At issue is whether the requirement that limits museums that do not capi-talize their collections to using proceeds from the sale of collections only for the acquisition of new collections is as absolute as Hart and Simmons state.

A careful reading of FASB 116's history and language shows that it is not. Additionally, reading the Standard in such a strict manner creates a disconnect between accounting standards and museum best practices—a problem for museums that FASB did not intend. Considering FASB's current work on revising other portions of its standards and AAM's forthcoming guidelines on direct care, this is an opportune time to revisit this issue and to encourage the Board to realign the Standard with long-standing museum best practices.

   1. FASB 116's drafters intentionally aligned FASB 116 with AAM's contemporary standards and best practices, as embodied in AAM's then-current Code of Ethics, but subsequent policy revisions by AAM have resulted in a misalignment between FASB and the museum field which bears correcting.

FASB 116's purpose was to distinguish assets held for financial gain, which must be capitalized, from "collections" which are objects "held for public exhibition, education, or research in furtherance of public service" and need not be capitalized.[10] In order to make this distinction, the accountants at FASB looked to the museum field itself as the expert, relying on AAM policies to ascertain what conditions would demonstrate a commitment to maintain collections. As FASB 116's "Basis for Conclusions" states:

> This Statement's definition of a collection is based on the American Association of Museums' *Code of Ethics for Museums* (1991) and its "Accreditation: Self-Study" (1989). *The definitions in those documents are widely used by the kinds of organizations for which the Board believes the relevant cost and benefit problem exists.* The Board decided that having an organizational policy that requires that the proceeds from collection items sold be used to acquire other items for collections demonstrates a commitment and a probability that the collections will and can be maintained. The Board believes that commitment is particularly relevant to its considerations about both the benefits and costs of providing information about those assets.[11]

AAM's policy documents, particularly its *Code of Ethics*, was (and remains) an appropriate basis for FASB's criteria. AAM represents all[12] of the many and varied institutions in the American museum field—zoos, science museums, planetaria, natural history museums, historical houses and museums, children's museums, botanical gardens, art museums, and aquaria—each of which have different collections and concerns, but all of which look to AAM's *Code of Ethics* as a source of best practices and professional expectations. Additionally, some types of institutions have more logistical difficulties with capitalization than others. While capitalization of its collection may be neither desirable nor appropriate, it is at least generally possible for an art museum, which may have thousands of objects with ascertainable fair market values; however, capitalization of, for example, a natural history museum's collection of tens of millions of specimens is nearly impossible, as many of its objects (jars of mites, study skins of endangered species, fossils excavated from government lands, bird nests, etc.) have no intrinsic fair market value or cannot be legitimately sold on the open market. FASB was promulgating one standard for the entire, diverse museum field, and so it looked to AAM because AAM's policies took this diversity into account and were widely accepted in the field as an authority.

FASB 116 was published in 1993, and, as noted above, it specifically relied on the then-current 1991 AAM *Code of Ethics for Museums*, which restricted the use of proceeds from the sale of collections to the acquisition of collections.[13] However, a year later, in response to strong pushback from museum professionals, AAM modified its ethics code in 1994 to allow such proceeds to be used for direct care as well as acquisition:

> Disposal of collections through sale, trade or research activities is solely for the advancement of the museum's mission. Proceeds from the sale of nonliving collections are to be used consistent with the established standards of the museum's discipline, but in no event shall they be used for anything other than acquisition or direct care of collections.[14]

Had FASB promulgated FASB 116 two years later, it is quite probable that it would have followed AAM's policies and included direct care, as well as acquisition. FASB wanted to reflect the museum field's best practices, not impose new policies where it lacked expertise, as long as those existing practices were consonant with FASB's goals and principles.

Even though AAM has revised its ethics code since 1994 (most recently in 2000), the provision allowing direct care has not changed since 1994 and remains in effect today.[15] Many museums have aligned their collections policies with this position. And, while the exact definition and boundaries of "direct care" continues to engender much discussion within the museum field, direct care is and is likely to remain widely accepted as an appropriate use of sale proceeds.[16]

Notably, the Association of Art Museum Directors ("AAMD") requires that proceeds from the sale of collections be used only for the acquisition of collections and not for direct care.[17] AAMD's *Policy on Deaccessioning* provides extensive criteria and sound rationales for deaccessioning for the health of a museum's collection, but it, somewhat strangely, offers no such discussion of its limitation on the use of sale proceeds to acquisitions only.[18] The policy does, however, specifically reference and incorporate the language of

FASB 116, which may be the origin of AAMD's limitations on the uses of sale proceeds.[19] Thus, AAMD's deaccessioning policy relied on FASB 116, which, in turn, had relied on AAM's 1991 *Code of Ethics*, even though the Standard was already misaligned with the museum field's standards with regard to direct care as a suitable use of sale proceeds. AAMD may have valid reasons for requiring its members to use proceeds from the sale of collections only for new acquisitions, but the Standard should not be the foundational justification for such a stricture. Rather, AAMD should articulate its policies regarding the use of sales proceeds based on its expertise and its sound ethical and museological rationales, not accounting standards.[20]

FASB drew from contemporary AAM standards in 1993, explicitly adopting AAM's position on the disposition of proceeds.[21] FASB should continue to rely on AAM's policies as the authority for museum best practices for the wider museum field. The Standard was properly aligned with the state of the field in 1993, but it has failed to evolve. Direct care has been entrenched in AAM policy for more than twenty years because AAM and the museum professionals it represents have recognized that direct care is necessary for the preservation of a collection in perpetuity. Revising the Standard to allow for both acquisition and direct care would bring it back into alignment with long-standing AAM policy and the expectations of the many museums that adhere to these best practices.

2. *Direct care is consistent with a holistic reading of the Definition and the Standard's overall purpose to provide conditions that demonstrate collections can and will be maintained and are held in furtherance of public service rather than financial gain.*

Bringing the Standard back into alignment with AAM's current *Code of Ethics* and best practices by revising part (c) of the Definition to explicitly include direct care (A) is consistent with a holistic reading of the Definition; (B) promotes FASB's collections maintenance and reinvestment goals; and (C) addresses FASB's concerns about financial gain.

A. A holistic reading of the Definition supports the inclusion of direct care.

FASB's definition of "Collections" referenced in ASC 958 establishes conditions under which collections need not be capitalized. These conditions are ones that demonstrate that the collections are held for the purpose of public service rather than financial gain; as FASB 116's Summary statement provides: "Contributions of works of art, historical treasures, and similar assets need not be recognized as revenues and capitalized if the donated items are added to collections held for public exhibition, education, or research in

Lori Breslauer and Sarah Ebel

furtherance of public service rather than financial gain."[22] These conditions, as stated in the Definition, are

> Works of art, historical treasures, or similar assets that meet all of the following criteria:
> a. They are held for public exhibition, education, or research in furtherance of public service rather than financial gain.
> b. They are protected, kept unencumbered, cared for, and preserved.
> c. They are subject to an organizational policy that requires the proceeds of items that are sold in order to acquire other items for collections.[23]

The Standard requires that each of these three conditions be met. However, the relationship between parts (b)—requiring protection, care, and preservation of the collection—and (c)—requiring an organizational policy that requires sales proceeds to be used for acquisition—is ambiguous and, possibly, conflicting. Given that museums have limited resources, it is not in their best interests to require organizational policies that prioritize acquisitions over collections care and preservation. Allowing use of proceeds for direct care specifically satisfies part (b) of the Definition and resolves the potential conflict between parts (b) and (c). Further note that the organizational policy requirements of part (c) do not state that proceeds may be "used *only* to acquire other items for collections" or "the organization *may not* apply proceeds from the sale of collection items to any other purpose." The language does not explicitly exclude the use of proceeds from the sale of collection items for other activities; the expression of one acceptable use (i.e., acquisitions) does not necessarily exclude all other possible uses (e.g., direct care). A holistic reading of the Definition resolves ambiguity between the sections and is also consistent with FASB's original intent for the Standard.

FASB's original intent was not to promote new acquisitions or to prevent direct care—its intent was to distinguish between items held for financial gain and those used for public service. FASB specifically sought conditions leading to the maintenance of and reinvestment in collections, which is the essence of the mission of collections-based organizations; investment in collections and their protection, care, and preservation is at the core of direct care. An organizational policy that allows the use of proceeds from sales of collection items for both direct care and acquisition should fall within a broader reading of ASC 958 that is inclusive of Definition conditions (a), (b), and (c). Such a reading is appropriate given the Definition's language and construction and is consonant with the overall goals of the Standard and with the interrelated history of FASB 116 and AAM's *Code of Ethics*.

B. Inclusion of direct care promotes FASB's collections maintenance and reinvestment goals.

Again, FASB's main goal is to distinguish assets held for gain from collections held for public service. FASB finds collections maintenance and reinvestment to be particularly relevant in determining whether a collection should be capitalized. It explains that

> The Board decided that having an organizational policy that requires that the proceeds from collection items sold be used to acquire other items for collections demonstrates a commitment and a probability that *the collection will and can be maintained.* The Board believes *that commitment is particularly relevant* to its considerations about both the benefits and costs of providing information about those assets.[24]

And, in specifically discussing the noncapitalization conditions contained in paragraph 11(c) of FASB 116, it states that

> Some museums that endorse the provisions of paragraph 11(a) and (b) but are not committed to reinvesting proceeds for sales of collection items to acquire other items for collections (paragraph 11(c)) asked the Board to allow nonrecognition of their collection items. *Having an organization policy and demonstrated commitment to reinvest in collection items is particularly relevant to the Board's conclusions about collection assets.*[25]

These statements demonstrate FASB's goal of promoting reinvestment in and maintenance of collections, both as a whole and in the items that make up those collections. However, expanding a collection through acquisitions is only one way in which museums maintain and reinvest in their collection; the other is to engage in the direct care of existing collections, which is reinvestment in individual collections items. Being limited only to expansion through acquisition may actually make it more difficult for an organization to properly maintain its collection, stretching resources for care and conservation ever thinner. Acquisition *and* direct care are appropriate, complimentary means of reinvesting in collections. A broader, holistic reading of the standard (or the explicit inclusion of direct care in the definition) would allow museums to choose between acquisitions or direct care or pursue both, depending on their specific and evolving collection maintenance needs.

C. Inclusion of direct care addresses concerns about financial gain.

FASB is firm in its belief that collections items are assets, which normally should be capitalized.[26] But it allows an exception for collections items held "in furtherance of public service rather than financial gain."[27] Allowing use of proceeds from the sale of collections for direct care would not run afoul of this concern. The reinvestment of proceeds into direct collections care, like the reinvestment of proceeds into in an acquisition fund, does not lead to "financial gain" by the institution. Rather, investment in collections care allows for the furtherance of public service by ensuring that collections items are accessible to the public and preserved for generations to come.

CONCLUSION

To distinguish between assets that must be capitalized and collections that need not be, the Board sought evidence demonstrating a commitment and probability that a museum's collections can and will be maintained in furtherance of public service. Museum policies that adhere to AAM's current *Code of Ethics* can and do demonstrate such a commitment; FASB's Standard should be realigned with this long-standing best practice. Specifically, part (c) of FASB's definition of "Collections" should be revised as follows: "c. They are subject to an organizational policy that requires proceeds of items that are sold to be used *only for direct care or* to acquire other items for collections."

Revising the Definition to specifically state that proceeds from the sale of collections may be used for both acquisitions and direct care would bring FASB's Standard back into alignment with current, long-standing AAM standards and best practices and with expectations common in the museum field. Moreover, inclusion of direct care is consistent with ASC 958's intent and overall purpose because it promotes FASB's goal of ensuring collections are protected, unencumbered, preserved, and cared for in furtherance of public service, encourages reinvestment in and maintenance of existing collections as an alternative and compliment to collections growth, and preserves FASB's prohibition on using noncapitalized collections for financial gain.

On June 26, 2018, the Financial Accounting Standards Board (FASB) issued a proposed update to its definition of collections based on the change suggested in this paper: allowing entities that do not capitalize their collections to use deaccession proceeds for both direct care and acquisitions. The paper was presented to the FASB Not-for-Profit Advisory Committee (NAC) in March 2016 by Jim Croft, former Field Museum CFO and current NAC member. Richard Cole, NAC Supervising Project Manager, provided technical expertise, consulted with museum professionals, and helped advance the project. A final decision is anticipated in late 2018.

8

Monetizing the Collection

The Intersection of Law, Ethics, and Trustee Prerogative

Mark S. Gold

There is no greater flashpoint—real or imagined—in the relationship between trustees and museum professionals than the monetizing of the collection, defined as the use of the proceeds of deaccessioning for purposes other than the collection and its care or, even worse, deaccessioning to raise money for operations or other institutional expenses.

Underlying the distrust and disaffection, frequently, is a lack of appreciation for the legal status of the ethical rule that proscribes monetization and a lack of appreciation for the duties and responsibilities that are vested in trustees as a matter of law.

Although the language of the rule differs slightly from association to association, it is a universally accepted ethical principle of museums and museum professionals that the proceeds of deaccessioning may be used only for acquisitions and direct care of the collection.

In the case of American Alliance of Museums, the ethical rule was a reaction to an initiative of Financial Accounting Standards Board to require the financial statements of museums to list their collections at fair market value. The enactment of the ethical rule was more about avoiding the capitalization of collections than it was about preserving collections. Regardless, it has become sacrosanct, and condemnation of violators is swift and unequivocal. While the professional museum associations have no legal authority, they seek to turn the offending institution (even if not an association member) into a pariah, often encouraging other museums to refrain from intermuseum loans with the offender.

With some very limited exceptions in a few states, and assuming there are no donor-imposed restrictions on any particular object, however, there are no laws or regulations on a federal or state level that prohibit the sale of objects from the collection nor restrict the use of the proceeds from those sales. There is nothing illegal about monetizing the collection.

If monetizing the collection were illegal, the Attorneys General would be enforcing the prohibition. In the United States, oversight of public charities (and the decisions of their boards) is vested exclusively in the office of the Attorney General of the state having jurisdiction over the institution. In performing that function, they are considered to act as guardian of the public's interest. The very rare exception occurs in those situations in which someone has such an intimate relationship to the specific object at issue (the donor of a recently accessioned painting, for example) that the courts might allow that person to participate in the process. Generally, though, it is only the Attorney General who has standing to challenge museums on their disposition-related decisions.

That oversight is limited to ensuring that the board, in taking the action at issue, has met its fiduciary duties and obligations to the institution and has complied with any applicable donor restrictions. It is not a matter of substituting the judgment of the Attorney General for the judgment of the board in the good faith exercise of its decision-making power.

If one examines the cases of monetization, a common thread is the very limited extent, if at all, to which Attorneys General have entered the fray to oppose the transaction. Indeed, in the massive deaccessioning for operations by New-York Historical Society in 1994–95, the Attorney General of New York helped structure the transaction. In the recent case of Fisk University, the Attorney General of Tennessee was a very active participant but the dispute centered on an interpretation of a donative document and not on whether Fisk University otherwise had the legal authority to sell an interest in the collection to support the operations of the university. In Virginia, there was no question that Randolph College had the legal right to sell paintings from its Maier Museum of Art and, accordingly, the Attorney General of Virginia did not get involved. Had the dispute over the Rose Art Museum at Brandeis University not been settled, the involvement of the Attorney General of Massachusetts would ultimately have been limited to ascertaining if any of the objects to be sold were subject to donor restrictions.

Unquestionably, professional associations have authority to create a system of rules for their members and impose sanctions on those that violate them. Although the associations, admirably, do not seek to confuse their members into believing that the rules have the force of law, one would be hard pressed to find any of the associations making the distinction. The mistaken perception as to the status of the rule does nothing to help museum professionals think about the issue of monetization and respond thoughtfully when it takes place.

The unwillingness of the museum community to recognize the legal right of museums to monetize their collections lies not just in the misconception that the ethical rule has somehow acquired the status of law but, more importantly, is encumbered by a failure to appreciate the legal obligation and prerogatives of the governing boards of museums—the trustees.

The principles are stunningly simple and logical. There are two duties of trustees that are relevant to this discussion—the duty of due care and the duty of obedience. Almost every articulation of the duty of due care shares the following language or concept:

> A director . . . shall perform his or her duties as such in good faith and in a manner he or she reasonably believes to be in the best interests of the corporation, and with such care as an ordinarily prudent person in a like position would use under similar circumstances.[1]

Marie C. Malaro and Ildiko Pogány DeAngelis describe the duty of due care as follows:

> At the very least, the board should be under obligation to institute policies reasonably designed to further the mission of the organization and should also be able to demonstrate good-faith efforts to monitor such policy.[2]

Malaro and DeAngelis describe the duty of obedience as "the obligation to focus on the specific mission of the organization" and continue with the following elaboration:

> Also, although a museum board has discretion in deciding how its mission is to be accomplished, careful adherence to the duty of obedience means selecting goals carefully. The question should not be merely, "Is this goal relevant to our mission?" The harder question needs to be asked: "Is this a wise goal in light of our anticipated resources?"[3]

Both in theory and in practice, it is all about mission and the legal obligation of the trustees to deploy institutional resources to support the mission.

For most freestanding museums, the mission goes far beyond possession and care of a collection. The museum community is justifiably proud of the evolution of museums into sites for education and community dialogue. A museum without programming is little more than the proverbial cabinet of curiosities. The mission statements of most museums are expansive articulations of the several benefits that the institution provides to its defined community.

When the museum is part of a parent organization, the collection is of even less prominence. The typical college or university will cast its mission in terms of education and, in some cases, research. One is not likely to find a college or university that includes the collection, preservation, exhibition, and interpretation of objects in its mission statement.

Although there may be a predilection on the part of a college or university to maintain a museum and its objects for the prestige it can bring to the institution, the only basis on which any academic museum will fit into the mission of a college or university is as part of the educational process.

That educational mission is the seminal justification for college and university trustees thinking about the museum and its collections differently than if they were museum trustees. The academic museum is just one component of an array of resources and strategies available to meet the mission of the organization, which is broadly educational and not limited to the care, preservation, and interpretation of the collection owned by the museum on campus.

Similar issues pertain to other parent organizations such as foundations, municipalities, and other governmental entities.

Regardless of whether a museum is freestanding or part of a parent organization, when there are insufficient resources to support its mission, a prudent board of trustees will, in addition to seeking other sources of revenue and reductions in expenses, look to programs that can be eliminated and, perhaps, assets that can be monetized—all within the context of fulfilling its mission.

When the Randolph College community was informed that the trustees were considering a monetization of the collection of its Maier Museum of Art, the interim president clearly articulated the legal obligation of the trustees, as follows:

> The art is, of course, an issue of great concern. By many valuations, the art collection is more valuable that the College's endowment. In carrying out their fiduciary duty, trustees must determine that the College is deploying all the assets available to it in a fashion that will best enable the College to fulfill its mission of educating students in the liberal arts and sciences.[4]

The tension between law, the ethical rule, and trustee prerogatives has real-life implications. The Berkshire Museum in Pittsfield, Massachusetts, is an excellent example.

The Berkshire Museum hosts around 85,000 visitors per year with an array of exhibitions and programs. It boasts a natural science collection, objects from ancient civilizations, and a collection of American art. Few students leave the public schools of Berkshire County without experiencing at least one field trip to the Berkshire Museum.

In 2008, the museum deaccessioned three Russian paintings that had no relevance to the collection and had never been exhibited in more than fifty years of ownership. The museum netted about $7 million in proceeds at public auction—a significant event in the life of an institution with a $2 million operating budget. The proceeds were placed in an account restricted to acquisitions and the direct care of the collection, as the rule requires.

Although the Berkshire Museum is lean, efficient, and well managed, staff reductions to meet budget shortfalls could impair the museum's ability to be the educational and cultural resource so valued by the community. The collection, on the other hand, is well cared for, and there is no interest in expanding it in a new direction.

The mission of the Berkshire Museum is to "bring people together for experiences that spark creativity and innovative thinking by making inspiring education connections among art, history, and natural science." Although the museum possesses a collection of over 30,000 objects, the word "collection" is not even mentioned in its mission statement.

Since the proceeds are otherwise unrestricted as to use, if the trustees were to apply those proceeds to fund operating or capital expenses for the museum, all in support of its articulated mission, they would unquestionably be within their legal right to do so. Indeed, one might speculate that at some point, if conditions became dire, they would be violating their fiduciary duties to the institution by declining to do so.

Conditions did, in fact, become dire. Dealing with an estimated six to eight years of remaining financial viability with declining demographics of its communities and strong competition for a limited philanthropic base, the Board of Trustees made some strategic decisions. A shift in the museum's strategic plan to reinvent the museum to more aptly serve its community, and to create an endowment that would ensure the financial sustainability of the museum, included the proposed deaccession of artwork, including two works by artist Norman Rockwell. The proposal sparked much controversy and discussion in the museum world and in the museum's immediate community. There is no stronger case for the use of the proceeds of deaccessioning than when the survival of the museum hangs in the balance.

On March 26, 2014, the Delaware Art Museum announced that it would deaccession and sell four works of art from its collection of 12,500 objects. The museum's stated goal was to raise $30 million to pay off the bond debt of $19.8 million incurred in connection with renovation and expansion of its Kentmere Parkway building and to replenish the endowment to secure the financial future of the museum.

The following statement issued by Elva Ferrari-Graham, President of the Board of Trustees, is an articulate expression of how thoughtful governing boards will weigh priorities and deploy resources:

> This decision was made with heavy hearts, but clear minds. While the Trustees fully understand and respect museum best practices, we couldn't bear voting to

close our beloved Delaware Art Museum—a local treasure with a century-long legacy of uniting our community and cultivating a deep connection to art. This decision today will help us achieve financial stability and allow us to channel all of our collective energy back into our tradition of being a cherished community resource. Our unique collections provide educational opportunities, access to art for all ages and the chance to experience learning and creativity. In addition, the Museum fosters innovation, drives economic development and tourism and adds to the quality of life in our region. The Trustees and staff will work tirelessly in 2014 to support our new educational initiatives, our thriving Studio Art program, our new Membership program and the exciting exhibition schedule.[5]

Mike Miller, Chief Executive Officer of the Delaware Art Museum, could not have summarized the issue more precisely:

> After detailed analysis, heavy scrutiny and the exhaustion of every reasonable alternative to relieve our bond debt, the Trustees had two agonizing choices in front of them—to either sell works of art, or to close our doors. While today's decision is certainly hard to bear, the closure of this 100-year-old museum would be, by comparison, unbearable.[6]

The Berkshire Museum and the Delaware Art Museum are situated at the intersection of law, ethics, and trustee prerogative. They are not alone.

The ethical rule is all about collections to the exclusion of all else. A thoughtful and informed trustee will put the collection into the context of the broader institutional mission. The trustee will recognize that the rule does not rise to the level of law and that the trustee's legal obligation is to deal with the collection as one of several resources to fulfill the mission of the museum and, indeed, ensure the survival of the museum. In being so transparent about their decision and in articulating their rationale so clearly, the trustees of the Delaware Art Museum have contributed significantly to highlighting how this can and should operate in the real world.

A failure by museum professionals to understand the legal obligations and prerogatives of trustees, and their persistent opposition to the use of the proceeds of deaccessioning to support the mission of the museum, risks rendering them irrelevant in the important discussion on the deployment of limited institutional resources.

9

Flying under the Radar

What Does Direct Care of the Collection Really Mean?

Ashley Downing

INTRODUCTION

This essay examines some of the rudimentary problems that exist when museums choose to sell items that have been deaccessioned from their permanent collection. It presents an analytical review of more than one hundred current museum professionals regarding the definition of "direct care" of objects, how this has influenced the decision to sell artifacts, and how proceeds were spent. By exploring the mindset of current professionals from a myriad of museums across the country, this analysis provides an understanding of the trying effects of deaccessioning, and the logic behind one of the most important yet misunderstood procedures in the museum world.

For the past twenty-five years, the absence of a definition for direct care of objects has led many museums to interpret the meaning of the phrase and its inherent responsibilities differently. Even with strong guidance from the American Alliance of Museums (AAM) and other governing organizations, the ethical boundaries have been blurred as museums across the country struggle to understand the parameters of direct care.

DIRECT CARE

Over one hundred museum professionals throughout the United States were asked to answer questions related to "direct care" and deaccessioning activities that have occurred at their institutions within the past ten years. Almost half of the respondents came from small institutions (classified as a budget of under \$250,000). The remaining individuals provided an almost equal mix of medium to large institutions.

Fifty percent of those that participated came from an institution with a paid staff ranging from one to five individuals (with part-time staff counting as half a person). Only 15 percent of those surveyed work at an organization with over fifty paid individuals.

The survey was broken down into three parts: the first focused on the institution, the second questioned deaccession activity, and the final section specially asked about the American Alliance of Museums' phrase "direct object care."

First appearing in the AAM's Code of Ethics in 1993, "direct care" has been without a definition for almost twenty-five years. In 1993, when the code was put into place, it only permitted the proceeds from the deaccessioning and disposition of collection objects to be used for "acquisition or direct care of collections," a phrase left open to interpretation. Any other use of the proceeds would violate ethical standards and could result in sanctions and/or a loss of AAM accreditation.[1]

The definition was expected to evolve through practice in the field, but no clear definition has emerged over the past two decades. Without clarification or parameters, the interpretation of "direct care" has been left to interpretation and applied inconsistently within the field.

The AAM recently released a multidisciplinary template to assist with interpreting the ambiguous term. In 2016, *Direct Care of Collections: Ethics, Guidelines and Recommendations*, a white paper that defines direct care as "invests in the existing collections by enhancing their life, usefulness or quality and thereby ensuring they will continue to benefit the public," and an accompanying matrix were released by AAM. The matrix provides a guiding principle and criteria for decision-making, without providing a definitive yes/no list, thus allowing for differences within the museum field where one standard may not be appropriate for a myriad of organizations.[2]

The survey probed to see whether museum professionals thought the new definition of "direct object care" was clear. Knowing the difficulty in trying to gauge a response about a term that has been vague for over twenty-five years, respondents were allowed to comment and expand on their position of the term, its definition, and even its uses within their own organization.

While using the AAM's new definition, over half of those surveyed indicated that the definition was clear enough for their institution. Forty-eight percent felt that the definition was not clear or that there was still a lot of gray area around its interpretation. A few of the respondents stated that they had never heard the phrase or the definition prior to the survey.

The definition of "direct care" is relatively fresh within the museum field, having only been in place a short time. With almost half of the professionals still uncertain about the phrase, it indicates that the definition is still too new to be fully comprehended and applied or that it may still be too obscure of a term.

One survey response concluded that "[direct care is] somewhat vague with potential for multiple interpretations. However, having a field-wide standard (AAM White Paper) is helpful in advocating for ethical collections care practices."

THE PROCESS

When to Deaccession

Deaccessioning upsets some of the long-standing traditions in the museum field with regard to providing good stewardship. In Carol Neve's book, Patricia Ainslie argues "deaccessioning is about making difficult but realistic decisions in the interest of the museum and its community. Stewardship means being entrusted with the management of another's property and preserving that inheritance. It does not mean keeping everything in a collection for all time."[3]

Based on Ainslie's argument, good stewards realize that their role is to safeguard the collection, sometimes from itself. Although there aren't clear statistics for American museums, in European institutions, which can be assumed to be similar, museum collections grow at a 1 to 2 percent average per year; storage space, dedicated collection staff, and conservation needs do not reflect a balanced growth.[4] Accepting too many items into the collection without the space or staff leads to mismanagement and overcrowding. With an average cost of $50 per year to preserve an item, the financial pinch can be felt by museums across the country.[5] Museums must evaluate the cost of investing in each item within their care; decide if the collections support the museum's mission or are becoming a burden, draining the museum's resources; and determine if action is needed to hone the collection.

Deaccessioning can be seen as a natural next step within the museum field. Over 80 percent of survey respondents indicated that they either participated in deaccession activities in the past ten years or had plans in place to implement them in the near future. This general practice implies that deaccessioning is a common activity that occurs throughout the country and at museums of all sizes.

The number of objects removed from the collection varied between surveyed institutions.

From the individual museums that deaccessioned, almost half removed between one and fifty artifacts from the collection. Another 10 percent

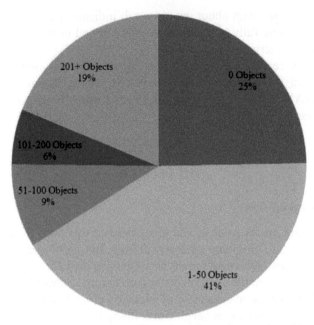

Figure 9.1. How Many objects have been deaccessioned in the last ten years?

responded that over two hundred artifacts have been removed in the past ten years. The remaining 15 percent that deaccessioned fell within the middle of these two figures. However, the survey did not question the reason for deaccessioning objects. Further, the survey does not indicate the size of the permanent collection or the available storage space and if storage informed the decision to deaccession.

How to Deaccession

There are multiple categories of deaccession, including destruction of the object, loss, transfer to educational collections, or for use as material for conservators. However, the most common type of deaccession is when an object is completely removed from the museum's collection in a variety of ways.

Many of the organizations that were surveyed varied in terms of the final step in the deaccession process, how the objects were dispersed. Many participating museums utilized at least two different types of deaccession activity. Over 60 percent transferred or donated artifacts to another nonprofit organization. Twenty-five percent returned the items to the donor or the donor's family. A few objects were transferred within the organization to an educa-

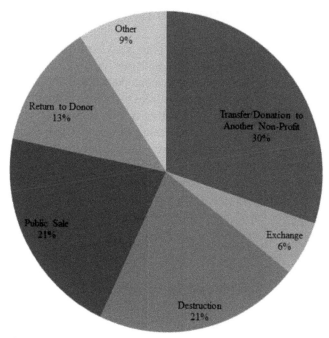

Figure 9.2. After deaccessioning where did the objects go?

tion or reproduction collection. Almost half of the museums represented in the survey either destroyed the objects or sold them at public auction. Only a few museums elected to sell the objects through a private sale.

The deaccession and disposal process is labor intensive and time consuming. While many museums grapple with the financial pressure of today's environment, organizations struggle to afford the process of deaccessioning. Those with qualified staff may not have time to dedicate to the labor-intensive process, and those that require outside expertise may not have the available funds to pay a consultant.

The final step in the process involves finding a long-term placement for deaccessioned artifacts. Survey respondents noted that some items that were deaccessioned still remained on site, pending transfer to other institutions. It was not clear if another institution had accepted the objects and objects were stored awaiting transfer or if the organization was still searching for a permanent placement.

Storing the objects in limbo requires additional space, ideally away from the permanent collection. Because many museums are bursting at the seams, using additional square footage to house deaccessioned objects for an indeterminate amount of time can pose a challenge.

POLICY AND PLAYERS

A main component in the deaccession plan is laying a strong foundation by articulating protocol in a museum's collections policy. AAM recommends that the museum's collections management plan detail the deaccessioning process and the criteria for the proceeds from the sale. Listing the members of the professional staff and governing authority who should be involved in the decision-making process is a key component.[6] Outlining details for the deaccession process in the collection policy allows alignment of both board and staff.

Respondents noted that there was an almost equal split between staff and board members making the decision to deaccession. A little over half of those surveyed either had or created a deaccession committee. The survey did not ask whether staff or board members made the ultimate decision of what items were to be deaccessioned.

SELLING MUSEUM ARTIFACTS

The Ethics of Deaccessioning

The AAM policy on the ethics of deaccessioning artifacts and the use of the proceeds from the sale states that the funds may be used for the purchase of new artifacts or for the direct care of objects. Participants thought that an acceptable use of proceeds included restoration of artifacts (most acceptable) followed by the purchase of new artifacts and/or archival materials. One respondent noted, "It would be clearer if actual guidelines were issued about acceptable and unacceptable activities, particularly for non-professionally trained staff." Many who participated in the survey shared this thought.

Because the survey did not ask if deaccession had occurred recently, it is hard to know if the AAM's definition of direct care and its accompanying matrix were consulted. Therefore, it is impossible to know if the white paper helped staff and boards to make informed decisions.

Unethical Deaccessioning

There are very clear lines as to what activities constitute unethical behavior for museums considering object deaccession. All guidelines state that revenue generated from deaccessioned material cannot be used for general operating or capital costs, including utilities, facilities maintenance, administration, and new construction.[7] A total of 35 percent of participants disagreed with the AAM's ethical guidelines and were in favor of several activities

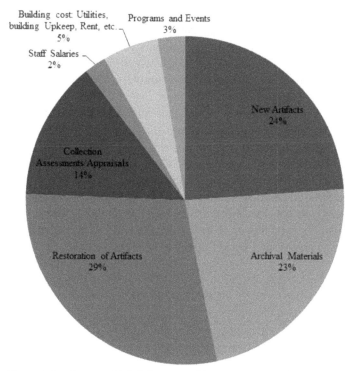

Figure 9.3. Do you think it is acceptable to use money from sale of museum artifacts for the following?

that AAM determined an unethical use of deaccessioned funds. Respondents did not indicate if they used deaccession funds for any unethical activities as defined by AAM.

During the recent recession, museums across the country considered selling objects for operating expenses, while several museums made the news when their objective to deaccession to raise operating funds was revealed. In times of financial hardship, museum boards must make difficult decisions regarding the future of their institutions. Thought it is not illegal, selling items for operating expenses goes against the museum's fundamental responsibilities and violates the museum's core value. As organizations continue to view collections as liquid assets, they may depend on the collection to save the museum and stop researching alternative means of bolstering revenue.

Of those surveyed, 17 percent elected not to answer the question targeting reasons for deaccessioning at their institution. Of those that answered, only 5 percent of survey participants stated that their objective in selling the items was financially motivated. The survey did not question if there was any backlash from their communities or if the sale of objects did in fact help ensure fiscal stability at the organizations.

The remaining 95 percent of participants that answered said that deaccessioning was not for financial reasons, which indicates that other factors influenced the decision process. It is unknown if these reasons fall within AAM's ethical parameters.

The AAM policy names activities that cannot be funded in this manner, including staff salaries or maintenance costs. According to participants in this survey, at least one quarter of them found it acceptable to use deaccessioning funds for these activities. As one respondent stated, "I think it should include staff salaries. Staff cares for collections directly. We have so few resources available for staff salaries and this one seems arbitrary. If you have to deaccession and you have to sell, put the money where you need it to keep the doors open." In fact, this opinion is common and has been put into practice by museums across the United States.

CONCLUSION

AAM's direct care policy has come under scrutiny across the museum field since its inception over twenty-five years ago. Museum professionals have grappled with the gray area around use of funds from the sale of deaccessioned artifacts. As organizations across the country have applied the term to their own institutions, many have crossed ethical boundaries and faced backlash from communities and museum organizations.

By representing professionals across the country, this survey examined some of the common misconceptions about deaccessioning. Most museum professionals have participated, in some form, in deaccessioning activities at their institutions. A majority of museum professionals surveyed indicated that their organization has used deaccession funds in an ethical manner. Some stated that revenue had been applied to activities that are considered unethical by most museum governing bodies.

As a way of creating a more streamlined and cohesive understanding across the entire field, the AAM created a matrix to help organizations understand the challenges of deaccessioning and use of funds. AAM also created a definition for direct care intended to reduce ambiguity and allow for professional standards on deaccessioning to be implemented in museums across the country. Time will tell if the definition and matrix prove useful to the museum community and if changes will be needed that make the process of deaccessioning more easily understood and consistent across the entire field.

IV

CASE STUDIES

VI

10

Building a Legacy for the Liberal Arts
Deaccessioning the Newell Bequest, Wheaton College

Leah Niederstadt

INTRODUCTION

In October 1966, Wheaton College received notice of a bequest from the estate of Adra Marshall Newell (1885–1966). Although works of art had been on campus since Wheaton Female Seminary was founded in 1834, when news of what came to be known as the Newell Bequest arrived, the college lacked a gifts-in-kind policy and did not think of itself as possessing an art collection of any significant pedagogical or financial value. Not surprisingly, therefore, faculty, staff, and administrators struggled to process both the gift and its implications. Administrators and staff saw the gift as a potential boon to the then current capital campaign, but faculty in the Art/Art History[1] and Classics Departments fought strongly against efforts to sell the Newell Bequest only to benefit the college's operating budget.

Advised by the Art Visiting Committee, Wheaton eventually decided to deaccession most of the ancient glass from the Newell Bequest, and in December 1978, several hundred pieces of ancient glass from Newell's collection were auctioned off at Sotheby Parke-Bernet in New York City.[2] The proceeds from the sale were used to establish the Newell Bequest Fund, an endowment for the acquisition and care of the objects. Since 1981, when a *Greek Black-Figure Attic Amphora*[3] was acquired, the Fund has been used to purchase twenty-three objects. Along with the items kept from the Newell Bequest, students in dozens of courses and numerous disciplines have used these objects. In addition to this legacy, the Newell Bequest provided the impetus to form the Wheaton College Permanent Collection in the mid-1970s.

Today, Newell's gift serves as an example of an effective deaccessioning, one that helped build an extraordinary teaching collection for generations of students. It also adhered to what is now considered the ethical rule[4] for deaccessioning, enshrined in the Code of Ethics for the American Alliance of Museums (AAM),[5] as the proceeds were restricted to acquisitions and direct collections care.

THE NEWELLS

Comprising more than a thousand Greco-Roman and Egyptian antiquities, including alabaster and glass vessels, bronze figurines, textiles, ceramics, and coins, Adra Marshall Newell's collection was primarily compiled during her marriage to Edward Theodore Newell (1886–1941), an internationally renowned numismatist, who served as President of the American Numismatic Society (ANS) from 1916 to 1941. Yet, until 2013 when research on Adra began in earnest, little was known about her or her reasons for donating to the college.[6] Unfortunately, much of Adra's personal history remains a mystery, primarily due to a decision taken by George Miles, who was Executive Director and Chief Curator of the ANS at the time of Adra's death. As her husband's primary heir and executor, Adra inherited Edward Newell's papers, which included his half of their personal correspondence, as well as his correspondence with other individuals, and various documents and works-in-progress. When Adra died, Miles "selected all of [Edward] Newell's notebooks, manuscripts . . . some correspondence, and anything else of scholarly interest."[7] Unfortunately, he did not choose to retain the bulk of Edward's correspondence files, and they were presumably destroyed, as were the majority of Adra's papers.[8] This may also explain why the only image of Adra known to exist was a 1911 bronze medal cast by Theodore Spicer-Simson, featuring her in profile.[9] It is not clear why Adra designated Wheaton as a beneficiary of her estate. Furthermore, contrary to numerous descriptions of Adra as "just a wife" focused on preserving her husband's legacy, Adra was a collector, much like her famous husband.[10] She, too, had a legacy to leave.

Adra Nelson Marshall was born in Jersey City, New Jersey, on May 31, 1885, to Grace Nelson Marshall (1852–1927) and William Armstrong Marshall (1850–1887). She had two older sisters, both of whom predeceased her: Grace Nelson Marshall (1879–1881), who was named after her mother, and Edythe Nelson Marshall (1883–1958).[11] Adra's mother was one of eleven children born to Samuel Cogswell Nelson (1819–1883) and Eliza Jane Watson (1820–1915), both of whom were born in New York. Watson's parents immigrated to the United States from Ireland,[12] but the Nelson family had long roots in the New York region, extending back to both the American Revolution[13] and the founding of New Netherland.[14] According to US Census records, Samuel Nelson was a "ship's chandler," a merchant who sold supplies to the shipping industry.[15] He worked his way up in the business, eventually owning the firm Martin and Nelson.[16] In 1860, Nelson reported owning $15,000 in real estate[17]; but by 1870, when he identified as a "retired merchant," he reported $400,000 in real estate and $15,000 in other assets, a personal wealth equivalent to more than $10 million today.[18] In 1880, three years before his death, Adra's maternal grandfather served as Comptroller of Jersey City,[19] a position indicative of the family's political and economic status.

Samuel and Eliza Nelson's daughter, Grace, was raised in New York City until the age of fifteen, when the family moved to Jersey City.[20] There, Grace met Adra's father, William, about whom relatively little is known. His parents, David and Mehitable, were both born in Ireland, circa 1820, and eventually immigrated to New York, where William and his younger sister, Mary, were born.[21] By 1870, the family had settled in Bergen, New Jersey, which had recently been annexed into Jersey City, and William was working as a "traveling clerk."[22] He married Grace Nelson on April 29, 1878.[23] The couple lived in Jersey City, New Jersey, where William worked as a "mayors [*sic*] clerk."[24] He died in 1887.

After her husband's untimely death, Grace Nelson Marshall and her daughters lived with her mother, Eliza, primarily in Jersey City.[25] Little is known about Adra's childhood, including where and how she and her sister Edythe were educated. Their aunt, Lucy F. Nelson (1850–1934), with whom they also lived after their father's death, was a music teacher by profession[26] and President of the Womans [*sic*] Choral Society,[27] so music education was presumably part of their schooling. At some point during her childhood or as a young woman, Adra met Edward Newell, to whom she became engaged on March 5, 1909. The *New York Times* announcement of their engagement identified the couple as "childhood sweethearts."[28] Adra's 1923 passport application indicated that they had known each other for twenty years, placing a late date for their meeting to 1903, when they were both in their late teens.[29] No direct connection between the families has yet been identified; however, the young couple likely met at a social function in New York City or in New Jersey. Edward's mother, Frances Cecelia (née Bain) Newell (1849–1907), moved to the region from Kenosha, Wisconsin, when her husband died in 1901. She resided in New York City[30] "with the exception of summers, which she spent at the family's estate in Bernardsville, NJ,"[31] where she died in 1907.

Edward Theodore Newell was born on January 15, 1886, in Kenosha, Wisconsin, to Frederick Seth Newell (1845–1901) and Frances Newell. The couple already had a daughter, Marjorie Moyca Newell (1881–1968). Frederick Newell helped run the Bain Wagon Company, which was owned by his wife's family. "By the early 20th century it had grown into the world's largest manufacturer of wagons. . . . [and] was able to proclaim justifiably that it produced 'the best wagon in the world,'"[32] making Frances Newell an extraordinarily wealthy woman. Edward was interested in coins and antiquities from a young age, a passion encouraged by his parents and made possible by the family's economic status, which, as their passport applications attest, allowed them to visit Europe several times when their children were young.[33] His collecting practices appear to have begun early, as an archival photograph of him as a child is inscribed on the back, "Edward started his coin collection in N. Africa at this stage in his career."[34] In addition to the education provided by overseas travel Edward was taught by private tutors who traveled with the family,[35] and he briefly attended the Harvard School in Chicago.[36] In 1903, two years after his father's death, he entered Yale University, his father's alma mater. Frances Newell's death in 1907, while he was still an undergraduate, left Edward an extremely wealthy young man. At the time of his engagement, Edward's personal fortune was estimated at $3 million.[37] He graduated from Yale in 1907 with a bachelor of arts, having focused his studies on history and ancient languages,[38] and returned home to Kenosha, Wisconsin, for a year, ostensibly to visit the family business.[39] Choosing to leave the management of the family business in the hands of others and pursue his interests in archaeology and numismatics, Edward left Wisconsin to travel for several months in North Africa and Europe before returning to Yale in 1908 to earn his master of arts in archaeology and Oriental languages.[40]

Edward's relationship with the ANS began during his time at Yale. In 1905, right around his nineteenth birthday, he became a member of the Society and began visiting almost weekly, quickly assuming a role as assistant to its curator.[41] In 1910, he was elected to the Society's governing Council.[42] In 1916, he was named President, a position he held until his death on February 18, 1941, at the age of fifty-five. During his lifetime, Edward was considered to be the world's leading expert on the coinage of Alexander the Great and his successors, although "his scholarly and collecting interest were catholic, embracing the entire ancient world."[43] He was a prolific author, publishing dozens of monographs and articles during his lifetime and leaving numerous unpublished manuscripts.[44] His coin collection (of more than 87,000 coins) was considered to be the largest collection of Greek coins held in private hands.[45] He also collected Babylonian tablets and seals, donating 2,500 tables to Yale during his lifetime[46] and a "collection of Sumerian, Babylonian and similar seals,"[47] which one expert described as "one of the largest and finest groups of such objects in the world."[48] In his estate, Newell bequeathed the bulk of his coin collection to the ANS, and it remains the largest single donation ever given to the Society.[49]

In his last will and testament, Edward detailed bequests to the ANS, Yale University, and various friends and family, including his wife of nearly thirty-two years, Adra. Article VI of his will specified that Adra be allowed to choose "such articles from my collection of seal cylinders, engraved stones, coins, Numismatic books, furnitures, rugs, and other antiquities, now contained in the building of the ANS . . . provided that her selection of coins shall be limited to not more than 1,000 in number."[50] Per Article VI, any items not chosen by Adra would be bequeathed to the ANS, placing Edward's widow and the Society in direct competition for items from his estate. This meant that Adra arguably had to rely on her own expertise in selecting objects from her husband's collections, further indication of the knowledge she possessed of ancient art and of coins, in particular. The list of items she selected from Edward's estate is fifty-seven pages long and does not include the tangible property and funds otherwise bequeathed to her directly or as part of the residuary estate.[51] In addition to claiming Edward's stamp collection, Adra selected thousands of objects, ranging from Persian miniatures to an eighteenth-century Hepplewhite armchair, as well as the aforementioned 1,000 coins and Edward's entire collections "of approximately 150 Greek, Roman, and Egyptian statuettes, amulets, Ushebti, fibula implements and miscellaneous small articles and ornaments in bronze, faience, terra cotta, etc." and "of approximately 650 Babylonian and Hittite and Sumerian and Tassamian and other cylinders, seals and tablets of hematite, jasper, lapis, carnelian, aget and other hard stones, each with incised helioglyphic and cuneiform inscription."[52] She was also named executrix of her husband's estate, further solidifying her relationship with the ANS and its staff. Edward's decision to allow his widow such control over his estate is not surprising, given the close partnership the couple developed over the course of their thirty-two-year marriage. As ANS archivist David Hill wrote,

> Edward must have delighted to have in Adra, his childhood sweetheart, a lifetime companion with whom he could share his love of all kinds of venerable old objects. Attentive to their mutual interests, he made certain, for example, that when [ANS Secretary Sydney P.] Noe sent the latest issue of *Art and Archaeology* to him in Washington, he also sent one to his wife at the Halesite, Long Island home.[53]

Such requests, along with Edward's estate planning, are also indicative of the respect he had for Adra as a fellow collector and collaborator.

Adra became a member of the ANS in 1910, a patron in 1925, and a benefactor in 1952.[54] In the quarter-century between Edward's death and her own, Adra "became a much more active presence [at the ANS], serving at times as

[Edward's] surrogate, and ruffling more than a few feathers along the way, to the point where her actions would come to be seen as a threat to the harmonious governance of the society."[55] Among other complaints, she expressed concern about ANS Secretary Noe's handling of her personal mail and about access to and the lack of drinking water at the Society's Audubon Terrace headquarters.[56] She also fought unsuccessfully against plans to renovate the Western Hall at Audubon Terrace, taking her complaints to the Society's then President Louis West.[57] Her often-contentious relationship with ANS administrators and staff was arguably tolerated out of respect for her husband and his legacy, as well as the Society's interest in retaining access to his research materials, which she controlled. Perhaps most importantly, however, the ANS wanted the coins Adra had been allowed to select from her husband's collection. Despite being seen as lacking expertise or connoisseurship, the one thousand coins Adra chose from Edward's collection were among the very best in his collection, including a number that were described by one scholar as "exceptional."[58] Although the exact nature of the negotiations between Edward's widow and ANS staff remains unclear, an agreement was quickly reached so that the coins never left the ANS head office, then at Audubon Terrace. Adra was named "Honorary Curator of the Newell Collection" and given a private room to which she had one of only two keys.[59] In this space, she housed the coins as well as her own collections, including "antique pottery and glassware,"[60] most of which was bequeathed to Wheaton. As Hill writes, she was also "made chair of the Society's Greek Coin Committee in 1948" and her "decision was final on all matters relating to her husband's unpublished works, since she in fact owned the notebooks and manuscripts."[61] Between 1941 and 1966, Adra remained actively involved in the ANS and in preserving her husband's legacy, generous with her time, money, and opinions. In his article on the Newells, Hill acknowledged, "We have Adra to thank for, among much else, saving and passing on Edward's research notes and notebooks, many of which are inscribed, 'Property of Mrs. Edward T. Newell.'"[62] Mrs. Newell collaborated with ANS staff to publish Edward's unfinished manuscripts and, in the end, bequeathed to the Society the one thousand coins she had chosen from his collection. She clearly saw herself as caretaker and steward of her husband's legacy, but what of her own?

THE BEQUEST

On July 13, 1953, Harry Hoffman of the law firm Guggenheim and Untermeyer wrote to Wheaton College[63] regarding a client who was considering a bequest to the college.[64] Describing her as "a lady interested in numismatics," Hoffman explained that she was "considering leaving a portion of one of her smaller collections, as well as certain Greek and Coptic embroideries or tapestries" should the college "have a Department into which these would fit, or in case you are interested in starting such a Department in a small way."[65] Three days later, then President Howard Meneely replied that the institution would be happy to accept a gift of coins and Greek and Coptic textiles and embroideries whenever the donor wished to make the gift.[66] We now know that the "lady client" to whom Hoffman referred was Adra Marshall Newell.

While Edward clearly began collecting as a child during his travels abroad, little is known about when and why Adra began collecting, although it appears to have been after their wedding. The couple spent their honeymoon in Europe,[67] and, occasionally accompanied by family members,[68] they traveled extensively throughout their marriage, with the exception of a period during World War I when Edward was stationed in Washington, DC. A review of their passports issued from 1914 through 1923 indicates that the Newells regularly traveled to Europe, the Middle East, and North Africa.[69] Their passport applications and other records indicate that they visited Austria, Denmark, Egypt, France, Germany, Great Britain, Greece, Italy, Palestine, Russia, Switzerland, Syria, and Turkey, often for months on end. Archaeological research was usually listed as the purpose of their travels, although Edward's passports sometimes include mention of "business for [the] Amer. Numismatic Society."[70] While the extent to which Adra participated in hands-on archaeological fieldwork remains unclear, she actively collected during her travels abroad and when home in the United States. Her will makes a clear distinction between her collections and those "bequeathed to me by my late husband"[71] and also indicates at least one dealer, Dikran Kelekian,[72] from whom she acquired objects.[73] Correspondence with Wheaton administrators in the 1960s also reveals Mrs. Newell acquired objects from John S. Khayat, an antiquities dealer based in New York City, who specialized in ancient glass. Khayat claimed that both Adra and Edward were his customers and that "almost one hundred per cent [of her collection] came from me."[74] While his claim was likely exaggerated, unless he was referring solely to Adra's collection of Greek and Roman glass, later correspondence indicated Khayat's knowledge of her collection, as he provided a detailed overview of it and offered to purchase "all the objects that you care to dispose of."[75] As shall be explored further below, Khayat was not the only individual to indicate an interest in acquiring objects from Adra's bequest to Wheaton.

At the time of Hoffman and Meneely's 1953 correspondence, what is now referred to as the Wheaton College Permanent Collection (hereafter, Collection) did not exist. Its origins stretch back to 1834 when Wheaton Female Seminary was founded and the Wheaton family gave landscapes and portraits to decorate the first campus buildings.[76] Among the collections that arrived at Wheaton during the nineteenth century are several dozen Japanese prints, plaster cast reproductions of ancient Greek and Roman sculpture, and study collections of bird skins, botanical specimens, and shells.[77] By the late nineteenth century, if not earlier, objects were used as pedagogical tools; they also served to enhance the aesthetic environment on campus and to remind community members of the Wheaton family's legacy.[78] Photographs from the period reveal artwork displayed in a variety of campus settings, including lecture halls, smaller classrooms, parlors, and the Principal's office. Documents now held in the Marion B. Gebbie Archives and Special Collections (hereafter, Gebbie Archives) reveal that the plaster busts and casts were used to inspire students in art making, help them master technique, and educate them about ancient art. Most objects were donated by faculty, students, or staff or acquired by founder Eliza Baylies Chapin Wheaton (1810–1905), who sometimes asked alumnae traveling in Europe to purchase artwork for the Seminary on her behalf.[79] In 1907, the Board of Trustees approved the first known expenditure of Seminary funds for the acquisition of artwork, and by the late 1930s, a collection of nineteenth-century paintings had been donated and an art rental collection had been established.[80] Throughout the nineteenth century and into the late twentieth century, art and ethnographic objects that arrived on campus were used as needed, for display, teaching, and research.

In the mid-1970s, Dr. Ann H. Murray, who taught modern and contemporary art and served as Gallery Director, was tasked with organizing several of the collections scattered around campus. In addition to items housed in the library, the Gebbie Archives, and the Art/Art History and the Classics Departments, objects were discovered in attics, basements, barns, and garages, as well as in offices, classrooms, and faculty and staff housing.[81] Today, the Collection holds approximately seven thousand objects ranging from Greco-Roman and Egyptian antiquities to twenty-first-century contemporary art.[82] Acquisitions occur primarily through gifts and bequests from alumni and their families or other friends of Wheaton, or through objects found as part of an ongoing inventory. The collection has four endowed acquisition funds and the Ann H. Murray Art Conservation Fund, which although not endowed receives annual donations from an alumni group known as the Friends of Art.[83] Housed in Watson Fine Arts, the Collection's mission is:

> to reinforce connections between the arts, humanities, sciences, and social sciences and among people and cultures across time and geography, and enhance the aesthetic environment at Wheaton. The collection provides students with practical experience in collections care and management and exhibition design and inspires their work as artists and scholars.[84]

Adra's bequest, which comprises the majority of the Collection's holdings from the ancient Mediterranean world, is the single largest gift of objects ever received by the college.

Despite the wealth of material held in the Collection, and the generosity of the alumni and other donors it represents, limited funding and staffing have negatively affected how all of Wheaton's campus collections have been documented and managed. It is, therefore, difficult to understand their origins and early use and to trace their provenance, especially as none of them have been fully inventoried. For example, since February 1967, when the Newell Bequest arrived on campus, numerous other antiquities have been attributed to it and at least eight different accession numbers have been assigned to objects in the bequest.[85] Adra's gift was not immediately and completely catalogued when it arrived on campus because the college had "never before faced such a mass of material."[86] To this day, we remain uncertain which of our antiquities came from Adra and which came from other sources, e.g., the Classics Department. An ongoing project aims at identifying objects in the Newell Bequest using a 1967 appraisal created for probate by Samuel Marx, Inc., an appraisal firm based in New York City.

Responsibility for determining how best to handle the Newell Bequest fell on the Art/Art History and the Classic Departments and on the Art Visiting Committee, an advisory board primarily comprised of alumni and outside experts with expertise in the art and museum fields. In October 1961, the Art Visiting Committee (AVC)[87] was created[88] to support the Art/Art History Department, which would move into the newly built Watson Fine Arts Center that December.[89] Soon thereafter, the Friends of Art (FoA) was also founded. Charged with raising funds and friends to support the activities of the department's faculty and students, the FoA remains in existence today. The AVC had a different mission, one focused on providing advice and support to the department's faculty and to the administration. Its goal was not focused on fundraising "but to serve as a moral booster."[90] The AVC's founding members included Dorothy Adlow, art critic for the *Christian Science Monitor*, and James S. Plaut, trustee and past director of Boston's Institute of Contemporary Art, as well as several alumnae, including Monawee Allen Richard, Class of 1934, who had worked for the Museum of Modern Art in New York City.[91] Agnes Mongan, who was "affiliated with [the] Fogg Museum [and was an] authority on prints and drawings," initially chaired the committee.[92]

Faculty and administrators often attended AVC meetings during which members were asked to advise on a range of topics. Among the early issues addressed by the AVC were how to improve teaching in large lecture courses, how best to make use of the new Watson Gallery, and how to develop an effective teaching collection. At their October 1964 meeting, members discussed "problems of how to acquire works of quality and how to handle gifts," with then Wheaton President William (Bill) C. H. Prentice responding that the college's Gift Committee "decides on the acceptance or rejection of gifts."[93] AVC

Chairman Mongan countered that "it would be desirable to have a committee of experts to pass on gifts of art."[94] This latter issue, in particular, remained a topic of discussion for many years. The minutes for the April 1969 meeting state that the Art/Art History Department and the AVC "should be able to screen gifts and to make recommendations to the gifts committee. . . . Yet the college must be free to reject worthless gifts, for example a fake Renoir, and to sell a real Renoir if it wished."[95]

In 1967, the AVC's focus shifted when news of the Newell Bequest arrived on campus, as the AVC was charged with determining how best to handle the gift. First mention of the bequest at a committee meeting occurred in the afternoon of October 12, 1967, when the "recent gift to the college, the Newell Bequest, was introduced, and Mrs. (Professor Dorris Taylor) Bishop of the Classics Department, who was most informed about it was asked to explain the extent and contents of the bequest."[96] The committee was asked to provide "guidelines with reference to the gift as a teaching collection."[97] After significant discussion, the committee's members

> agreed that it was impossible to make a decision without careful study of the objects, and allowing sufficient time for consultation with experts and to test their usefulness of objects in teaching. . . . A motion was made by Miss Mongan that the Newell Bequest be kept by Wheaton College *in toto* for at least five years and that it be made available for use in the classroom, for study and research to any member of the Faculty and to scholars in the area. Mr. Hirschland amended the motion to add that students be involved in the work of cataloguing, study, and research, connected with various categories of objects represented in the Collection.[98]

The amended motion passed unanimously[99]; and the AVC's two-page report[100] was forwarded to President Prentice from Agnes Mongan on October 25, 1967.[101] In his reply, Prentice thanked the committee members for their service and accepted their recommendations regarding the bequest,[102] giving administrators, faculty, and the committee time to think about and engage with the "mass of material" Adra had left to the institution.

Although the college gained time to determine how best to handle the Newell Bequest, the AVC's work was far from over, both in regard to the bequest and to other matters. As soon as members voted in that October 1967 meeting they "then turned to a more precise consideration of the role of a teaching collection."[103] For several years, likely driven by the opening of Watson Fine Arts, the Art/Art History Department had expressed desire for such a collection.[104] Given the number of objects that had already found their way on campus by the early 1960s, it seems clear that the college already owned a teaching collection, albeit one that was not recognized as such by administrators or faculty.[105] As one member commented, "To teach history of art without objects is like teaching chemistry without a laboratory."[106] In unanimous agreement that such a collection would be useful, "attention focussed [*sic*] on ways of acquiring objects through purchase or gifts. At the present high cost of works of art, an acquisition by means of purchase was deemed unrealistic."[107]

The Newell Bequest must have been, therefore, very appealing both to the AVC and the faculty, as it provided the college with an extensive teaching collection at relatively little cost. This is reflected in the committee's preliminary report to President Prentice, which demonstrates that its members were already considering how to house, display, and make use of objects in the Newell Bequest. For example, the report made it clear that "in accepting the bequest, the college in no way commits itself to a museum program" yet indicated that "there does exist adequate storage space for the objects in Watson [Fine Arts and] that a small controlled study area, where a changing group of objects would be readily available for study, could be set up in the art seminar room, or in some such area, with little expense."[108] It also addressed the collection's potential for use in teaching and in Wheaton's gallery and the negative publicity that could result from "selling a bequest that is widely known among scholars before its usefulness to the college can be tested."[109]

Yet, in recognition that Wheaton's administration may choose to dispose of the Newell Bequest, either in part or in its entirety, AVC members discussed early on how best to dispose of it, once its pedagogical and research potential had been assessed. Minutes from the October 12, 1967 meeting state, "If the Newell Bequest were sold, would the money go to the Classics and Art Departments? Some members thought it should, others disagreed. It was hoped, however, that it might be possible to exchange duplicates or less useful objects with other institutions."[110] This is reflected in the preliminary report, as the fifth of its eleven guiding "principles" states:

> After five years, if parts of the collection do not prove useful to the educational program of the college, efforts should be made to exchange objects with other institutions, which would make the collection more valuable to use. If this cannot be, expendable items should be given to a reputable auction house, such as Parke-Bernet, to be sold anonymously. Objects should not be sold through a dealer.[111]

Over the next five years, the AVC continued to discuss Adra's gift, but only briefly. They focused instead on other matters including the department's curriculum, conservation of the nineteenth-century painting collection, and support for the college gallery and the department's library.

Professor Doris Taylor Bishop, who chaired the Department of Classics in the late 1960s, had been tasked with reviewing the bequest at the ANS and organizing its shipment to campus. Given her role, she became Wheaton's expert on the Newell Bequest, at least until her death in 1969, when her husband, a fellow Classics faculty member, informally assumed the role. Professor J. David Bishop claimed to have found evidence that Adra Newell's estate may have been governed by an outdated will. The version of her will that went through probate was signed on August 10, 1953.[112] In a handwritten note, David Bishop wrote that Mrs. Newell had been in the process of updating her will, following the 1958 death of her sister Edythe, who was named as a major beneficiary in the 1953 will.[113] He does not, however, explicitly state the source of his evidence, beyond "Doris's files on the Newell Bequest"; and a review of his wife's faculty file in the college's Gebbie Archives did not contain additional information on this topic.

It is difficult to determine the extent of Adra Newell's estate. Copies of the will held by the American Numismatic Society and Yale University only contain the pages relevant to the gifts made to each institution and Wheaton's copy of the will has yet to be found, so it is difficult to determine the extent of Adra's estate. Yale's copy indicates that she left gifts of tangible property and/or cash to ten institutions and five individuals.[114] It is clear that the ANS received a cash gift of $15,000 and tangible property, most notably the one thousand coins Adra selected from Edward's estate. Yale University received a significant bequest that included twenty-five objects now in the Yale University Art Gallery: twelve Tanagra terracotta heads[115]; an ancient Greek gold and glass necklace[116]; a Roman marble relief (Head of Flamen by altar)[117]; a marble portrait head of a woman[118]; among other objects.[119] The Metropolitan Museum of Art (Met) received several small metal figures, including two Byzantine weights[120] and a bronze Iranian pendant,[121] and a standing stone Buddha,[122] while the New-York Historical Society was to receive "two items of antique clothing."[123] Various cousins, trusted friends, and household staff, as well as charities, including the Salvation Army and the American Schools of Oriental Research, received bequests of cash, artwork, and household furnishings.

In terms of the number of items of tangible property, Wheaton received the largest bequest. According to the appraisal made at the time of probate, the college received: approximately 520 coins; more than 1,000 books; approximately 365 glass items, including fragments; two dozen Coptic textile fragments; some 40 alabaster objects; various bronzes; and numerous pieces of Egyptian jewelry.[124] At the time of the bequest, the collection was appraised at $55,000 with the coins and glass receiving the highest values of $17,851 and $14,400, respectively.[125] While responsibility for and control of the bequest legally fell to the college's Board of Trustees, then President William C. H. Prentice looked to the AVC, the Art/Art History Department, and the Classics Department for advice and guidance. The AVC's role in preserving Adra's legacy cannot be understated, as various administrators and faculty argued that the bulk of the bequest should be sold and the proceeds used to cover general operating expenses, endow scholarships, or pay for departmental expenses, such as adjunct faculty. Once the decision had been made to deaccession objects, the debate continued, as both academic departments argued for control of Adra's collection and, more importantly, the endowed fund created from the sale of objects.

On October 28, 1972, the AVC met to decide on its final recommendations regarding the Newell Bequest. At the time, S. Lane Faison Jr., an art historian who then served as Director of the Williams College Museum of Art, led the committee.[126] Faison joined the AVC in 1965, although he does not appear to have regularly attended meetings until 1969. He was elected to serve as Chairman for the 1972–1973 academic year, a role he continued to hold until the 1979–1980 academic year,[127] when the committee was disbanded by then Wheaton President Alice F. (Tish) Emerson. Faison thus led the committee during the critical period in which the college's administration decided to move forward with deaccessioning objects from the Newell Bequest. During that October 28 meeting, AVC members who were advised by faculty from the Art/Art History and the Classics Departments, considered a list of eight options for dealing with the Newell Bequest. The list included recommendations to "1. keep everything and take no action 2. sell everything 3. sell a portion to be determined."[128] The other items on the list focused on how to use the proceeds from a sale, should one be recommended, which seemed inevitable given the inclusion of five options for spending the funds raised from a sale.

Several weeks prior to the October meeting, Faison wrote to Wheaton President Bill Prentice indicating that the committee was likely to recommend[129] what became the third option on the list, with a focus on selling Edward Newell's numismatic library, transferring or selling "the finest [pieces of glass to] important collections open to the public" and taking a similar approach to the coins.[130] Faison also reminded Prentice that Mrs. Newell's gift had been made before the college had a gifts-in-kind policy, which was not developed until 1969, and that this be taken into account when considering "the moral implications . . . in respect to the donor's wishes,"[131] particularly as they applied to the use of funds from any sale of bequest items. In his reply, Prentice stated that the college "has higher priorities [than acquiring a collection] and should therefore turn the gift into cash for such priority purposes."[132] He also compared the Newell Bequest to a gift of IBM stock, which the college "would unhesitatingly have sold."[133] At the AVC meeting later that month, Prentice reiterated his position but also recognized the complicated nature of the Newell Bequest.[134] After a lengthy discussion, the committee voted for the third and sixth options on the list, namely that a portion of the bequest be sold and that "the proceeds should divert to the Art and Classics Departments primarily for acquisitions of Graeco-Roman art" and for an endowment to maintain the collection.[135] In reporting the AVC's final recommendation to Prentice, Faison made clear that

> several persons loath to sell, or sell very much, were won over by the argument that disposition of Newell items could make possible such additions to the [Art/ Art History and Classics] Departments' teaching facilities. It was clear that this consideration was paramount in their decision; without it, they would not have supported what turned out to be the [AVC's] position.[136]

Faison's report also listed the categories of objects in the 1967 appraisal of the bequest and detailed the committee's suggestion for each one, including the recommendation that Adra's collections of alabaster and of Egyptian jewelry be sold.[137] (This suggestion does not appear to have ever been considered by the college.) The AVC Chairman recognized that "our recommendations are purely advisory. Still, we do want to advise to the best of our abilities"[138] and he highlighted the need to keep objects in the public domain if possible.[139] Finally, Faison emphasized Wheaton's moral commitment to honor what were perceived as Adra Newell's wishes, especially given the lack of a gifts-in-kind policy at the time of the bequest. "That moral commitment, we are persuaded, should preclude reversion of the proceeds of sales to the general funds of the College."[140]

While the Art Visiting Committee seemed to promote, from the beginning, what are now widely accepted best practices for deaccessioning (e.g., attempt transfer to or exchange with another public collection before moving to public auction as a last resort), the administration was not always in agreement, as Prentice's aforementioned comments make clear. Tension between college officers, faculty in the Art/Art History and the Classics Departments, and committee members is evidenced by minutes from a meeting held on October 14, 1969. They noted that administrators felt "that the [Art] Visiting Committee should meet for the purpose of discussion rather than decision making."[141] In fact, the decision to sell the ancient glass at a public auction only came about when other options fell through, including a 1974 attempt to sell some of the coins,[142] as the college regularly "receive[d] inquiries from potential buyers"[143] once news of the bequest had been made public. In addition, several attempts were made to sell most of the glass to private collectors. In June 1977, the Executive Committee of the Board of Trustees voted "to authorize the President to sell to Mr. Richard C. Reedy the collection of ancient glass bequeathed to Wheaton College by Adra M. Newell for a sum of $70,000 less than the appraised value of any pieces retained for teaching purposes."[144]

In hearing of the proposed sale to Reedy, Faison wrote, "Hooray for the Newell Sale. Whew!"[145] His response may seem surprising, given the AVC's goal of keeping objects from the Newell Bequest in the public domain.[146] At one point in the debate over what to do with the bequest, Faison had cited John Canaday, an art historian and art critic who wrote for the New York Times: "Even when sales from public collections (or those open to the public) are justified, they should remain in the public domain." He went on to explain that the AVC felt that "the College should retain a few pieces for study purposes and try to place the finest ones in important collections open to the public."[147] As a well-known collector of ancient glass and both a fellow of and donor to the Corning Museum of Glass, Reedy expressed his intention to keep Adra Newell's glass collection available to the public by donating "much of it" to the museum in his name.[148] Had it gone through, the sale would have had the effect of keeping the glass in the public domain and saving the college the hassle of organizing an auction. The proposed purchase price was also appealing, as administrators had long made clear their eagerness to raise as much money as possible from the sale of objects in the bequest. As President Prentice once wrote, "We must consider the respective value to Wheaton of the collection and of the cash that it would bring."[149] Raising funds from the sale of objects in the bequest clearly appealed to administrators, faculty, and staff, albeit for different reasons. By December 1977, the private sale of the glass had been cancelled, as Reedy was unable to follow through on the purchase;[150] and the college decided to move forward with a public auction, "unless . . . a private buyer [could be found] in the next few weeks."[151] Despite concerted efforts to arrange another private sale,[152] the college had to proceed with plans to auction most of the glass from Adra Newell's collection.

The objects donated by Mrs. Newell were eventually accessioned into the Collection, under the auspices of the Art/Art History Department. Management of the Newell Bequest Fund (hereafter, Fund) is shared by both the Art/Art History and the Classics Departments. The decision to divide governance of the Fund between the two departments was based on the incorrect belief that Adra had made such a large bequest to Wheaton College because of the relationship she and her husband had with Dr. Eunice Work, Professor of Classics from 1925 to 1955. The extent of their relationship remains somewhat unclear, due to the aforementioned destruction of the Newells' correspondence, which may have revealed if the couple and professor had a personal friendship in addition to their professional one. Professor Work (1894–1961) was a member of the ANS in the 1930s and 1940s and was among those who sent condolence cards to the ANS (and presumably Adra) at the time of Edward's death. Professor Work taught at Wheaton for three decades, and a review of her faculty file reveals that she conducted research at the ANS in the summers of 1931 and 1932.[153] Work also supervised Wheaton students on a project supporting the Society's files, which resulted in the ANS giving the College a group of twenty-eight coins.[154]

It is now clear, however, that Adra Newell chose Wheaton College as the primary repository for her collection in honor of Heather Young Gsell, Class of 1953. An English major, Heather Young married Cyrill C. Gsell in June 1953, soon after her graduation.[155] Gsell's father, Fred J. Young, was "the trusted advisor and friend of Mrs. Newell for many years prior to her death"[156] and served as co-executor of her estate. On October 26, 1966, soon after news of the bequest reached campus, Arthur D. Raybin, Director of the Office of Development and Public Relations, wrote to Guggenheimer & Untermyer, the law firm handling Mrs. Newell's estate, to request an explanation for the gift. Murray Friedman, on the firm's lawyers, replied two weeks later on November 9, 1966. Apologizing for the delay, which he attributed to the firm's due diligence regarding the request for information, Friedman wrote that Mrs. Newell "made the bequest to the College because of the great affection she had for Heather Young (now known as Heather Gsell)."[157] In a memorandum dated November 11, 1966, Raybin shared this information with President Prentice and Professor Doris Taylor Bishop.[158] The news proved somewhat difficult for Professor Bishop and her husband David Bishop to accept. On a copy of Raybin's 1966 memoir, he penned a handwritten note that read,

> Mr. Friedman may be partly right, but Doris's letter of Nov. 1, 1966 is solidly based on Miss [Professor] Work's known connections and work with, at, and for the Amer. Numismatic Society of which Mr. Newell was president. It is inconceivable that friendship for Miss Work is not the basic reason [for the bequest].[159]

In the late 1960s, the college attempted to learn more about Mrs. Gsell's relationship with Adra Marshall Newell,[160] while also searching for evidence to support the argument that the bequest was made because of Professor Work and her connection to the ANS and thus, the Newells. In November 1966, Doris Taylor Bishop wrote to Mrs. Gsell, inquiring if Mrs. Newell knew Professor Work and requesting "information which might throw light on their relationship."[161] She also asked for any information "on the manner in which Mrs. Newell selected her antiquities."[162] No record of a reply has been found in Wheaton's Gebbie Archives or in files held by the college's Office of Advancement; and Heather Young Gsell died in 1989, ending the possibility of learning more from her. The refusal to believe the explanation of Adra Newell's lawyers stuck fast, and belief that the bequest was made in memory of Eunice Work was often reiterated by college administrators[163] and by members of the Classics Department,[164] driven in large part by Professor David Bishop. His wife's untimely death, only two years after the Newell Bequest physically arrived on campus, arguably left him eager to protect both her legacy and his own, as he later co-authored a catalogue of Wheaton's Greek and Roman coins, the vast bulk of which are from the Newell Bequest.[165] He was, also, undoubtedly eager to protect his department's interest in Adra's collection and, later, the endowed fund that was created when objects from the bequest were sold at auction.

On December 14, 1978, most of the ancient glass Adra bequeathed to Wheaton was offered for auction at Sotheby Parke-Bernet in New York City in sale number 4196, *Important Egyptian, Greek, Roman, and Western Asiatic Antiquities*.[166] The sale was scheduled to coincide with *Treasures of Tutankhamun*, the blockbuster exhibition that opened at the Metropolitan Museum of Art the following day. "The auction . . . was an important event for many collectors from all parts of the world, many of whom were in New York to also see the Tutankhamon [*sic*] exhibit. This 'coincidence' was cleverly planned by Sotheby, Inc."[167] Approximately 250 glass objects were offered in 161 lots and sold quickly.[168] "The most valuable piece sold was a colorless glass dish dating from the second or third century AD. This tray-shaped dish, thought to have come from Egypt, sold for $11,000 to a Japanese collector. The value of the dish is derived from its unusual shape and design."[169] Other lots were acquired by buyers based in Europe and North America. An *Opague red bowl*[170] made its way to German collector Erwin Oppenländer before being sold by his son to the J. Paul Getty Museum in 2003.[171] Several pieces were acquired by the British Rail Pension Fund and then sold nearly two decades later at Sotheby's London office.[172] As the *Wheaton News* reported on February 8, 1979, "The auction was a great success. Most of the glass was sold at prices higher than appraisal estimates. The total amount gained for the collection was $174,525 (gross.) This money will be used in buying artifacts and works of art to be used as teaching aids in the art and classics departments."[173] Once expenses, e.g., photography, packing, transport, insurance, and commission, were paid, the proceeds from the sale were used to establish the Newell Bequest Fund early in 1979. The language that described the fund made clear the constraints under which it could be used:

> Both the endowment and the income will be restricted to art objects that can be used for teaching purposes and their maintenance. This could include the acquisition of art objects or rare books, and first preference should be given to items that relate to Classical Studies and Ancient Art.[174]

The remains of Edward T. Newell's numismatic library were sold in December 1989 for $21,000 and the proceeds were added to the Newell Bequest Fund.

We do not know what happened to all of the remaining pieces of ancient glass bequeathed to the college by Mrs. Newell. Twenty-two glass vessels still held in the Collection have been identified as belonging to the bequest, based on the measurements and limited descriptions listed in the 1967 appraisal. These include a *Pale Blue Spherical Bottle with Bronze Loop Handle*[175] and an *Ancient Egyptian Deep Blue Glass Perfume Bottle*.[176] Numerous pieces of Egyptian glass jewelry, included bracelets and beaded necklaces, also remain part of the Collection, but these appear to have been listed under "Jewelry" in the appraisal. Fragments of several glass objects were found in a small box alongside the glass vessels that have since been identified with the bequest. Therefore, we surmise that these were once part of Adra's collection, either the original "small fragments" listed in the appraisal or pieces of vessels that were broken after they arrived on campus. The fate of dozens of other glass objects that were listed in the appraisal but not sold at auction remains unidentified.

A LASTING LEGACY FOR THE LIBERAL ARTS

As mentioned above, in October 1967, members of the Art Visiting Committee passed a motion that Adra's bequest "be made available for use in the classroom, for study and research" and that "students be involved in the work of cataloguing, study and research" of the collection.[177] Now more than a half-century later, her gift has been used for all of these purposes and for others that were, perhaps, not imagined by the committee. In addition to serving as pedagogical tools and as primary sources for researchers on- and off-campus, objects in the bequest or purchased with the Fund have been exhibited in Wheaton's galleries and incorporated into fundraising and marketing campaigns. They have also been used to train several generations of work-study students, many of whom have gone on to graduate study in related fields and/or to work in museums and galleries.

The first purchase using the Fund was made in 1981 when a *Greek Black-Figure Attic Amphora*[178] was purchased from a gallery in New York City. Classics faculty, who, prior to notification of Adra's bequest, had asked the Wheaton administration for funds to acquire high-quality antiquities for teaching, had long coveted such an item. Once the decision had been made to sell most of the glass in the collection, faculty in the Art/Art History and the Classics Departments drew up a list of high-priority items for acquisition. A "Black-Figured Greek vase of quality" topped the list, followed by a "Red-Figured Greek vase of quality [and] a good example of Greek marble sculpture, perhaps a head" as well as a Roman or Hellenistic portrait bust; an example of a Roman wall painting and of a Roman mosaic; a few small Egyptian items; and examples of Bronze Age artifacts.[179] In the decade that followed, the departments held to this list, acquiring a third-century-CE marble *Head of Gallienus* in 1985,[180] a Roman mosaic floor fragment depicting Terpsichore,[181] and a Greek marble head of a child.[182] Over the next twenty-six years, nineteen more objects were purchased, including a sixteenth-century *Book of Hours*[183] and a complete thirteen-volume set of Ulisse Aldrovandi's *Opera Omnia*.[184] Most recently, in 2013, the fund was used to purchase Grant Wood's *Sultry Night*, a 1937 lithograph printed as part of a subscription offered by Associated American Artists.[185] This latter purchase is somewhat unusual, given that the language of the endowment indicated, "first preference [for acquisitions] should be given to items which relate to Classical Studies and Ancient Art."[186] The acquisition of *Sultry Night* was justified because the work, which features an image of a nude male farmhand, could serve as a contemporary example of the ancient Greek practice of depicting male nudes.

As of October 1972, when use of the Newell Bequest was reported to the AVC and Wheaton's administration, three articles had been published on the Newell glass: two articles by Israeli archaeologist and numismatist Dan Barag[187] and a 1971 article by American archaeologist Elsbeth B. Dusenbery, who argued that the "material suggests the collector was as much, or more, interested in shape than in surface technique."[188] Nearly a decade later, Wheaton's J. David Bishop and Brown University archaeologist R. Ross Holloway published *Wheaton College Collection of Greek and Roman Coins*, which included all of the Greek and Roman coins donated by Adra. The 1972 report also listed two independent research projects and nine courses, including Art 101: Introduction to Art History and Religion 315a: Ancient Near Eastern Religions, that had made use of the bequest. Objects had also been displayed in the gallery in 1970 and 1972 and in the exhibit cases housed in Watson Fine Arts.[189]

Aside from these examples, it is unclear how often items from the Newell Bequest were exhibited at Wheaton between 1967 and 2007, when campus displays began to be tracked in the collection database. Between 2007 and 2017, Newell-related objects were used in six student-curated exhibitions[190] mounted in the Beard and Weil Galleries[191] and two mini-exhibitions displayed in cases in Mary Lyon Hall and in Watson Fine Arts.[192] Each of these provided students with opportunities for experiential and object-based learning, as they designed and installed the exhibitions, researched the objects, and authored interpretive materials, including object labels, brochures, catalogues, podcasts, and/or wall texts. Faculty then used the student-curated exhibitions for a variety of assignments, including formal analysis and sketching objects as inspiration for monoprints.

Class use of the Collection was not consistently tracked until 2002, when a part-time registrar was hired to work in the newly renovated Watson Fine Arts building, which houses a climate-controlled and alarmed collections storage room. Since then, more than sixty individual courses have used the Newell Bequest or objects acquired with the Fund. These include courses in art history, anthropology, classics, English, history, religion, and studio art, as well as seven different first-year seminars.[193] Newell objects have been incorporated into a wide variety of assignments. Students enrolled in Greek and Latin courses have translated the text found on ancient coins and in the *Opera Omnia* and the *DuBourg Book of Hours*, while French students have translated the French text handwritten on the endsheet and flyleaf of the *Du-Bourg Book of Hours*. Faculty have guided students in explorations of how objects were used in Ancient Greece and Rome and how accurately objects reflect visual conventions of the cultures in which they were created and/ or consumed. Students enrolled in an introductory museum studies course have used objects donated by Mrs. Newell or purchased with the Fund to better understand the antiquities trade and the international community's response to it. They have also conducted provenance research on nearly twenty of these objects, one of which was featured in *The Provenance Project*, an exhibition mounted at the Attleboro Arts Museum in Attleboro, Massachusetts in February 2018.[194] Two faculty members have studied the *Opera Omnia*, which was acquired in 2009, and the history of the bequest has been the subject of faculty-student research that led to this contribution.[195]

In addition to pedagogical use, faculty research, and display, various administrative offices have made use of Newell Bequest objects. In spring 2014, the many ways in which Adra's gift has been used at Wheaton were detailed in "Gifts at Work: 'Founders All Are We,'" an article published in the fundraising brochure *Generations: What Will Your Legacy Be?* It included an image of the *Etruscan Antefix*[196] purchased with the Fund. Alumni, prospective students and their families, and staff occasionally tour the Collection Storage Room,[197] and such visits prominently feature objects donated by Adra or purchased with the endowed fund. For example, in fall 2017, the *Cycladic Figure*[198] and *DuBourg Book of Hours* were both incorporated into an Office of Admissions tour for prospective students and their parents, introducing them to campus-based arts resources. Such tours share Adra's legacy with an audience beyond Wheaton faculty and students. Finally, it is worth mentioning that the arrival of the Newell Bequest forced the college to develop its then nascent gifts-in-kind policy and to make at least some effort to consolidate the various collections scattered across campus.

CONCLUSION

Much about Adra Marshall Newell remains unknown. We may never know where, how, and by whom she was educated or when and why her passion for collecting began. Given the destruction of her personal papers and the lack of direct heirs, we are unlikely to learn more about these aspects of her life. Yet researching Mrs. Newell's life and her collection reveals a great deal about the history of Wheaton's Permanent Collection and about the myriad ways in which her bequest has been used to educate generations of students—on topics ranging from collecting in the early modern period to the illicit trade in antiquities. It also speaks to the politics of academia and of gender and marriage in the early to mid-twentieth century, both of which are topics for continued research.

The final decision to deaccession only the glass and Edward T. Newell's numismatic library can be summed up in a quote Lane Faison Jr. wrote in a letter to Wheaton President Bill Prentice: *N'oubliez jamais la possibilité de l'imprévu.* (Always leave room for the unexpected.)[199] As Faison had argued earlier that same year, Wheaton needed to "consider usefulness to the College from a long-range standpoint: not merely what is clearly 'relevant' just now, but what may gain in interest with changing styles of education."[200] In choosing to retain the bulk of Adra's collection, even during what were "clearly agonizing [economic] conditions of the present,"[201] Wheaton allowed for the unexpected and followed what has become established best practice in the field.

The twenty-three objects that have been purchased since 1981 have been used by dozens of courses and hundreds of students, and these acquisitions, as well as objects from the original bequest, have been displayed multiple times, engaging and educating members of the public and the Wheaton community. Researching the Newell Bequest has helped train more than twenty-five students in archival and provenance research and in using objects as primary sources, while reconciling Wheaton's antiquities with the original Newell Bequest appraisal has taught students how to catalogue objects and has illuminated some of the challenges collections and museum staff encounter on a daily basis. It has also made clear that, in addition to being "just a wife," Adra Marshall Newell was a collector and a generous benefactor. Her legacy lives on—at the Metropolitan Museum of Art, at the Yale University Art Gallery, and at Wheaton College.

BIBLIOGRAPHY

American Alliance of Museums. 2000. "Code of Ethics." https://www.aam-us .org/programs/ethics-standards-and-professional-practices/code-of-ethics-for-museums/.

American Numismatic Society. "Newell, Edward Theodore, 1886–1941. Biographical or Historical Note." Accessed August 5, 2017, https://numismatics.org/authority/newell.

Barag, Dan. 1970. "Glass Pilgrim Vessels from Jerusalem: Part I." *Journal of Glass Studies*. Vol. 12, pp. 35–63.

———. 1971. "Glass Pilgrim Vessels from Jerusalem: Parts II and III." *Journal of Glass Studies*. Vol. 13, pp. 45–63.

Bassett, Mary Cooley. 1912. *Lineage Book National Society of the Daughters of the American Revolution*. Volume XXXIII. Telegraph Printing Company: Harrisburg, PA.

Bishop, J. David, and R. Ross Holloway. 1981. *Wheaton College Collection of Greek and Roman Coins*. American Numismatic Society: New York.

Buchanan, Briggs. October 1968. "The Newell Collection of Oriental Seals: An Important Addition to the Yale Babylonian Collection." The *Yale University Library Gazette*. Vol. 43, no. 2, 91–97. http://www.jstor.org/stable/40858181.

Ciccone, Joseph. Winter 2004. "Young Edward Newell." *ANS Magazine*. http://numismatics.org/magazine/author/admin/page/20/.

"Doves and Dolphins on Greek Coins." April 30, 1932. *Wheaton News*.

Dusenbery, Elsbeth B. 1971. "Ancient Glass in the Collections of Wheaton College." *Journal of Glass Studies*. Vol. 13, pp. 9–33.

"EDWARD T. NEWELL TO WED." March 11, 1909. *New York Times*.

Giniewicz, Jayne. February 8, 1979. "Glass Sold at Auction." *Wheaton News*. Vol. 56, no. 8.

Gold, Mark S. 2015. "Monetizing the Collection: The Intersection of Law, Ethics, and Trustee Prerogative." In *The Legal Guide for Museum Professionals*, edited by Julia Courtney. Rowman & Littlefield: Lanham, MD.

Hannah, Caryn, ed. 2008. *Wisconsin Bibliographical Dictionary*. State History Publication: Hamburg.

Heath, Sebastian. Winter 2004. "Arras Coins at the ANS." *ANS Magazine*. http://numismtaics.org/magazine/arraswinter04/.

Herringshaw, Thomas William, editor. 1922. *The American Elite and Sociologist Blue Book*. American Blue Book Publishers: Chicago, IL.

Hill, David. 2014. "The Newells: Two Big Personalities and an Enduring Legacy." *ANS Magazine*. American Numismatic Society: New York, NY.

IMPORTANT ANCIENT GLASS FROM THE COLLECTION FORMED BY THE BRITISH RAIL PENSION FUND. 1997. Sotheby's: London, England.

IMPORTANT EGYPTIAN, GREEK, ROMAN, AND WESTER ASIATIC ANTIQUITIES. 1978. Sotheby Parke-Bernet Inc.: New York.

Jandl, Stefanie S., and Mark S. Gold. 2015. "Keeping Deaccessioned Objects in the Public Domain." In *The Legal Guide for Museum Professionals*, edited by Julia Courtney. Rowman & Littlefield: Lanham, MD.

Malouin, Kayla, and Leah Niederstadt. 2009. "Collecting Art, Creating A Legacy: A History of the Wheaton College Permanent Collection." In *The Problem of Sources in Women's Memory*. Women's Library and Information Centre: Istanbul, Turkey.

Martin, Audrey. February 8, 2018. "Wheaton students do some sleuthing for Attleboro Arts Museum." *Attleboro Sun Chronicle*.

"Miss Heather Young Engaged to Marry Ensign Cyril Gsell." March 5, 1953. *The Rye Chronicle*.

Ogden, Mary Depue, editor. 1915. *Memorial Cyclopedia of New Jersey*. Vol. II. Memorial History Company: Newark, NJ. https://archive.org/stream/memorial cycloped02ogde/memorialcycloped02ogde_djvu.txt, accessed May 10, 2017.

"Visiting Committees." October 13, 1961. *Intercom*. Wheaton College: Norton, MA.

Witschonke, Rick. Winter 2008. "Better Late than Never: Newell Manuscript Finally Published." *ANS Magazine*. American Numismatic Society: New York, NY.

11

Digital Deaccessioning

An Exploration of the Life Cycle of Digital Works in Museum Collections

Katherine E. Lewis

In recent years, museums have demonstrated increased interest in the acquisition of digital works of art for their collections and have been challenged to apply traditional acquisition and accessioning techniques and policies to this ever-evolving medium. To date, there are no known deaccessioning controversies involving a digital work or collection of digital works, but given the relative ease with which some may view digital accessions, one can see a not-too-distant future where concerns of overlap, duplicity, and adequate resources needed for massive, data-driven art collections might lead to consideration and implementation of digital deaccessions.

Acquisitions of new media works are not altogether new: museums have been acquiring audiovisual works and recordings for some time, and these acquisitions offer similar challenges as newer, source code–based mediums do, and the lessons learned from these earlier works are valuable and viable. For example, when attempting to establish objective migration criteria, one can likely look to the artist to identify certain technological criteria that should be convertible to new or different platforms. Similar to how video artists will identify a particular number of frames per second, projection size, volume decibel, etc., a digital media artist working in augmented reality might establish certain system, sound, and installation requirements that the museum would have to maintain in any migration to a different platform or service in order to preserve the artistic intention.

Digital works take on increasingly diverse forms, including audiovisual works, video games, augmented reality works, virtual reality works, mixed media and immersive experiences, software as art, software as a component of art or experience, and mixed hardware/software works to name just a few. For purposes of this essay, a baseline assumption will be that the digital works at issue are comprised primarily of or originating from a computerized or automated origination, and while there may be some physical manifestation in the form of hardware, these physical elements merely serve to facilitate access to and use of the work.

To put the concept of digital deaccessioning into context, this essay begins by providing two examples of pioneering museums engaging in digital accessioning. The essay then applies traditional concepts of accessioning and deaccessioning to unique characteristics of digital works to explore opposite sides of the same coin and offers suggestions in developing best practices to address questions of ownership, licensing, and due diligence on the front end and describes certain contractual remedies that can be built in at acquisition to help clarify questions of ownership and restrictions during a later determination of appropriate deaccessioning and disposal processes.[1]

PIONEERS IN DIGITAL ACQUISITIONS

The following are two examples of large art institutions acting as pioneers in digital art acquisitions. Others are certainly following suit; however, these will serve as examples to frame the current discussion.

As part of an ongoing commitment to "the study and interpretation of video games as part of the national visual culture,"[2] the Smithsonian American Art Museum (SAAM) has become a leader in museum collection of video games, acquiring many video games for its permanent collection over recent years and exploring the concept through a regular exhibition schedule. It was one of the first, if not the first, national museum to recognize video games as an art form. Video games are complex works with layers of musical, illustrated, and software source code content, all of which when combined also create an independently copyrightable work. Older video games were embedded in physical cartridges played on a hardware console. Newer games are software-only products, still accessed and played on a gaming console, but subject to software licensing agreements.

In 2010, the Museum of Modern Art (MoMA) added the @ symbol to its collection, a digital asset with no ownership ties or entanglements as it has long been in the public domain. Leaving aside the discussion of "What is Art" and sticking with the present question of management of digital acquisitions and conversely, deaccessioning the same, this acquisition was an interesting departure from the physical to digital collections practices for a number of reasons. Later, in 2016, MoMA added to its growing digital objects collection of typography and video games, acquiring an emoji library for the museum's permanent collection. Paola Antonelli, the Senior Curator leading the acquisition, perhaps put it best when she said of the @ acquisition, "[The acquisition] relies on the assumption that physical possession of an object as a requirement for an acquisition is no longer necessary."[3]

ACCESSIONING AND DEACCESSIONING: OPPOSITE SIDES OF THE COIN

Accessioning, as a term of art, means the formal process used by a museum to accept and record an item as a collection object.[4] A museum may assume possession of an object in a number of ways, including through gift, loan, purchase, or even abandonment; however, possession does not always mean that the museum owns the object. Furthermore, "ownership," particularly in the context of digital works, is not always a clear-cut determination: by their nature, digital works are often layered with content owned or controlled by multiple parties.

In order for an object to be deaccessioned, it must have first been accessioned. Meaning, if a digital work has come into the possession or use of a museum through some other means and has not otherwise been accessioned into the museum's permanent collection, deaccessioning procedures would not apply to the disposal of that digital work.

The museum community accepts one thing without question: once an object has been accessioned into a collection, the museum has a host of corresponding fiduciary and care obligations to the object and donor. What is unique about digital works? The answer to this question will vary based on the exact medium(s) used in the digital work, but some general considerations come to mind with respect to both the digital work itself and the state of the museum's digital collection:

> Does the duty of conservation and preservation mean the museum must maintain the digital work in a form and condition such that it may be experienced at any given time in the manner that the artist intended? If that is so, and without any limitations, that obligation could potentially be imposing very burdensome requirements on the museum and requires that the museum secure certain rights and permissions (ideally at the point of acquisition) from the artist in order to meet those obligations.

> Are there end user license agreements (EULA) that will be applicable to the use of the digital work, which will have to flow down to the museum's visitors when

the work is exhibited? If yes, has someone reviewed the EULA to determine whether there are any legal or business concerns that need to be addressed?

In order to accommodate the digital work, or collection of digital works, does the museum need to secure additional server space? Can it meet those obligations by storing the digital content locally on its own servers, or does it have to seek third-party support (e.g., Amazon Web Services) to provide server space? What obligations, if any, are there to the donor or artist if the museum uses a third-party service provider?[5]

Once the digital collection reaches a certain size or significance, does the museum need to hire staff (e.g., software developers, information technology experts, etc.) to help maintain and support those collections, similar to how a museum may employ certain curatorial support for other unique collections?

Should collections management policies include specific processes and procedures for digital works? Should these include data management policies?

Should accompanying hardware be treated as part of the accession, or does this unnecessarily restrict the museum from disposing and updating hardware as needed to maintain the underlying digital work?

If a museum maintains a large enough collection of digital works, would the cost of keeping the lights on; the temperature and humidity controls in check for on-premises servers and systems; the payment of third-party vendor agreements necessary to host, use, and display the digital works; and/or payments for maintenance and support plans continue to be considered operational costs? Or is there a reasonable argument to be made that those are legitimate costs related to the direct care of the digital collection?

Accessioning and deaccessioning processes and procedures are commonly set forth in the museum's Collections Management Policy. Standard accessioning considerations apply equally to digital accessions, but unique as demonstrated in part above, considerations can be encountered at nearly every stage of the accessioning analysis from the determination of ownership, appropriate due diligence, intellectual property rights considerations, donor restrictions (and now potentially other third-party restrictions), public access and research, conservation, preservation, and ultimately the process for deaccessioning and disposal. For that reason, and given the increased interest and attention to digital acquisitions, it seems prudent to consider the development of customized guidelines in Collections Management Policies addressing the process and procedures particular to digital acquisitions, similar to how other special classifications might be treated (e.g., endangered species collections, indigenous peoples' artifacts, etc.).

OWNERSHIP AND DUE DILIGENCE

Determining ownership is part of the necessary due diligence in acquiring and accessioning a work and can impact any disposition or use of the work downstream, including deaccessioning or disposal. Ms. Antonelli tells us that physical possession of the object is no longer necessary for an acquisition of the object, which may be true, but how does that comport with our traditional understanding of title and ownership?

"Title" generally refers to who has legal ownership and the right to use a piece of property. This foundational concept is carried through to most types of property including real property, personal property (e.g., cars, boats, paintings, etc.), and intellectual property. Transfer of legal title is the transfer of ownership and the right to use the subject of the transfer exclusively. If the individual or company purporting to transfer title to the work at issue does not in fact own or possess the necessary rights to do so, the museum's ownership interest in the work will be undermined, which may lead to more serious issues in the future. In the case of digital works, it is very rare for a transfer of ownership to take place; rather, in most cases the rights to the work are licensed to the museum.

In digital works, it is more likely than not that multiple parties will have an ownership interest in the digital work, or components of the digital work. These parties may have assisted in the creation or production of the digital work; they may have licensed source code to the artist; they may have built the platform through which the digital work is transmitted, displayed, or performed. In some instances, the artist should have secured ownership rights, but it may also be appropriate for the artist to obtain only a license to use third-party content or services.

Traditional concepts of ownership and transfer of title would require securing a transfer of title and interest in each component (or assurances from the artist that they own all rights in and to the work) in order for the museum to retain ownership and title to the work; however, that is not necessary and is likely not to be achievable with a digital work. In large part, the transfer of ownership and rights in or to a digital work is akin to the transfer of intellectual property rights in and to a physical object: just because the museum acquires the physical work, does not mean it also acquired the right to exercise the intellectual property rights in the work. The main distinction is that digital works are almost entirely intangible collections of layered intellectual property rights. For that reason, it is important to parse the layers and perform some amount of due diligence at each layer when contemplating an acquisition of a digital work in order to fully understand the nature of the work and rights being granted to the museum. Doing so, and maintaining documentation of the process, will be an enormous help not only in the museum's later use and exhibition of the work but also when or if the museum comes to consider deaccessioning and disposal of the digital work.

One particularly helpful approach in tackling this analysis is to learn as much as possible about the artist's creative process in order to determine how many layers of rights there may be. Take, for example, an augmented or virtual reality work. There are a number of ways to develop these types of works, but let's assume three primary methods of creation for this portion of the discussion: (1) the artist is a software developer and is capable of creating not only the work itself but also the platform or service on which the work is experienced; (2) the artist hires someone with the aforementioned capabilities, who performs the services necessary to bring the artist's vision to life, inclusive of creating a custom environment or platform or service on which the work may be enjoyed; or (3) either scenario 1 or 2 is true, but in both instances, the platform or service is owned, controlled, and operated by a third party. In any of the foregoing scenarios, the artist may have used third-party source code (either by license, or more often by use of open source libraries).

In order to create a clear and thorough analysis and documentation of rights, develop a list of questions to consider in the acquisition of a digital work. Here are a few initial questions and accompanying explanations to get started:

Is the artist transferring ownership of the digital work to the museum, or merely a license to use the digital work?

Common practice in the donation or sale of physical works is that the artist will transfer title to the physical work and grant the museum a nonexclusive license to the necessary intellectual property rights, specifically, a limited license in the copyright and the artist's right of publicity (i.e., the right to use the artist's name, image, and likeness in connection with the work). Even in the context of a donation or sale of a physical work, artists are loath to assign or transfer title in the intellectual property rights in the work to the museum. As discussed earlier, with digital works, it is more likely than not that the museum will be granted a license to use the work, and absent acquisition of an accompanying physical component of the digital work, no transfer of title or ownership will occur.

How many parties claim authorship of the digital work? (e.g., how many artists are there?)

Certain digital works may have been a collaborative effort between multiple artists, artist collectives, and/or either of the foregoing and a for-profit corporation. Each of these parties will likely have some ownership interest in the work.

Did the artist develop the work himself or herself? Or did the artist create the concept and hire or otherwise engage third parties to execute the concept?

Artists may subcontract out development of a digital work, or portions of the digital work, to a third-party individual or company, and these relationships may be paid or unpaid.

- If paid, there should be a work for hire agreement.
- If unpaid, there should be an assignment of rights to the artist.

Did the artist and/or the artist's assistants use any third-party content or source code in the development of the work?

Third-party content might include images, sound, music, performance, videos, clips, or source code. If the answer is yes, did the artist secure the necessary third-party licenses and/or permissions for use of the content in the digital work? If yes, did the artist secure *sufficient* permissions to flow through to the museum? For example, if the work includes a song, did the artist secure the license to use and publicly perform the song? And if yes, in making the transfer of the digital work to the museum, does the museum also have the right to publicly perform the song in the context of displaying the digital work to the public, or must the museum secure its own license?

Third-party source code might include licensed libraries of source code or open source libraries. In each case, the licenses under which the source code was made available would be applicable to the museum's use of the digital work. If the artist used third-party source code, depending on the use of the work, the preservation and conservation obligations the museum pledges to undertake, it may be wise to request a list of any and all third-party source code libraries or applicable licenses.

After completing the foregoing analysis, the museum should have a list of the parties with an ownership interest in the digital work and a much better understanding of (1) the necessary licenses and permissions it needs and (2) any applicable restrictions on its use of the digital work (and for purposes of this essay, on the potential deaccessioning and disposal of the work).

In preparing the acquisition documents (including the applicable agreement), consider what the museum's obligations to each party is in accessioning the work. Conversely, consider what the museum's obligations are to each party in any possible deaccessioning or disposal of a digital work. Always keep in mind what the museum's objectives are in relation to the acquisition, meaning what the museum hopes to achieve with the work and how it would like to use the work. This will help in refining the scope of the analysis and in determining the rights needed to achieve those goals. Given the complexity of these works, it may even be wise to establish certain minimum commitments the museum is willing to assume with respect to conservation and preservation of the work and perhaps include a disclaimer relieving the museum of any obligation to maintain or support the work. The following sections provide some suggestions for securing the necessary rights, protections, and assurances in the acquisition of digital works.

SECURING NECESSARY RIGHTS IN THE DIGITAL WORK

Museums acquire works for their collections for the purpose of mission fulfillment, and what that means will vary from museum to museum. Irrespective of mission, once acquired and accessioned, subject to any limitations the parties might agree to, the museum has certain obligations to the digital work. The museum will want to use the digital work in its exhibitions and educational programs and perhaps make the work available for research purposes. Where digital works are concerned, these uses require specific language in the license grant provision of the agreement governing the license of the digital work, whether that be a Donor Agreement, Purchase Agreement, or other agreement.

Artists are generally unwilling to grant wholesale assignments or transfers of their intellectual property rights. In the case of digital works, with the exception of hardware, the entire work is comprised of intellectual property rights. That means, in a very real sense, that the heart of an acquisition agreement for a digital work is the license grant provision. The license is nearly always going to be a nonexclusive license, meaning the artist may grant a license to the digital work to others and may himself or herself use and display the work.

Some things to consider in drafting and negotiating the nonexclusive license provision include:

Scope of Use. There are two ways to approach the scope of use portion of the license grant: (1) only include the known and anticipated uses or (2) draft the license broadly to encompass both the known and anticipated uses and those which may develop in the future. The latter may be preferred to minimize the likelihood of having to return to amend, modify, or secure a separate license to use the work at a later date, which may include additional license fees. In addition to the traditional scope of use requirements, like the ability to use the work for noncommercial, educational, research, and museum purposes, the museum should consider the following:

(a) Ability and responsibility to maintain and support the digital work in perpetuity (this factor may depend on the level of the artist's involvement);
(b) Ability and responsibility to conserve and preserve the digital work, including the ability to migrate the digital work to another platform in the event the existing platform is unavailable, has been discontinued, or is no longer supported by the provider;
(c) Ability to make the work available to researchers or other third parties and how they would need to grant the necessary access.

Certain of the foregoing may require that the museum have a limited ability to sublicense the work and to reverse-engineer and make derivative works of the digital work. This may be worrisome to the artist, so the common suggestion is to ensure that these rights are limited solely to the purpose of conservation and preservation.

The specifics of this provision should be tailored to the digital work at issue and the needs of the museum, as these will both heavily impact the drafting of the license language. Also, particular digital mediums or mixes of digital mediums may justify more customized considerations.

Limited Number of Licenses. Is there some intrinsic value in the work that is diminished if the number of licenses to the work exceeds a certain amount? In the case of MoMA's acquisition of @ and the emoji collection, this was not likely a concern, as both were already and continue to be freely and frequently used by the public; but what if the work is a contemporary augmented or virtual reality piece by the most interesting living artist working today? Does the analysis change? Would the museum perhaps reevaluate its purchase price if the work was going to be made freely available to the world three months after execution of the Purchase Agreement?

Geographic Scope. Consider requesting a worldwide license in order to accommodate use on the Internet and inclusion of the digital work in traveling exhibitions.

Term. In most cases, it may be ideal to obtain a perpetual term, but this may vary depending on the nature of the digital work and the museum's desire to maintain, support, conserve, and preserve the work.[6] In either case, it would be best to secure an irrevocable license.

Third-Party Access; Sublicensing. Consider whether the museum needs the ability to grant third parties access to the digital work (e.g., public access, academic and research access, etc.). Question whether this use requires the museum to have the ability to sublicense the work in order to permit researchers to access the work or to permit subcontractors of the museum to make the work accessible through a museum-owned and -operated website or other digital application.

A Note Regarding Donor Restrictions in Digital Works. It is common practice for museums to resist donor restrictions on their use of the acquired work, and for good reason. However, when considering donor or artist restrictions on the use of digital works, keep in mind that the artist may be contractually obliged to impose these restrictions on the museum in order to comply with third-party licenses embedded in certain components of the work. If the issue comes up, the best thing to do is engage in a meaningful and informed discussion with the artist to determine the reason for the restrictions. The museum can then make an informed determination as to whether the restrictions are acceptable. Restrictions should be drafted with specificity in the agreement to avoid any doubt in interpretation.

SPECIAL CONSIDERATIONS FOR SOFTWARE

If the expectation of the donor or seller is that the museum will maintain the digital work in a condition similar to the original intent of the artist, then there are certain rights and access requirements the museum must have in order to meet this expectation. The following is a list of possible ways a museum may secure these rights:

- **A License to the Source Code.** The museum might consider requesting a license to the underlying source code of the digital work (as opposed to a license just to use and access the digital work). This may be interpreted by the artist as akin to requesting an assignment or transfer of ownership in the work, but it may be completely necessary for the museum to have access to the source code in order to exercise the license, particularly if it will be museum's responsibility to maintain, support, update, and migrate the work in order to keep the work accessible and usable.
- **Source Code Escrow.** If the artist is resistant to granting a source code license (some will be), and depending on the cultural significance of the acquisition and the relative level of importance the applicable digital work has in the scope of the collection itself, one possible alternative would be to agree to place the source code in the custody of a disinterested third party, subject to what is commonly known as a Source Code Escrow Agreement. The purpose of a Source Code Escrow Agreement

is to have the party granting the license deposit the source code into a third-party escrow account for the benefit of the licensee. There are ongoing costs associated with this option, as source code escrow entities charge fees for the service, but depending on the importance of the work, it may be an appropriate option to pursue. If the parties decide to enter into this type of arrangement, consider requiring the artist to update the escrow deposit whenever they update or upgrade the digital work so that the source code in escrow is always the most recent version. Again, depending on the nature of the digital work, this may or may not be a reasonable solution.

- **Artist-Provided Support and Maintenance.** If the artist will not agree to place the source code in escrow or to provide the museum with a source code license, the question of maintenance and support should be addressed somehow, and it should be the artist's obligation to secure and bear the cost of all required maintenance and support. If the work is not functioning, has bugs, operational errors, or requires an update or upgrade due to a corresponding update or upgrade to the platform on which it is hosted, then the artist should be prepared to provide assistance to the museum and pay the costs and expenses required to maintain the work and enable the museum to continue display and use of the work.
- **Museum Disclaimer.** If no mutually acceptable compromise can be reached, the agreement should include a disclaimer by the museum relieving it of any obligation to maintain or support the work and from any liability for deaccessioning and disposing of the work at any point in time where it becomes impractical for the museum to continue the use or to access the digital work as initially intended to be enjoyed and experienced.

WHAT ABOUT HARDWARE?

Digital works often require hardware to access and experience the work. Software as art requires a computer to display in live format (acknowledging that some software artists reproduce their works in tangible mediums); augmented and virtual reality works require mobile devices, glassware, headsets, and headphones. Consider whether the donor is also providing the requisite hardware or if it is the responsibility of the museum to acquire the hardware. If the artist is providing the hardware or is reselling the hardware to the museum, make sure the manufacturer warranties flow through to the museum. If it is the museum's responsibility, it is recommended that the museum require the artist or donor to provide a comprehensive and detailed list of hardware required to support the digital work and any installation instructions to ensure accurate replication of the intended experience.

SECURING NECESSARY THIRD-PARTY RIGHTS

As discussed at length, many digital works require access to and use of third-party platforms and services in order to operate. Determine which party will be responsible for maintaining the requisite licenses and making corresponding payments for the same. In many cases, the museum may be the likely candidate, but keep in mind that as the museum builds its digital collection, the need to pay for, maintain, and comply with a growing number of disparate third-party platform and service agreements may become a burden and possibly a liability down the road. Museums might consider including a provision in the digital acquisition portion of the Collections Management Policy addressing this issue. For example, are there certain software vendors or approved vendors that the museum staff can consider when identifying potential acquisitions? Are there minimum safety, security, and data privacy requirements a vendor must satisfy?

MINIMIZING MUSEUM OBLIGATIONS

As exciting as the digital art space may be and as necessary as it is to include and preserve these works in an art historical context, there does need to be an acknowledgment that museums are not in the business of software or information technology development or maintenance, and certain of the undertakings referenced above are entirely beyond the means and resources of many museums. Some museums have robust information technology departments, and a select few have begun building new media and technology departments. Many other museums simply do not have the resources to build these departments and may even rely on volunteers to perform some of these functions. Should that mean that they should not engage in acquisitions of digital works? Certainly not. Rather, these museums should consider ways in which to (1) obtain only the rights they need to achieve the intended use of the digital work; (2) where possible, secure artist commitment to support and maintenance of the work; (3) determine whether the artist or donor is willing to donate the resources necessary to maintain any required third-party subscriptions or permissions necessary to use and enjoy the work; and (4) seriously consider including a disclaimer relieving the museum of any obligation to maintain or support the work, and from any liability for deaccessioning and disposing of the work at any point in time where it becomes impractical for the museum to continue the use of or access to the digital work as initially intended to be enjoyed and experienced.

SECURING PROTECTIONS IN THE DONOR AGREEMENT OR PURCHASE AGREEMENT

From a legal perspective, it is absolutely necessary to complete appropriate due diligence on the digital work to understand and document the different layers of ownership interests in the digital work in order to ensure that the museum's use and display of the digital work does not violate the rights of a third party, and thereby expose the museum to unnecessary risk of a third-party lawsuit. It is also necessary because the primary hurdle in deaccessioning and disposal of a work is a determination of ownership, restrictions, and potential liability. Digital works, more than any other medium, are reliant on multilayered ecosystems of intellectual property assets, and therefore the exposure to third-party claims is higher than most other mediums.

If at any point in the due diligence process the museum discovers a flaw in the ownership or licensing chain of the digital work or a component of the digital work, it should engage in discussion with the artist to determine the best way to correct the flaw and, assuming a reasonable agreement can be reached and the necessary rights secured, the parties may then continue with the transaction.

Regardless of how in-depth the museum decides to go in completing its due diligence, it should still include certain basic protections in the Donor Agreement or Purchase Agreement to ensure the museum will be held harmless in the event there is a third-party claim arising from its use or display of the digital work. This includes securing certain representations, warranties, and indemnification from the artist and/or the gallery where possible.[7]

In practice, museums tend to take one of two drafting approaches to the Donor Agreement: (1) include the necessary nonexclusive license as a section or provision of the Donor Agreement; or (2) attach a Nonexclusive License Agreement as an appendix of the Donor Agreement. The second approach tends to be more popular, perhaps due to the desire to separate what some perceive to be a business consideration from the charitable intention of the donor. For most works of art, this approach works well (or at least is not harmful) because more traditional mediums generally include a transfer or donation of a physical object, and the licensing of the accompanying intellectual property rights is treated as separate from the physical object. In the case of digital works, that distinction becomes less practical and in combination with the increased potential risk of third-party claims arguably inherent in digital works, it would seem more advisable to take the first approach and enter into a single Donor Agreement that includes the following legal provisions.[8]

REPRESENTATIONS AND WARRANTIES

Representations and warranties often go together and are sometimes mistaken for having interchangeable meanings, but in reality a representation is a statement of past or present fact and a warranty is a promise that the fact is true. Often there is little distinction between the two in an agreement because generally if something is important enough to represent in writing at the time of the agreement, it is equally important that it be true.

A Donor or Purchase Agreement for a digital work should include representations and warranties from the artist to the museum that (1) they either own or have secured the necessary intellectual property rights to grant the rights contained in the agreement to the museum, (2) that they have not infringed the intellectual property or other rights of any third party in the creation of the work, and in the case of the gallery (3) that they are (a) the legal representative of the artist and (b) are authorized to enter into the agreement and bind the artist to the agreement. If the museum is unable to secure the foregoing from the gallery, it should request that the artist sign the agreement personally, as contracts are generally only enforceable against the party(ies) who sign them. If the digital work is a software program, consider adding standard software representations and warranties that the work does not include any malicious code, Trojan horse, time bombs, bugs, errors, etc., that might damage the museum's systems.

As artists grow to be more sophisticated in the creation of digital works and particularly if the artists are coming from a software development background where contracts with representations and warranties are more standard industry practice, it may become more commonplace to see disclaimers of warranties, particularly if the museum is requesting warranties and representations. If that happens, consult with an attorney on the review and negotiation of any warranty disclaimers, as these may negate other protections in the agreement and will certainly have an impact on the museum's rights and remedies in the event of any legal claim down the road.

INDEMNIFICATION

Indemnification is a special protection that requires a party to compensate the other party for damages, costs, and losses (including reasonable attorneys' fees) incurred as a result of the actions of the other party. Ideally, both the representation and warranties and indemnification provisions are tailored to the transaction and should be reasonably related to the perceived risks involved. If a party is required to not only indemnify, but also to defend and hold harmless, the protection is broadened to include the costs of defense. The latter is preferable because whether or not a third party has a basis for a claim, they can still commence a legal proceeding, which requires the museum to respond, incurring costs and expenses to do so. By including the requirement to defend, indemnify, and hold harmless, the museum is requiring the artist or gallery to step into their shoes and fully protect the museum against the type of claims identified in the applicable indemnification provision.

In the case of digital works, it is reasonable to request indemnification from the artist for third-party claims arising from a breach of its representations and warranties (of particular concern are third-party claims and intellectual property infringement claims). Some level of pushback and even refusal should be anticipated, particularly if the digital work is a gift. In the case of a gift, the donor's position will likely be that they are making a donation, and including an insurance policy in the form of indemnification for the museum is beyond the limits of their generosity. In these scenarios, it is advisable to engage in an informed discussion with the donor, and to do the maximum amount of due diligence on the work in order to make a comprehensive and informed assessment of the risk to the museum in proceeding without indemnification. Consider also the level and type of insurance coverage the museum may be able to rely upon. In the case of a Purchase Agreement, the museum may have more leverage to secure these protections with less fuss. One thing to keep in mind in either scenario is that, as nice as it is for the museum to have an impressive digital work in the permanent collection, it is also nice for the artist and/or donor to be part of that collection.

Whether or not to include this provision is ultimately a risk assessment for the museum to make. However, one could argue that because digital works implicate so many third-party rights and, particularly in the case of software, carry additional risk exposure to the museum's own systems that will host the program to make it accessible to the public, the artist is in the best position to understand, control, and mitigate those risks as between the parties and should be responsible for any negative result.

DIGITAL DEACCESSIONING

Deaccessioning is the "process of removal permanently of an object from a museum's collection or to document the reasons for the involuntary removal (one required by law or due to circumstances not controlled by the museum)."[9] Deaccessioning is generally governed by internal policy with legal obligations triggered by restrictions associated with the object and, in some cases, by a deaccessioning action that catches the attention of the state's Attorney General's Office.

Many of the traditional reasons for deaccessioning may also apply to digital collections. Similar to physical collections, management can be a challenge. Brick-and-mortar museums are excitedly engaging in the acquisition of digital works and collections, and it is reasonable to predict that in an environment where a collection is suddenly free of more traditional physical storage constraints, that collection might balloon quickly in size. Overlap; duplicity in objects; resources to devote to storage, upkeep, and maintenance, including hosting services; staffing support; and third-party software maintenance and subscriptions are all potential reasons that a museum may look to deaccession digital works or digital collections.

When considering the deaccessioning of a work within the collection, the initial question is one of ownership, with a corresponding need to identify any applicable restrictions on the object's disposal. Other considerations include the method of disposal, the use of proceeds from the disposal, and any potential donor notification requirements (whether as a matter of courtesy or as required by interpretation of the documentation accompanying the object).

OWNERSHIP AND RESTRICTIONS

Assuming museums take the position that the act of accessioning can occur absent a complete transfer of title, provided the license is perpetual and sufficiently broad that the museum ostensibly has meaningful ownership-like rights, then the threshold deaccessioning question (usually understood as one of "ownership") now becomes an analysis of the web of intellectual property rights and licenses underlying the digital work, with a corresponding need to identify any applicable restrictions and obligations that might be contained in the agreements governing the gift or purchase of the digital work. It should be kept in mind that in the context of digital works, restrictions may not only be donor-imposed restrictions but third-party license restrictions as well.

The earlier discussion of ownership centered on licensing because, in the context of digital works, it is unlikely that the artist or donor would assign or transfer ownership in the work completely to the museum. Even in cases where such a transfer might occur, there is still the consideration of applicable third-party rights entangled in the digital work and which are likely subject to a license grant and certain use restrictions. Several methods to ensure that the museum has secured the necessary rights, assurances, and protections for the museum to not only carry out its obligations as caregiver of the digital work in the public's interest, but also to create clear documentation as to the ownership and licensing structure for any potential deaccessioning or disposal needs in the future, were discussed at length earlier in this essay.

By establishing and complying with best practices in the acquisition of digital works at the time when the interest in such acquisitions is on the rise, museums will be making compliance with the corresponding documentation required as a best practice for deaccessioning and disposal of the work at a later date much easier, as trying to restructure this information years later may be a monumental task.

If, however, a museum faces the question of deaccessioning a digital work and has not, up to that time, completed its due diligence and analysis of the digital work's ownership and restrictions, consulting with this essay will provide helpful insights on the questions to consider and the provisions of the Donor Agreement or Purchase Agreement to review for further information.

METHOD OF DISPOSAL AND USE OF PROCEEDS

Although (hopefully) able to satisfy the challenge of ownership in the context of accessioning and, therefore, deaccessioning, the question of the method of disposal is tied firmly to the license grant underlying the digital work. Where, in more traditional mediums, the Donor Agreement or Purchase Agreement would have dealt with a physical object as separate from the accompanying intellectual property rights, in the context of digital works, the entirety of the work is a bundle of intellectual property rights with no physical manifestation (other than perhaps hardware, which is best treated as separate from the accessioned work, unless there is some reason to do otherwise[10]). In the case of a physical work, subject to any applicable and legally binding donor restrictions, the museum is presumed to have title in the object itself and may dispose of it in any number of ways, including through auction and sale. The museum's ability to transfer any associated intellectual property license would be entirely dependent on the language of the license grant.

Digital works, in contrast, being entirely subject to license grants and restrictions, are likely to be further restricted with fewer available methods of disposal. For example, it is likely that the license granted to the museum restricts the museum from transferring or sublicensing the work to third parties. It's also likely that the museum would have agreed to only use the work for noncommercial purposes. The sale of a digital work is therefore not likely to be an available method of disposal.

Katherine E. Lewis

It is highly recommended that if a museum is contemplating the sale of a digital work as a means of disposal, it consult with legal counsel prior to doing so, in order to engage in an analysis of whether the museum possesses the requisite rights to do so or may otherwise be putting itself at risk of a breach of contract claim or intellectual property infringement claim.

DEACCESSIONING BY INVOLUNTARY REMOVAL

The concept of deaccessioning by involuntary removal is traditionally considered in the context of allegations of theft and where cultural heritage objects may be subject to removal by operation of law.[11] Referring back to the working definition of deaccessioning referenced above, involuntary removal might include removal either as required by law or due to circumstances not controlled by the museum.

In the context of digital works there are a few specific scenarios one might anticipate triggering deaccession by involuntary removal, including:

As required by law: An intellectual property infringement claim against the artist that results in the digital work being found by a court to be infringing a third party's rights; and/or

Due to circumstances not controlled by the museum: The server hosting the digital work fails permanently and the digital work is not able to be recovered; or, the artist or other responsible party fails to provide the necessary updates or upgrades to the digital work as needed and the museum does not otherwise have the rights or access to the source code of the digital work to do so themselves.

In either case, the museum would seem to have a legitimate reason to support deaccessioning and disposal of the digital work from the collection and should follow its established policies and procedures for documenting involuntary removal of objects from the collection.

CONCLUSION

The primary distinction between digital works and nearly every other medium of creative expression is the fact that the artist is no longer the sole creative source; rather, they are part of a larger collective of multiple sources of content, which leads to a more complex analysis of rights, ownership, and restrictions. Artists will continue to push the envelope and create other ways to channel the diverse nature of technology into creative expression. Collection Management Policies, including portions thereof addressing accessioning, care, conservation, deaccessioning, and disposal, should attempt to address some common considerations by creating guidelines that are both practical enough to be helpful and flexible enough to accommodate the near daily evolution of digital medium expression.

Due to both the necessity and complexity of analyzing multiple agreements and third-party licensing in making these determinations, it is highly recommended to engage legal counsel in both the acquisition of and any deaccessioning of digital works to ensure that the museum is securing the rights, protections, and assurances it needs to carry out its responsibilities to the digital work as part of its collection on the front end and to ensure that the museum is not in violation of third-party rights or inadvertently subjecting itself to a breach of contract to infringement claim in the process of deaccessioning and disposing of the digital work.

12

Higgins Armory Museum and the Worcester Art Museum

A Case Study in Combining and Transforming Mature Cultural Institutions

James C. Donnelly Jr. and Catherine M. Colinvaux

On December 31, 2013, Worcester, Massachusetts's beloved John Woodman Higgins Armory Museum closed its doors after eighty-three years of exhibits organized around one of North America's greatest collections of arms and armor.

Three months later, on March 29, 2014, the Worcester Art Museum (WAM) opened its *Knights!* exhibition, marrying treasures from the John Woodman Higgins Collection and old-world masterpieces from WAM's renowned collection. Shown side by side, the art elevates the armor, highlighting its grandeur and elegance and the magnificence of its craft. And the armor elevates the art, creating new and compelling connections with relevance to a broad, modern audience. Severely bodiced Elizabethan women with prim headdresses are revealed as "armored" in their confining costumes as they glance side-eyed toward their metal-clad courtiers. And the courtier knights are suddenly less conclusively masculine and warlike as we see reflections of the women's finery in the tracing, gilt embellishments, and wasp-waists of their armor "corsets."

In the next *Knights!* gallery, helmets spanning four continents, nearly 2,700 years, and cultures as diverse as Ancient Greece, sixteenth-century Japan, and the Ottoman Empire form a "roundtable" of heroes under the watchful eye of a once-and-future (dark) "knight" in the form of Batman. In further galleries, there are spaces dedicated to children and to exhibits that juxtapose historical weaponry with reminders of modern warfare in the form of a stylized Arc d'Triomphe and photographs from the Pulitzer Center on Crisis

151

Reporting. As the *Huffington Post*[1] observed, the combination is a "a tour de force assemblage elevating WAM to international status" while providing a crowd-pleasing and "admirable job" of "connecting past to present and real to pop culture . . . [a]s Knights were once the 'Super-heroes' of their day."

The *Knights!* exhibit signals a revitalization of previously, purely stately WAM, most especially in WAM's approach to audience engagement and children. The opening, which included a Renaissance Faire with family-friendly offerings to engage visitors of all ages, attracted an average month's worth of visitors in only its first weekend. Children flocked not just to the *Knights!* exhibition galleries, but to the entire museum in unprecedented numbers.

Yet as successful as it has been and continues to be, *Knights!* provides only a taste of things to come. Over the next few years, the exhibit will be continually refreshed with new armor, new presentations, and new interpretative experiences, providing a laboratory and a template to learn from the best of the Higgins Armory and expand family-friendly programming across the entire Museum. Within five to seven years, WAM will make a permanent home for the Higgins Collection, creating a four-thousand-square-foot multilevel gallery dedicated to its display and interpretation in ways that enhance and connect the collection to the wider world of art. At the same time, WAM will continue and expand programming to attract new audiences with an emphasis on the family audiences that traditionally loved the Higgins Armory; it has hired key Higgins Armory employees, including the Armory's curator; and it will conserve, steward, and enhance the Higgins Collection in ways that were beyond the Higgins Armory's capacity.

Although a transformational triumph for WAM, the *Knights!* opening represented a bittersweet moment for the Higgins Armory. The Armory had announced only a year before the *Knights!* opening that the Armory must close, and for a grueling final nine months, a skeleton staff had labored around the clock to honor and celebrate the Armory in public exhibitions and programming, while performing behind the scenes the myriad legal and practical tasks necessary to wind down the Armory Museum as a business and to steward the Higgins Collection to a new home.

That final year of celebrations and farewells, itself, marked the beginning of the end of a multiyear process. For more than thirty years, Higgins Armory's trustees and directors had struggled with systemic and existential challenges, including a minimal endowment, insufficient donor support, and extraordinary expense associated with an iconic landmark building that is difficult to maintain. The decision to close was neither sudden nor accidental: it followed years of creative but ultimately unsuccessful lifesaving measures, and in that context, represented a careful, realistic appraisal of the Armory's circumstances and of the last, best opportunity to steward its collection into the future: to protect the collection itself, honor the legacy of the Higgins Armory's founder, and preserve for the people of Worcester, Massachusetts, one of their greatest treasures.

This article reviews the challenges that led the Higgins Armory Museum's trustees to the seemingly unthinkable decision to close a beloved institution, the hurdles that WAM trustees confronted in deciding whether it would be prudent to accept the challenges of safeguarding the Higgins Collection, and the collaboration that preserved and will eventually enhance a precious cultural legacy. This article intends to describe the history and process in ways that will inform the judgment of other institutions in similar situations.

A SHORT HISTORY OF HIGGINS ARMORY AND WAM

If, in the words of Justice Oliver Wendell Holmes, a page of history can be worth a volume of logic,[2] then the Higgins Armory Museum is a case in point. For Worcesterites, past and present, it is almost impossible to think of the Higgins Collection of Arms and Armor as anything other than an organic, quintessential piece of Worcester history. Worcester industrialist John Woodman Higgins and several of his friends founded the Higgins Armory Museum in 1928 to exhibit what had been Mr. Higgins's private collection of arms, armor, and other interesting metalwork. Mr. Higgins's love for metalwork grew out of his avocation as president and owner (together with other family members) of Worcester Pressed Steel Company, and Worcester Pressed Steel was, in turn, among the core industries, many of them involved in steel and metalworking, that made Worcester an industrial capital in the nineteenth and early twentieth centuries.

In the early 1900s, Worcester Pressed Steel developed modern methods for mass-producing stamped metal objects. As the nation prepared to enter World War I, the War Department considered how to design and mass-produce military hardware to meet the demands of twentieth-century warfare. Making the perhaps questionable assumption that Renaissance armor could provide models, the War Department engaged Bashford Dean, the legendary first curator of arms and armor at New York's Metropolitan Museum of Art (the "Met"), to assist in designing helmets for the modern army.[3] Mr. Dean, in turn, engaged Mr. Higgins and Worcester Pressed Steel to produce prototypes of a design derived from Renaissance helmets. The War Department ultimately rejected the historical models and settled on the more prosaic "doughboy helmet," but Worcester Pressed Steel remained an important participant in the war effort, manufacturing nearly two hundred thousand helmets and many other munitions by war's end.[4]

Figure 12.1.   A split image of a knight and portrait of a woman, reflecting similarities in clothing design, courtesy of Worcester Art Museum.
Worcester Art Museum

Mr. Higgins's involvement with the war effort and his associations with Bashford Dean transformed a preexisting interest in arms and armor into a passion. After the war, Mr. Higgins began to collect in earnest, guided in part by Mr. Dean. In the late 1920s, Mr. Higgins and his wife Clara traveled extensively in Europe. Although Mr. Higgins's own fortune had survived the Great Depression, the political and economic aftermath of the war forced many European noble families to sell assets. Mr. Higgins seized the opportunity to assemble a world-class collection of arms and armor, which he augmented with purchases from great American collectors such as William Randolph Hearst and Jay Gould.

According to family lore, in the mid-1920s, Clara Higgins told her husband that there was too much armor in their stately William Street home and that Mr. Higgins must find another site to store his growing collection. Mr. Higgins was prompted to action. In 1928, he, his wife, and six other relatives and friends chartered the "The John Woodman Higgins Armory, Inc." In 1929, Mr. Higgins retained a Boston architect, Joseph Leland, to give form to Mr. Higgins's own idea to create an entirely new type of building that would be beautiful and practical, but would also reveal its industrial skeleton. By 1931, the building and Museum were opened to the public: "As a correspondent to the magazine *Steel* observed at the time the Museum opened, Higgins 'sought to build a structure of advanced design which in addition to its value as a place in which to work might be at the same time a steel building for a steel man, a monument to the industry to which he has given his life, and to which his own products might contribute.'"[5]

Built in part with labor and technology from Worcester Pressed Steel, and co-located with the steelworks, the first two floors of the dramatic art deco building housed Worcester Pressed Steel's corporate headquarters, and the top levels presented a grand, two-story faux-Renaissance "Great Hall" to house and exhibit Mr. Higgins's still-growing collection.

In 1931, when the building was complete, the John Woodman Higgins Armory Museum opened to the public with great fanfare, including a performance of the Boston Symphony Orchestra in the Great Hall. The Armory's archives include letters from celebrities of the times, including extensive correspondence from Norman Rockwell on the occasion of Mr. Rockwell's *Saturday Evening Post* cover drawing of a "knight watchman" having his coffee with one of the knights in the Higgins Armory Great Hall,[6] and a letter to Mr. Higgins from Groucho Marx, who quipped that while "there is no particular reason to bring me to Worcester, Massachusetts . . . if I ever get that far I will be happy to enroll myself as an Iron Knight, or any other knight that you may have around."[7]

For all its glory, however, the Higgins Armory Museum was always a "junior sibling" to the older, better known Worcester Art Museum. WAM was founded in 1896 by an earlier generation of Worcester industrialists and cultural elites, and it has its own illustrious history, including an impressive list of "firsts" and notable achievements placing it at the forefront of American art museums. The Museum houses renowned collections of Colonial American paintings, Revere silver, American impressionist watercolors, and early photography. As early as 1904, the Worcester Art Museum was exhibiting and collecting photography as fine art. In 1910, it became the first American museum to acquire a painting by Monet. In 1927, WAM was the first museum to bring a complete medieval building to America, and in 1932, WAM partnered with the Louvre and two other institutions in the professional excavation of Antioch, resulting in the Museum having the largest and among the finest Antioch mosaics on public display. More recently, WAM originated the first exhibition to focus on Judith Leyster, a rediscovered female Dutch painter from the golden age.

WAM has also been a leader in art scholarship, conservation, and audience engagement. Founded in the 1930s, WAM's Conservation Department remains one of the most respected conservation departments in any museum, and WAM directors have a remarkable history as leaders in the art world. Four of the now famous "Monuments Men" were directors or curators of the Worcester Art Museum, including George Stout and the illustrious Francis Henry Taylor,[8] who graduated from WAM to become one of the most famous directors of the Met. Currently, WAM is among the first art museums to redefine traditional curatorial and educational boundaries to better respond to the interests of twenty-first-century museumgoers.

As this parallel history may suggest, the relationship between the Higgins Armory and WAM had elements of sibling rivalry. If the two institutions saw themselves as members of the same Worcester family, then WAM was the privileged older sibling. Indeed, in one sense, the institutions' sibling rivalry was literal: John Woodman Higgins's older brother, Aldus Higgins, was himself a successful industrialist. Aldus Higgins was president and a principal owner of Norton Company, which in turn was older, larger, and more established than Worcester Pressed Steel. Although Aldus Higgins supported the Higgins Armory, he was better known in Worcester as a distinguished collector of art and a patron, benefactor, trustee, and sometime president of WAM.

Over the years, Higgins Armory and WAM collaborated on significant projects, but each sought to differentiate itself from the other in ways that siblings often do. WAM, befitting its senior status, was the more "serious" institution and became a founding member of the American Association of Museum Directors (AAMD), whose policies represent the "gold standard" in managing, exhibiting, and conserving museum collections.

Meanwhile, in contrast to its more staid, elder sibling, the Higgins Armory Museum continued to bear the personal touch of John Woodman Higgins, who (albeit with discriminating taste) purchased according to inclinations that did not necessarily correspond to current museum standards. For example, the Armory collection included high-quality reproductions with provenance from collections of William Randolph Hearst and Jay Gould, reflecting an era when reproductions were collected for decorative purposes. Similarly, Mr. Higgins's broad interest in pressed steel and decorative metalwork led him to collect a wide variety of iron and steel objects, ancient and modern, with no apparent relationship to one another except for the material used in their creation. Mr. Higgins collected Roman scalpels, Dacian arm bracelets, a Piper-Cub airplane, modern mass-produced utensils, automotive parts, and art deco forged metalwork. Other objects that did not belong in a museum collection were also occasionally assigned accession numbers. One notable example is Mr. Higgins's personal office desk, which, although a lovely piece of furniture, does not belong in a museum collection, particularly a museum of arms and armor.

Mr. Higgins's personal touch extended to interpretation and exhibition. He considered the steelworks themselves a part of the Museum. Museum visitors were encouraged to enter the factory to observe workers in action complete with museum labels explaining the workers' activities.[9] In his later years, Mr. Higgins delighted in personally conducting tours for visitors, especially children (who sometimes came to the Museum on their own after school to spend time with their "friend," Mr. Higgins). Norman Rockwell's *Nightwatchman* charcoal study for the *Saturday Evening Post* cover, which is part of the Higgins Collection and currently on exhibit at WAM, captures the whimsy of this era in its depiction of a museum guard balancing a sandwich in his lap and pouring coffee from a thermos while perched on the base of a mounted knight, the horse mannequin looking on askance.

THE END OF AN ERA:
JOHN WOODMAN HIGGINS EXITS THE STAGE

By 1978, however, the Armory's circumstances had changed. Mr. Higgins died in 1961. His son, Carter, who had succeeded him as president of Worcester Pressed Steel, died not long after. The Armory remained under family control through the 1960s, but it began to focus more consistently on its strength in arms and armor. At the same time, tax law changes made the operation of private museums increasingly difficult. The Armory became a private "foundation." Although Worcester Pressed Steel could no longer fund it directly, the Armory continued to receive much of its financial support in the form of rents from Worcester Pressed Steel, which continued to occupy the Armory building's lower floors. Partly for tax reasons but also to preserve the Armory's independence and its legacy, the Higgins family sold Worcester Pressed Steel in 1971. In 1974, Worcester Pressed Steel went bankrupt, and the Higgins Armory, which had no significant endowment, lost its most important revenue source.[10]

NEW BEGINNINGS:
THE MIXED BLESSINGS OF INDEPENDENCE

In 1979, governance of the Higgins Armory passed for the first time to an independent board of trustees, including Higgins family and friends. The new trustees were mostly from the Worcester area, and none were collectors of arms and armor. Mr. Higgins's surviving descendants wanted the Museum to continue, but neither they nor the remaining trustees filled the financial void left by the loss of the Worcester Pressed Steel rents. The Armory was running a significant annual deficit, and it was forced to consider for the first time how to support itself through admissions, programming, and auxiliary Museum activities.[11]

At this critical juncture, WAM made the first of several overtures to acquire the Higgins Collection. Under the 1979 WAM proposal, the two museums would have merged, and the Higgins Collection would have been placed in storage until a new building could be financed and built to house it. After six months of intensive negotiations, final merger papers were drafted and the WAM and Higgins Armory trustees were asked to vote to recommend the merger to the larger voting body of "incorporators."

Both the WAM and Higgins Armory boards of trustees recommended acceptance; however, the Armory trustees' vote was deeply divided. Deciding factors for the Armory trustees favoring the merger were the Armory's deepening financial losses and the trustees' fear that the Higgins Collection would be dismantled and lost to the City of Worcester if the deficit continued to mount. A smaller group of trustees, led by Higgins family members, strongly opposed the merger. The dissenting trustees believed that the Armory had not made a sufficient effort to become viable as an independent institution.

Under Massachusetts law, the merger could not be approved without a two-thirds vote of a much larger group of stakeholders called the "incorporators." As the Higgins Armory incorporators' vote approached, John Woodman Higgins's two surviving children—both Armory trustees—agreed to cover the Armory's anticipated operating deficit for the next ten years. With this additional financial assistance guaranteed, the incorporators ultimately voted down the merger.

The incorporators' vote rejecting the 1979 WAM merger proposal granted the Armory time and freedom to develop as an independent museum. Although other unsuccessful acquisition overtures followed from both WAM and Boston's Museum of Fine Arts, Higgins Armory remained resolutely independent for another three transformative decades.

Following leadership changes, the Higgins Armory carried on more or less successfully into the twenty-first century. Despite challenges and periodic reverses, the trustees, directors, and staff did what can fairly be described as an extraordinary job in difficult circumstances. Lacking sufficient endowment to provide substantial operating support, Higgins Armory became known for creative programming that attracted a loyal following and generated the revenue necessary to stay in business. Operations became increasingly lean and efficient, and the Armory became "opportunistic" in the best sense: it became expert at seeking out and seizing opportunities and at making the most of its physical and human assets.

Chief among the assets was, of course, the collection of arms and armor. The Higgins Collection was (and still is) the second largest collection of arms and armor in the Western Hemisphere, second in size only to the collection of the Met, and preeminent in its own right. The collection spans a period from circa 4,500 BCE to the modern era and includes objects from every continent. It is also "magnetic" in the sense that it strongly attracts visitors. After 1979, the Higgins Armory refocused on this core strength. It deaccessioned valuable art deco metalwork and other material that the trustees considered outside the scope of an arms and armor collection. Proceeds from such deaccessioning created a collections fund that enabled the Armory to make new purchases, further enhancing the collection.

In 1990, Higgins Armory initiated a capital campaign that raised over $2 million and allowed the Museum to convert the former Worcester Pressed Steel offices into useful space for programs, a Museum store, a "hands-on" gallery for children, a temporary exhibition gallery, a classroom, secure storage for those portions of the collection that were not on display, and offices for the curatorial, educational, and administrative staff. A compelling collection, engaging programming, and clever marketing ensured strong attendance. The Armory earned accreditation from the American Association of Museums (AAM).

Notwithstanding two persisting weak points (the unsuitable building and the inadequate endowment), the Higgins Armory became a stronger, more vital, and more resilient institution. Still, the Higgins trustees recognized much more needed to be done. Although the Armory was successful by many measures, it continued to rely too heavily on revenue generated by attendance, programs, and the store.

In the late 1990s, under the leadership of an energetic new director, the trustees began to assess the Armory's strategic needs, which, they concluded, were very substantial indeed. There was still no true endowment. Although the Armory had accumulated investments that it loosely called an "endowment," the amounts were modest and provided only limited support. The Armory struggled to make ends meet, let alone to update technology or undertake new initiatives. When times were good, the budget appeared to balance, but in reality, the Armory's finances depended largely on external events, such as the economy, which no museum can control.

The landmark Armory building was itself a part of the problem. In its unmodernized condition, it was expensive, both in terms of energy consumption and maintenance of its steel and glass exterior. Even more concerning was an engineering study, which revealed that the existing building could not under any foreseeable circumstances provide a suitable climate to conserve the collection.

To address these challenges, Higgins staff and trustees considered another capital campaign. They estimated the true need at $65 million. Sensing that such a large campaign was unrealistic, the Armory engaged fundraising consultants to assess the feasibility of a more modest $10 million campaign to fund essential facility and program initiatives and strengthen the Armory's endowment. Recognizing that Worcester alone could not support a campaign of even this magnitude, the study had a national scope with particular emphasis on Boston- and New York-based donors.

The results of the study were disappointing. The analysis indicated significant challenges, including a narrow base of existing donors, and advised the trustees to "field test" a campaign with a goal of only $5 million, representing just half the already pared-down perception of immediate $10 million need. Even at a reduced $5 million level, the evidence of feasibility was inconclusive. Nevertheless, the trustees of the Higgins Armory resolutely embarked on the recommended $5 million campaign.

Then, as fate would have it, the events of 9/11 intervened. The aftermath of 9/11 challenged almost all nonprofit institutions; but for Higgins Armory, which had struggled even in the preceding boom times, the combined economic and societal impacts of 9/11 were devastating, both on the newly launched campaign and on day-to-day operations. A mood of uncertainty overtook the nation, infecting the Armory's audiences and funders alike. Donors became more cautious. Local foundations continued, dutifully, to offer support, but at reduced levels. Potential donors outside the Worcester area retreated, and private philanthropists retrenched. At the same time, public budgets shrank, further reducing grant opportunities and even curtailing school visits, which had become a critical revenue staple for the Armory.

In these already straitened circumstances, the financial crisis of 2008 and the Great Recession that followed were the final nails in the Armory's coffin. After years of effort, its critical needs campaign was exhausted at $2.6 million, well short of the $5 million "field test" target, and only 4 percent of the true estimated need.

THE UNPLEASANT AWAKENING:
HIGGINS ARMORY CONFRONTS DIFFICULT CHALLENGES

In 2008, the Armory's treasurer expressed concern that converging post-9/11 trends, compounded by the financial market crash that began in 2007, presaged serious financial challenges. In addition to diminished philanthropic support and reductions in public spending that depressed visitation, the Armory's already limited endowment had itself suffered a serious decline. The ongoing need to draw the same amount from its investments to maintain even a lean operation was forcing the Armory to consume what endowment it had. The continuing draw exacerbated market losses and, if sustained, would entirely deplete the Armory's investments within just a few years. In short, the combined circumstances were unsustainable and would very soon threaten the Armory's existence.

At the same time, an independent factor, ultimately as important as the economic threats, complicated matters. The Higgins Armory had been without a permanent director for three years. It had plugged along in the meantime under a part-time interim head. But in mid-2008, after a long search, the Higgins Armory had engaged a new Executive Director. The trustees were optimistic that the new director would lead a turnaround, and hopes were raised as a temporary exhibit, mainly targeted to family audiences, proved popular and stimulated attendance. Unfortunately, the reprieve was illusory. The underlying financial challenges remained. Attempts to restart the fundraising campaign failed. Human resources were stretched to the limit, and within a little more than two years the new director resigned to pursue other opportunities.

At that point, Higgins Armory engaged a nonprofit consultant to become its Interim Director and to work with the board of trustees in charting the Armory's future. Further financial analysis led the trustees to conclude that the persistent challenges were insurmountable. The Armory's economic circumstances were unlikely to change. Existing donors had begun to express "fatigue" and question what the future could hold. Based on the fundraising feasibility study of 2004 and subsequent experience in the failed $5 million campaign, the trustees determined that it would not be prudent to begin a new campaign.

After careful deliberation, the trustees concluded that the Armory must undertake what they euphemistically called "strategic structural change."

THE HIGGINS DECISION-MAKING PROCESS: MAKING THE BEST OF A DIFFICULT SITUATION

Having accepted that the Higgins Armory could not continue as an independent museum, Armory staff and trustees worked together to establish principles to guide their search for a solution for the Museum and its collection. Ultimately, they settled on four "desired outcomes":

1. Provide for long-term stewardship of the Higgins Armory Museum's "Core Collection" by ensuring that the Collection would be kept intact, valued, preserved, studied, and used;
2. Keep the Core Collection in Worcester if reasonably feasible, and if not, then as close to Worcester as possible;
3. Seek a partner for the Core Collection that would embrace a transfer of the Higgins educational philosophy and approach to interpretation; and

4. Assure that any resulting integration with another institution would be transformative and sustainable and not merely a transfer of assets.

Next, the trustees and staff identified and tested the feasibility of various alternative structures. Under some, Higgins Armory might have continued to exist in some form and partner with another institution. Under others, the Armory would close and transfer its assets after negotiating agreements to fulfill the desired outcomes. Confidential overtures tested the interest of possible strategic partners or acquiring institutions in Worcester and beyond, including not just the Worcester Art Museum, but also various colleges and universities and other cultural institutions.

Possibilities for a partnership that would allow the Armory to continue as an independent entity were quickly exhausted. No other institution was prepared to assume responsibility for the Higgins building or operate the Museum as a separate campus, and the benefit of combining administrative services was insufficient to offset the Armory's fiscal challenges.

Moreover, the preliminary inquiries identified stumbling blocks that deterred other institutions. Although deaccessioning had been under way for well over ten years, the process was gradual. The Armory's still-remaining collection of 4,500 objects had not yet been refined to a "Core Collection" that met the standards of the Armory's own Collections Management Policy, let alone the standards of other institutions not principally focused on arms and armor. Even if refined to a much smaller "Core Collection," the resources required to acquire, conserve, exhibit, and house the collection would be very substantial indeed! At first, no institution would offer more than a token exhibit while most of the collection would be stored for a decade or more pending fundraising to pay the cost of a permanent exhibit. And there was at first little willingness to consider adopting the Armory's educational and interpretational philosophy.

Despite these challenges, WAM remained the most likely prospect. After all, WAM and Higgins were members of the same "family" of Worcester cultural institutions, and WAM had unsuccessfully invited Higgins to merge on three prior occasions.

LOOKING A GIFT HORSE IN THE MOUTH: WAM REJECTS HIGGINS ARMORY'S "MODEST PROPOSAL"

Leaders of Higgins Armory approached WAM during the summer of 2011 to explore again the theoretical possibilities of combining the Armory with WAM. However, the renewed courtship between WAM and the Armory at first seemed as ill-fated as that of Romeo and Juliet, or perhaps more aptly, Beatrice and Benedick in Shakespeare's *Much Ado About Nothing*.

The Armory's overture came at a moment of important change for WAM. In fall 2010, WAM was considering the shape of its own future. The Great Recession had also taken its toll on WAM's investments, revealing weaknesses in WAM's other revenue streams. Despite what many institutions would consider an enviable endowment, WAM's trustees were starkly aware that they must strengthen fundamentals—including visitation and development—in order to ensure a sustainable economic future. At the same time, a beloved longtime director had announced his retirement, and WAM's board was preoccupied with the search for a successor.

In September 2011, after several months of exploratory discussion authorized by both the Armory and WAM boards of trustees, Higgins Armory's leadership presented a formal proposal to WAM's trustees to "consolidate" WAM and the Armory. Emphasizing the Armory's attraction to family and tourist audiences and the anticipated fundraising and operating efficiencies of consolidation, the Higgins proposal suggested that WAM provide gallery space to create a "Higgins at WAM." The institutions would combine operations in stages over a period of years. Ultimately, WAM would employ the equivalent of twelve former Armory employees, repurpose existing WAM galleries to house the Higgins Collection as an "Age of Chivalry" curated by Armory staff, and provide space to host the Armory's existing "Castle Quest" interactive gallery. The Armory and WAM would work together to sell or repurpose the Armory building with the realized assets supporting both institutions, and both institutions would revise their missions and philosophies to create a new harmonized entity. WAM would benefit from the additional Armory assets and from the visitation and "brand loyalty" of Higgins Armory enthusiasts. And Higgins would benefit from WAM's strong endowment and its climate-controlled galleries.

Understanding well the magnificence and attractions of the Higgins Collection, and having long been interested in a partnership with Higgins, one can imagine that the WAM trustees would have been strongly interested in the Armory's proposal. Many WAM trustees were themselves longtime residents or supporters of the City of Worcester, and it is likely they shared a sense of the importance of keeping the Higgins Collection in Worcester. The WAM trustees likely also appreciated the Armory's courage in facing its economic realities and developing an exit strategy.

At the same time, the Armory's proposal seemed to require WAM to assume significant Armory costs (including the twelve additional employees), take on large parts of the Armory's operations, give up significant gallery space to the detriment of its own collection, and reinvent itself in a new and untested model. Although WAM's revenues and visitation were not as strong as WAM desired, the Armory's proposal was conjectural, rather than the product of detailed analysis and due diligence. It seemed to require, at a minimum, possible redirection or addition to WAM's core mission, and it came, coincidentally, at the exact same meeting where the WAM trustees chose a new director, a director, who, it could be argued, should be given the opportunity to consider and direct the Museum's future unfettered by an unexpected, last-minute plan to consolidate operations with another institution.

Perhaps, not surprisingly in these circumstances, the WAM trustees did not accept the Armory's proposal. Although the WAM board allowed informal conversations to continue, WAM made clear to the Armory that it was not interested in a consolidation similar to the September 2011 proposal and that even a revised approach might not be considered.

Frustrating as WAM's rejection may have been to Higgins, hindsight clearly shows it was a prudent exercise of fiduciary judgment that ultimately produced a better outcome. WAM's rejection forced a greater level of planning, ensuring that the eventual agreement was supported by thorough due diligence that addressed the needs of WAM as well as Higgins. Indeed, the process that the institutions followed after this first rejection helped WAM revitalize and "jump-start" its own mission while allowing the Armory to meet its "desired outcome" of providing an economically secure and sustainable future for the Higgins Collection.

THE WAY FORWARD: SIBLINGS LEARN TO COLLABORATE AND RESOLVE CHALLENGES

Following WAM's September 2011 rejection, informal conversations continued. WAM's new director took over in November 2011. Within months, he and the WAM board had formulated a bold new vision statement. Trumpeting "relevance" and "sustainability," WAM sought to increase its visitation threefold by 2020, while helping to revitalize cultural life in Worcester.

Gradually, WAM's new director was introduced to the Higgins Armory and the theoretical potential of bringing a world-class collection of arms and armor to the Worcester Art Museum. Although WAM continued to feel strongly that it could not engraft the Armory's mission, employees, and collection as an essentially freestanding museum within a museum, the new director and the WAM trustees began to consider integration possibilities that could draw on the Higgins's greatest strengths—its collection, popularity, and success at engaging audiences—in ways that would ultimately enhance WAM, improving rather than altering WAM's core mission of collecting, conserving, exhibiting, and interpreting world-class art. Thinking creatively, a first breakthrough came when WAM identified space that could potentially be converted to arms and armor galleries without diminishing exhibit space for the WAM's own thirty-six-thousand-piece collection.

Figure 12.2. A knight displayed in the gallery at the Worcester Art Museum, courtesy of the Worcester Art Museum.
Worcester Art Museum

At the same time, Higgins Armory scaled back its ambitions. WAM's re-action to its September 2011 proposal helped the Armory to understand that the "desired outcomes" could not be achieved unless the Armory accepted the need for fundamental change. In the meantime, the Armory continued to move purposefully to hone its still-unwieldy collection to a museum-worthy "Core," and it began to think not of a legal consolidation, but rather in terms of a complex gift, or asset transfer, including the Core Collection and a "dowry" to support it. To protect the Armory's most important goals, the gift would be conditioned on fulfillment of legal covenants, including covenants on naming, use of the dowry funds, and maintenance of the Higgins legacy.

Thus focused, discussions returned to the board level. On October 23, 2012, the WAM board unanimously adopted a resolution that expressed intent to accept the Higgins Collection, provided that the two institutions could satisfactorily resolve certain remaining issues. The resolution envisioned a Joint Committee with the Armory to identify and address the challenges of any proposed integration.

As if continuing the romantic comedy theme, a rare October snowstorm produced a travel ban that postponed an Armory board meeting to respond to WAM's resolution. However, the Higgins board met on November 5,

2012, and adopted a nearly identical reciprocal resolution. The resolutions listed key "threshold" and "implementation" issues, which the Armory and WAM negotiated to ensure that they echoed *both* the Armory's "desired outcomes" *and* WAM's requirement that any integration not endanger but rather strengthen WAM's revitalized vision and sustainability goals. If, and only if, these threshold and implementation issues were met, the reciprocal resolutions obligated the Armory to give and WAM to accept and accession the Higgins Core Collection.

The reciprocal resolutions served several purposes. They guaranteed the Higgins Armory a home for its collection if its "desired outcomes" could be met, and they transformed WAM into a partner in seeking to achieve those outcomes. The resolutions ensured that WAM would only accept the Higgins Core Collection under terms that would help fuel its own "jump-start," and they created a process for leaders of both institutions to work together to explore, review, and attain shared goals.

The Joint Committee authorized by the reciprocal resolutions comprised the presidents, directors, and treasurers of each institution, together with several additional trustees. It began meeting even before the resolutions were finalized and continued meeting almost biweekly for several months. Early meetings established a timeline for a possible integration and identified essential issues that must be addressed before an agreement could be finalized.

The timeline emerged quickly once it became clear and could be voiced that, in order to conserve dwindling resources, the Higgins Armory must close no later than December 31, 2013. Working backward, other dates fell into place. Legal and financial due diligence must be completed as quickly as possible to identify any obstacles. Negotiations had been and remained top secret through March 2013, but the clear need to provide Higgins's employees ample time to seek other employment and the necessity of obtaining a ratifying vote from the Higgins's incorporators mandated a publicity plan. A budget must be developed to support fundraising and inform ultimate negotiations over the "dowry"; the deaccessioning must be completed; and a plan must be developed to dispose of the building. The Joint Committee identified key issues and formed Subcommittees on Legal, Finance, PR/Communications, Facilities (WAM), and on the future of the Armory Building.

Under Massachusetts law, any transfer of substantially all the assets of a Massachusetts nonprofit corporation requires approval by the Office of the Attorney General and frequently by the Supreme Judicial Court of Massachusetts.[12] Recognizing that the Attorney General should be apprised of the contemplated transactions well in advance of a public announcement, Higgins Armory involved the Attorney General's office shortly after the reciprocal resolutions went into effect. This step proved to be critical. The Attorney

General's office provided guidance that informed, improved, and smoothed all of the legal processes that followed.

The Joint Committee also realized that it must maximize the public relations and fundraising momentum of the imminent public announcement by planning a year of farewell ceremonies at the Armory to be followed, as soon as possible after the closing, by a groundbreaking new exhibition and welcoming activities at WAM. Staffs of both institutions worked together to share and develop exhibits and programming. While WAM staff focused on preparing the transformational *Knights!* exhibit to open in March 2014, Higgins's staff enhanced programming to celebrate the Higgins Armory during its final year. A special exhibit recounted the story of John Woodman Higgins and his wonderful Museum. Visitors were encouraged to record their memories and thoughts, and the recordings are now part of WAM's archives.

Major donors strongly supported the transaction, recognizing that it would not only preserve the Higgins Collection but also revitalize and strengthen WAM. Within months of being advised of the integration plans, foundations and individual philanthropists pledged $6 million toward a $12 million campaign to fund the so-called "Higgins integration."

Another important, albeit unplanned, benefit of the Joint Committee and subcommittees was the trust they created. The value of the combination became clearer to each side, but just as importantly, each side came to understand and accept that the other was motivated by legitimate fiduciary concerns; that the final agreements would have to be mutually acceptable; and that this mutual acceptability would require creativity, goodwill, and compromise. Although the process was not always easy—emotions sometimes ran high, as they do in challenging circumstances, and occasional roadblocks seemed insurmountable—the Joint Committee had faith they were doing something necessary, important, and transformative for their institutions and for the city, and solutions gradually emerged.

THE THINGS THAT REALLY MATTER: DEFINING THE HIGGINS "CORE COLLECTION"

The fifteen months between the reciprocal resolutions and the closing of the Higgins Armory were busy, with details of the integration absorbing nearly full-time efforts from key staff and many trustees of both institutions. Many projects were undertaken jointly, but others were institution specific.

The most important of the institution-specific activities was the Higgins Armory's refinement of the entire existing Armory Collection to a Core Collection of objects that met the standards of the Armory's existing Collection

Management Policy. To be sure that no ethical walls were breached, WAM played no role in the deaccessioning.

The deaccessioning process began with a detailed, object-by-object review by the Armory's own expert curatorial staff, but then progressed to a formal peer review by arms and armor curators of the Met. The Higgins and Met curators' recommendations were then vetted by the Armory's Collections Committee, which itself included nontrustees with expertise in the field of arms and armor.

At each stage of the process, any object that was judged to be within the Armory's scope and worthy of remaining in a museum was retained. Only objects that did not meet preexisting Collections Management Policy criteria were culled, including some objects that were museum quality, but not properly included in a collection of arms and armor. Doubts were resolved in favor of retaining objects that required further evaluation.

Ultimately, the recommendations resulting from this process were presented to the Higgins's trustees for final approval. Deaccessioning ultimately reduced the Higgins Collection from 4,500 to 1,900 objects.

Although not appropriate for retention in the Core Collection, most of the deaccessioned objects were valuable. Disposition of the deaccessioned objects followed one of the three paths prescribed by the Armory's Collections Management Policy. The Armory engaged a leading specialist auctioneer to market and sell most of the objects at auction in London in order to attract international bidders. Some objects that had particular historical or other significance to the Worcester community were donated to appropriate local museums, such as the Worcester Historical Society, and a few additional objects were sold to museums outside of Worcester at negotiated prices in order to keep the objects in the public domain while nevertheless furthering the purposes of the integration.

THE IMPORTANCE OF PUBLIC PROCESS: BUILDING BOARD CONSENSUS AND CONDUCTING PUBLIC DISCOURSE

The reciprocal resolutions, the Joint Committee, and all other discussions between the Armory and WAM were, of necessity, confidential. The WAM and Armory trustees were informed, but sworn to secrecy. Knowing that the incorporators must ultimately approve any vote to close the Higgins Armory or transfer its assets, the Armory trustees had been educating the incorporators for several years about the financial challenges and need for radical change. However, the Higgins incorporators had not been told the identities of potential partners or the details of negotiations.

By February 2013, Joint Committee activity had advanced to a point where further progress could not be made without going public. Fundraising for the integration must begin in order to ensure funds could be received in time to assist with looming integration expenses; the public needed to be informed that fundamental change would be forthcoming; and WAM employees had to understand the goal of the work they were undertaking. As a result, the Joint Committee developed a tightly timed publicity "rollout" scheduled for the end of the month.

The burden of the publicity and communications fell more heavily on Higgins than WAM. The Armory advised its own employees on the morning of February 28. Later that same day, Higgins trustees and staff began to inform the Higgins incorporators through meetings and telephone calls, advising the incorporators of the Armory's anticipated December 31 closing, the reciprocal resolutions with WAM, and the work of the Joint Committee. On March 7, 2013, the Armory notified the public through press announcements, leaving the Armory's loyal followers nearly a year to visit, to mourn, and to celebrate the Higgins legacy.

Public reaction was understandably mixed. Higgins Armory was a unique and beloved institution that had touched many people in Worcester, throughout New England, and beyond. A majority sadly accepted the need for change. Some were initially skeptical of WAM's commitment to the Higgins legacy but accepted that keeping the collection at WAM was better than dispersing it or sending it elsewhere. However, a small but determined group led by a descendant of John Woodman Higgins vociferously opposed the transaction and publicly attacked the motives and performance of the Armory's trustees and senior management.

A special meeting of Higgins incorporators was convened on February 28, 2013, to provide information without yet calling for a vote. Opponents intensified their criticism and initiated a "Save the Higgins" website and campaign to raise funds. They proposed alternatives, all of which the Higgins board had already evaluated but rejected as impractical or imprudent. News media including the *Boston Globe* took up the story.[13]

By the time of the Armory's Annual Meeting on March 27, 2013, the battle lines were drawn. However, despite significant publicity, the Save the Higgins campaign had raised only $660. Financial help was *not* on the way. After passionate discussion, with news media waiting outside for word of the outcome, fifty-five of the sixty-eight incorporators who were eligible to vote approved the transaction. Ten voted against it, and three either abstained or were absent without proxies.[14]

The affirmative vote by 80 percent of all eligible incorporators comfortably exceeded the required two-thirds supermajority. However, the vote of incorporators was not the last hurdle. Through their vote, the incorporators conditioned the Armory trustees' authority to conclude the transaction on the satisfactory resolution of key points. Specifically, the final covenants must require that the Higgins Core Collection be accepted, managed, and conserved in accordance with WAM's policies and AAMD standards; that WAM satisfactorily exhibit the Collection; that WAM permanently identify the Collection as the Higgins Armory Collection; that WAM give appropriate consideration to hiring Armory employees; that the proceeds of Higgins non-collection assets be earmarked to support the transaction; and that WAM invite some Armory-approved representatives to join its own board of trustees.

ALL'S WELL THAT ENDS WELL: COVENANTS AND FUND ALLOCATION AGREEMENTS

In the months following the incorporators' vote, the public response to news of the Armory's closing was remarkable. Attendance reached all-time highs, but ironically, at revenue levels that nevertheless vindicated the Higgins trustees' conclusion that increasing the already robust attendance and program revenue could not possibly fill the economic gap in the Armory's finances.

As the Armory celebrated its final months, WAM and Higgins principals negotiated the final details of the transaction. The negotiations were exhaustive, lengthy, and distinctly arm's-length. Ultimately, the agreements reached were memorialized in two documents: the "Covenants for the Transfer of Assets of the Higgins Armory Museum to the Worcester Art Museum" and an "Agreement Concerning the Allocation of Monies to be Transferred . . . to the Worcester Art Museum."[15]

The Covenants include numerous provisions that protect the Armory's legacy. They require WAM to exhibit, conserve, and interpret the Core Collection, identifying it as the [John Woodman] Higgins Armory Collection. Through them, WAM agrees to endow a curatorial position to focus on the Higgins Collection, to recruit two trustees and a Collections Committee member acceptable to the Armory, and to give reasonable consideration to hiring Armory employees. The Covenants provide a Collections Fund to enhance the Higgins Armory Collection over time. Further, within five to seven years, WAM agrees to open a four-thousand-square-foot permanent exhibit displaying substantially the entirety of the Collection.

However, the Covenants are careful not to create a separate, siloed Higgins museum within the larger walls of WAM. They ensure, instead, that the Higgins Collection becomes equal and integrated into the Museum's collections as a whole. For example, the Covenants permit Higgins objects to be

Figure 12.3. Conservation efforts at the Worcester Art Museum, courtesy of the Worcester Art Museum.
Worcester Art Museum

displayed throughout the Museum, thereby enhancing curators' ability to tell stories and draw connections between artworks of many periods and cultures. Similarly, recognizing that the best museums are fluid and that standards for interpretation evolve over time, the Covenants also allow future generations of WAM leaders flexibility to reinterpret the manner in which the Collection is displayed and interpreted, so long as the new approaches honor the relationship of the objects and integrity of the Higgins Collection.

As such agreements must, the Covenants and Allocation Agreement direct WAM's use of the Higgins "dowry." Specifically, the documents create three new funds at WAM: (i) a Higgins Armory Collections Fund for the purchase of new objects for the Higgins Collection; (ii) a Higgins Armory Curatorial Endowment to support the Higgins Collection–focused curator; and (iii) a Higgins Armory General Endowment to help ensure WAM's long-term sustainability by providing additional support for operations, including increased costs resulting from the integration.

In November 2013, the Higgins and WAM Boards of Trustees voted unanimously to approve the Covenants and Allocation agreements. In December 2013, after attentive review of a substantial record, the Massachusetts Attorney General—and then the Commonwealth's Supreme Judicial Court—approved the agreements. On December 31, 2013, the Higgins Armory closed as scheduled after a glorious but bittersweet final day of fanfare, and on March 27, 2014, the Higgins Armory Collection began its renaissance with the opening of *Knights!* at WAM. Finally, within months of the Armory's closing, it was able to transfer $4.2 million to WAM under the Allocation Agreement, and more funds will be transferred over time.

THE FINAL TALLY

The final measure of the integration is the extent to which it compensates for unavoidable losses, such as the ambiance of the Armory Museum's Great Hall, by achieving goals that were beyond the Armory's capacity while simultaneously advancing WAM's transformation.

In this context, the *Knights!* exhibit, itself a strong start, is only the tip of the iceberg. The Core Collection is now securely housed in climate-controlled storage that could not be replicated in Higgins's iconic building under any circumstances. Every object in *Knights!* received conservation prior to installation, and conservation is ongoing. *Knights!* includes objects that could not be exhibited at Higgins because their condition prior to conservation did not allow it. The Armory's conservator is now a member of WAM's multidisciplinary conservation team with access to a staff scientist and technology that the Armory could only dream of. Other key Higgins personnel, including its curator, have joined WAM's staff. WAM continues to introduce Higgins-inspired programs that engage the essential family audience, which together with other initiatives have dramatically increased attendance. Through prudent monetization of noncollection assets, the future of the Higgins Collection will be secured by the three Higgins Armory funds called for in the Covenants (i.e., the Collections Fund, the Curatorial Endowment Fund, and the General Endowment Fund) that are expected to eventually top off at $7 million—representing nearly a fivefold increase over the Armory's eroding $1.5 million endowment prior to integration—thereby enhancing WAM's ability to exhibit and interpret the Collection. Foundations that loyally supported Higgins but had expressed concern over its future have contributed an additional $4 million to fund the cost of integration, and a new donor attracted to the synergy of the transaction donated an additional $2 million. Within five to seven years, the proposed two-and-a-half-story permanent gallery will exhibit *the entire Core Collection* of some 1,900 objects, not just the 450 selected objects that had been displayed in the Great Hall.

Had Higgins not confronted its systemic weakness at the moment it did, the result would have been slow death and with the risk that an irreplaceable collection would be forever lost. Had WAM not taken up the gauntlet, the Higgins Collection would, even in a "second-best case scenario," be in storage for at least ten years in some other city, and the Armory's legacy of family-oriented programming and audience engagement would inevitably have been lost. Fulfilling the entire potential of the Higgins integration is a challenge that will of course continue, but it will continue with resources that are the product of inspired collaboration. It would be false to say that nothing was lost, but much was gained. And perhaps most important, the looming catastrophic loss of the John Woodman Higgins Armory's Core Collection has been entirely avoided.

Although only a promise of things to come, *Knights!* fulfills WAM's and the Armory's commitments to one another, to their stakeholders, and to the people of Worcester, preserving and protecting the Core Collection, and shepherding it to new greatness.

13

Randolph College: A Study in Governance

Peter Dean and John E. Klein

Randolph College is a small liberal arts college in Lynchburg, Virginia, that was founded in 1891 as Randolph-Macon Woman's College to provide an undergraduate education for women equal to that of the best men's colleges.[1]

The college[2] has long been known for its excellent American art collection, which was started in 1907 with the acquisition of a portrait by William Merritt Chase of the college's first President (donated by the members of the class of 1907). Now consisting of more than three thousand paintings, drawings, and other works, the collection has been built over more than a hundred years of deliberate acquisitions, especially in connection with the college's Annual Exhibition of Contemporary Art, and donations.

In September 2006, more than a century after Randolph-Macon Woman's College embarked on its mission of educating women, the Board of Trustees voted that the college should become coeducational and admit men for the 2007–8 academic year. This decision was driven by the need to counter a sustained operating deficit and by the recognition that to do so the college had to broaden its enrollment base and increase its tuition revenues. As a result of the change to coeducation, the institution's name was changed to Randolph College.

In 2007, the Board of Trustees reluctantly but unanimously decided that, in order to strengthen the college's financial position, four paintings from the college's art collection should be sold and the proceeds added to the college's general endowment. The decision was controversial and has attracted some criticism from the museum community.

This chapter explores the decision to sell the paintings, the process by which they were selected, and the issues considered by the Board. This exploration is set in the context of information about the college's art collection, the purpose for which it is used by the college, how it has been displayed and housed, and the applicable accounting, legal, and other treatment of the collection as a college asset. An appreciation of these issues is essential to a full understanding of the college's decision-making process regarding the sale, and of the manner in which its art collection differs from collections held by many other institutions.

CREATION, OWNERSHIP, USE, AND MANAGEMENT OF THE ART COLLECTION

The genesis of Randolph College's art collection is attributable to a remarkable individual, Professor Louise Jordan Smith.[3] One of the first five members of the college's faculty, Professor Smith was an artist as well as a teacher, who believed strongly in the educational value of art and particularly of the importance of being exposed to original art. In 1900, she said:

> I should like to see the walls of the public school and academy filled with good reproductions of masterpieces; and in college I want an annual loan exhibition from one to two months open to all students. This exhibition must contain only the best work that is done anywhere. . . . As an inducement to these artists to lend their pictures it should be understood that the best pictures should be bought for a permanent collection, which will belong to the college.[4]

In 1911, Professor Smith began the college's Annual Exhibition of Contemporary Art with paintings selected from galleries in New York City. This annual exhibition reached its centenary in 2011 with the 100th Exhibition, and is believed to be the longest continuously run series of annual exhibitions of contemporary art at any American educational institution. Many of the works in the college's collection were acquired from one of the exhibitions as examples of contemporary art. Professor Smith's goal of establishing a permanent collection to be owned by the college was adopted by the Board of Trustees and supported by students and alumnae who contributed to an acquisition fund that was started in 1920. It is worth noting that even at that early date both the educational value of the art collection and its potential value to the college as an investment were expressly recognized:

> This collection seems desirable for many reasons; . . . it will be a means of education to many . . . and a more material consideration but an important one, the work we see in these exhibitions is that of men whose fame is steadily on the increase and buying these pictures will be a good financial investment.[5]

Ownership and Care of the Collection

Randolph College's art collection is owned outright by the college. Although the public may view works of art from the collection, the collection has never been dedicated to public use, and neither the art collection nor any other college assets are held in the public trust (see the "public trust" issue below). Control over the collection is exercised by the college administration on a day-to-day basis, principally by the staff of the Maier Museum of Art at Randolph College, but subject to oversight by the college's President and Board of Trustees.

The college, like any other owner of valuable assets, recognizes the artistic and historical significance of its art collection as well as its monetary value. The college follows recognized standards for the proper custody and care of works of art of the kind represented in the collection. The collection is insured.

Development and Use of the Collection

As with other college assets, the art collection is held by the college for use in support of the college's mission of providing an education in the liberal arts and sciences that "prepares students to engage the world critically and creatively, live and work honorably, and experience life abundantly."[6]

An appreciation of the fine arts has been an integral part of the college's curriculum since its founding. In keeping with Professor Smith's desire that students at the college should be exposed to the finest examples of original works of art on a daily basis, the paintings in the collection have always been on display and accessible to the college community. Works from the collection were originally displayed throughout the campus, especially in the library, main hall, and classrooms. Although the most valuable works, and all works not on display, are now held in the building known as the Maier Museum of Art at Randolph College, many original works from the collection are still displayed in public areas of the campus.

College faculty uses the paintings as teaching tools in many courses, not just art history. Some examples of topics studied are the imagery used in selected paintings (American culture); landscape paintings as indicative of attitudes toward nature and wilderness, and cloud formations (environmental studies); and use of light, color, and contrast (theater design). Students are encouraged to work as docents, to participate in the selection of works for inclusion in special exhibitions, and to curate and present entire exhibitions.

A Permanent Home for the Art

For more than thirty years the most valuable paintings in the college's collection have been displayed (and stored when not on display) in a building known as the Maier Museum of Art at Randolph College or more simply as the Maier. This building has an interesting history, which is relevant in this context.[7]

The Maier was constructed in 1952 on the college's campus in Lynchburg by the National Gallery of Art (with the support of the A. W. Mellon Educational and Charitable Trust) as a repository for the National Gallery's art collection in the event of a national emergency. The National Gallery never used the building, which was then generally referred to as the Art Gallery for that purpose, but portions of it were used from time to time for the display of art by the college.

Control over the building was eventually ceded to the college, and by 1977 the most valuable pieces of the college's art collection were transferred to the Art Gallery in order to display and keep them in a more secure location and to facilitate their study and conservation. In 1983, the Art Gallery building was renamed as the Maier Museum of Art in recognition of a substantial donation from the Sarah and Pauline Maier Scholarship Foundation, for the purpose of renovating the building and establishing an endowment to defray its operating costs. The name has since been revised to the Maier Museum of Art at Randolph College. Despite the use of the term *museum* in its name, the relocation of the paintings to the Maier did not effect any change in the purpose for which the college held them. The intention of Professor Mary Frances Williams, head of the Art Department and the first official curator of the college's collection, was to "[embrace] the challenge of creating through the gallery a viable art center for the community and for the college's art programs."[8] One of the purposes for the move was an educational one, to make it easier to study the paintings in relationship to each other.[9]

The Maier Museum of Art at Randolph College is not an entity that exists independently of Randolph College, but is an administrative department of the college that is responsible for the management of the art collection and the use of the Maier building. The director of the Maier reports to the President of the college. The Maier does not have a separate board of trustees or endowment, and its operating budget is determined by the college administration in coordination with the Maier staff, as part of the annual budgeting process for the college. Although most of the college's art collection is now housed in the Maier building for security, conservation, and display purposes, the move to the Maier did not alter the college's ownership of the paintings. That action reflected the recognition that the increasingly valuable art collection should be properly cared for, but it did not constitute a release by Randolph

College of any of its ultimate authority and control over its assets, including the collection and the Maier itself. Both the building and the department are sometimes referred to as the Maier or the Maier Museum, and that name is sometimes transferred informally to actions taken by Randolph College, such as a statement that "the Maier acquired a painting." However, to speak, as some have done, of "the Maier's collection" or "the Maier collection" is to use an expression of convenience that obscures the truth. Such expressions are misleading and do not mean that the Maier itself owns any art. Although the college has delegated the care of its art collection to the staff of the Maier, the collection remains an asset of the college, subject to the ultimate control of the Board of Trustees and the college administration. The Maier staff has published operating rules and policies from time to time,[10] but these departmental policies do not limit the authority or the governance and fiduciary responsibilities of the Board of Trustees.

The Maier is not an accredited museum, whether under criteria adopted by the American Association of Museums (AAM) or those of any other body.[11] Accreditation is a major step that requires compliance with many criteria, including the adoption of a statement of permanency with respect to the collection. The adoption of such a statement would require action by the Board of Trustees and has never occurred, nor (so far as we are aware) has it ever been proposed to the Board of Trustees by the college administration.

Although some have suggested that the Maier should become an accredited museum, that has never been the college's objective. The Maier falls short of the standards for accreditation in several respects, including the lack of a statement of permanency. Although its name incorporates the word *museum* and it is commonly referred to as the Maier Museum or the art museum, the Maier is not structured, and does not operate, as a museum in the full sense of the term.

The Maier is open to the public several days a week during the academic year (depending on the college calendar) and has shorter hours when the college is not in session. The Maier functions as a gallery where some of the best pieces of the college's art collection are on display, and special exhibitions are organized, such as the Annual Exhibition of Contemporary Art, exhibitions curated by the Maier staff and other members of the Randolph College community, and exhibitions of art by students and faculty; a teaching and performance space, where college classes and other education programs gather to study the paintings, students pursue internships and practicums in museum studies, and lectures and recitals are given.

The acquisition of a new work of art will occur either by purchase or as a gift. The college, either from accounts for the acquisition of art that are included in its endowment or from donations and are managed through the

Maier's budget, provides funds for acquisitions. Each new work of art is accepted as college inventory either into the campus collection or the museum collection, with the differentiation being based primarily on value. If displayed, items in the museum collection are hung in the Maier, and items from the campus collection are hung in other campus buildings.

There is no formal approval process for accession decisions, neither by a museum board (since there is none) nor by the college's Board of Trustees. The President of the college and senior staff are generally not involved. If funding is available, the decision whether a new work of art is to be added to the college's collection is generally made by the Maier staff with the assistance of members of the college's art faculty, and in accordance with guidelines adopted by the staff, which includes ensuring that gifts of art are not subject to restrictive conditions.

The Significance of FASB 116 and Capitalization of the Collection

Consistent with its purpose in establishing and using its art collection as an educational asset, but unlike many other institutions, Randolph College capitalizes its art collection for financial accounting purposes and discloses it as a general asset of the college on financial statements presented to institutional lenders and rating agencies. The collection is carried on the college's balance sheet as an asset valued at historical cost (in general, this represents the cost of acquired items and the value at the time of gift of donated items). In this respect the art collection is treated in the same way as other assets of the college that are used in support of its educational mission.

The college's practice of capitalizing its art collection long predates, but is consistent with, FASB Statement of Accounting Standards No. 116 Accounting for Contributions Received and Contributions Made.[12] It is important to understand the application of FASB 116, because it is this accounting rule that determines how collections held by nonprofit institutions, such as museums or colleges, are to be treated. FASB 116 prescribes two different, but equally legitimate, methods of accounting for collections.

The default method, which the college follows, is that a collection must be capitalized and shown as an asset on a nonprofit institution's balance sheet unless the institution elects not to capitalize the collection and also adopts certain policies. One of these policies (see clause [c] in footnote 12) requires the proceeds from sales of collection items to be used to acquire other items for the collection. If the institution does not formally adopt such a policy then the collection must be capitalized.

Most nonprofit institutions with significant collections, especially museums, follow the alternative method of not capitalizing or disclosing the value (even at cost) of their collections. To do this they must meet the conditions described in footnote 12.

A full discussion of FASB 116 is beyond the scope of this chapter, but it is worth commenting on at least one aspect of its history. The issue of the proper treatment of museum collections came under scrutiny in the 1990s, when the accounting profession was pressing for more complete disclosure of assets of nonprofit institutions, in the interests of providing better information about their financial condition. Members of the museum community argued vigorously against any rule that would require capitalization of a collection, because they did not want to disclose the value of their collections.[13] Several reasons were given for this position, including:

- the administrative burden of determining the value of an entire collection;
- the negative implications for fundraising;
- the temptations that would be placed on governing bodies and others from a disclosure of the value (even if not a current fair market value) of collections.

In essence, the argument made by many in the museum community was that if a museum could make an unequivocal commitment that its collection is not a freely saleable asset (even though that commitment might not be legally binding) then the collection should be ignored in assessing the solvency of the institution from an accounting perspective. This argument is based on the philosophical concept of the public trust, discussed below.

The "Public Trust" Issue

Why do museums generally adopt a practice of not capitalizing their collections, and why does Randolph College follow a different practice? The authors believe that one issue lying at the heart of the matter is the concept of the public trust.

The term *public trust* appears frequently in debates about nonprofit institutions, but it does not have a clearly defined meaning, either with respect to the public for whose benefit the trust exists, or the details of the trust. It is used sometimes as a policy justification for the tax exemption enjoyed by many nonprofit organizations, and at other times as support for an argument that an institution should refrain from some activity that is unwelcome to the proponents of the public trust. Despite the use of a legal term (trust), a public trust has little in common with the well-established legal concepts of a trust. Subject to some inapplicable exceptions, the establishment of a trust that would be recognized for legal purposes requires an express statement of purpose, a beneficiary for whose benefit the property is to be used, a trustee, and a description of the property subject to the trust. None of these apply to Randolph College's ownership of its art collection.

The college is a Virginia non-stock corporation and has qualified as a tax-exempt 501(c)(3) corporation under applicable Internal Revenue Service regulations. Its tax-exempt status is derived from its purpose as an educational institution, and not from its ownership of any class of assets or from a commitment to make any of those assets available to the public, or to hold them in trust for the public or any other group. Its primary mission and responsibilities are to provide an education for current and future students. The college is empowered and obligated to use its assets for that purpose, and must manage its assets prudently in order to fulfill that mission. As discussed further below, the Board of Trustees has a fiduciary obligation to govern and direct the college for these purposes, which do not include the amorphous concept of a public trust. That concept may be relevant to other kinds of institutions, but it has no application to Randolph College.

Expressed in another way, the college has an obligation to use its assets in support of its educational purpose. Its art collection is included in this directive, unless a legitimate reason were to arise that would justify diverting the collection from that purpose and restricting its use to some other purpose, such as display in a public museum. Such an act would not, and should not, be taken if in the judgment of the Board of Trustees it would make the collection unavailable as a source of support, and thus conflict with the primary goal of the college.

Policies Adopted by Museum Organizations

Organizations of museums and their directors, such as the American Association of Museums (AAM) and Association of Art Museum Directors (AAMD), have adopted detailed rules and standards that museums are encouraged to follow. These are often referred to as codes of ethics, though they have little to do with ethics in a philosophical or moral sense. Many of the standards relate to the management and care of art collections and are relevant to any institution or collector that owns art, while others apply directly to organizations that function as museums. Randolph College and the Maier staff follow recognized best practices with respect to collection management and care as published by such organizations, where applicable.

Other rules adopted by the AAM and AAMD are not necessarily applicable to all institutions that own art. For example, both the AAM and the AAMD have adopted rules relating to the sale or deaccessioning of items from a museum collection. Although the wording varies slightly, each of them has adopted a rule that requires an accredited museum (AAM) or a member museum (AAMD) to adopt a policy stating that proceeds of sales of a deaccessioned work should not be used for operations or capital expenses and should only be used for the acquisition of items for the collection or the direct care of the collection (AAM) or solely for the acquisition of other items for the collection (AAMD). Neither Randolph College nor the Maier (a department of the college) is an AAM-accredited museum or an AAMD member museum, nor has the college ever adopted such a policy.[14]

The AAMD also has a rule stating that member museums should not capitalize collections. As explained above, the college has always capitalized its art collection, which is permitted under FASB 116. The AAMD and some other organizations claim the right to censure or impose sanctions not only on members, but also on nonmembers, for alleged violations of their policies and codes of "ethics."

FINANCIAL ISSUES AND A DECISION TO SELL

Randolph College is an educational institution, and as such it must manage its assets to achieve the threefold goal of fulfilling its educational mission, upholding its educational and academic standards, and securing a financially sustainable position so that it can thrive and continue to educate students. By the early 2000s the evolution of undergraduate education in the United States, and especially the smaller number of female students who would apply to a single-sex college, limited the tuition revenue that the college could obtain from its enrollment, and that revenue was failing to keep up with its expenses.

As noted above, in 2006, after a long period of study and debate, the Board of Trustees of Randolph-Macon Woman's College voted for the college to become coeducational and to admit male students, starting in the fall of 2007. This necessarily meant that the college would have to change its name, and in July 2007 it became Randolph College.

The college had relied for many years on draws from its endowment to bridge the gap between its revenues (principally tuition revenues and donations to its annual fund) and its expenses. Although the college had a relatively large endowment for a small liberal arts college, this draw had increased to a level well beyond the 5 percent of endowment assets that is considered a benchmark for financial sustainability.

Recognizing that this trend was not sustainable, in addition to making the decision in 2006 that it should change its admission policy and admit male students, the college embarked on a study of ways in which the operating deficit could be reduced and the college could become financially sustainable.

However, it was projected that, even after the change to coeducation, the operating deficits would persist for several years until enrollment grew and tuition discounting to attract students could be reduced. Because continuing an excessive draw on the endowment could only cover the projected deficits, the Board recognized that it would be necessary to increase the size of the endowment, so that the sums withdrawn each year would be at or close to the sustainable draw benchmark of 5 percent.

To increase the size of the endowment would require substantial donations from alumnae and other donors, or the sale of selected college assets, in each case with the resulting funds being placed in the general endowment. The enlarged endowment fund would then be able to support the projected draws. Because of the expected controversy arising from the coeducation decision and the resulting name change, it was not considered feasible to raise the funds needed from alumnae donations. The college's research indicated that donations would fall initially and then start to recover as the necessary changes were made to achieve financial sustainability and as enrollment and tuition revenues improved. However, starting a capital campaign while in the midst of significant changes, without having had the time to demonstrate that the financial situation would improve, was not regarded as a strategy likely to succeed.

After a detailed review of alternatives, the Board came reluctantly to the conclusion that the necessary capital infusion to the endowment would have to come from the sale of selected assets or perhaps, in the case of the art collection, an arrangement to share some of the collection with another institution. No other group of assets owned by the college represented anything like the value of the art collection, so that became the principal focus of attention. While this process was under way, the situation was exacerbated by an action taken by the college's accrediting agency.

College Accreditation—SACS

As an accredited undergraduate college, Randolph College is bound to follow the rules and constraints of its accrediting agency: the Southern Association of Colleges and Schools (SACS). The Board of Trustees has a fiduciary responsibility for the management of the college. In addition to requiring compliance with applicable laws, this duty includes oversight of the process by which the college maintains its essential accreditation. Failure to remain in good standing with SACS, which conducts periodic and very thorough evaluations of every aspect of the college's operations, would lead to probation and eventual loss of accreditation, which would fatally damage the college. Although a college may from time to time disagree with actions taken by its accrediting agency, it cannot ignore them.

In December 2006, SACS placed Randolph College on warning and expressed concern that the college's financial situation was deteriorating and was not sustainable. This warning reflected awareness by SACS of the same aspects of the college's situation that had caused the Board of Trustees to approve the admission of men as undergraduate students—a persistent financial deficit that threatened the ability of the college to survive.

Although, as is customary, the SACS warning did not mandate any specific action (for example, the sale of assets such as art), it placed additional emphasis on the importance of the process for improving the college's financial stability that was already under way. Failure to get the SACS warning lifted would have resulted in the college being placed on probation, and eventually losing its accreditation. There is only a limited amount of time during which a college may remain on warning before being placed on probation.

Acknowledging that Randolph College's financial position had to be improved, and with the added impetus of the SACS warning, starting in 2007 the college implemented a series of severe expense reductions involving layoffs, early retirements, elimination of some academic departments, salary freezes, and reduction in benefits for staff and faculty. The college also initiated a thorough examination of the ways in which its assets could be used to generate funds for the endowment, including recourse to the art collection if necessary. As a result of the drastic measures taken by the college to improve its financial position, it was successful in persuading SACS in 2007 to remove the warning that had been imposed in 2006.

In 2011, the college successfully completed the rigorous process of earning reaffirmation of its accreditation from SACS. However, none of these welcome developments relieve the college from the burden of restoring financial stability. This task has become more challenging as a result of the 2008 financial crisis and its aftermath, which have adversely affected investment return on the college's endowment. Compliance with SACS standards remains a mandatory aspect of the college's governance and management and requires periodic reviews.

Decision to Sell Art

While Randolph College was engaged in the process of evaluating appropriate corrective measures, in December 2006 a proposal was submitted by several members of the college faculty, with the support of the art faculty and the then director of the Maier. They proposed that the college should explore the sale of a part interest in selected paintings to another institution, with the proceeds of sale being transferred to the college's endowment.

In pursuit of this goal, representatives of the college worked very hard for several months in 2007 to conclude an arrangement to share ownership of some of the college's art collection with another educational institution or art museum. The financial goal was to realize a substantial sum in cash proceeds that would be transferred to the college's endowment, but to retain a partial ownership interest in the paintings and the right to display them on the college campus on a regular and recurring basis.

This process involved identifying a core group of twenty-six significant paintings selected after obtaining advice from outside professionals, including directors of major art museums, concerning the integrity of the collection, as well as legal advice to ensure the absence of impediments. A total of eight museums and other institutions were approached, and serious discussions were conducted with two of them. Regrettably, it proved to be impossible to work out an acceptable transaction, and both institutions with which serious discussions were held declined to proceed.

This left the college with the difficult decision to select a smaller number of paintings to be sold outright, again with the proceeds being transferred to the college's endowment. The decision to sell any works of art from the college's collection, let alone any well-known ones, was taken with great reluctance by the Board of Trustees, and only after hard study of numerous alternatives in consultation with outside consultants and advisors. More than two-thirds of the Trustees were alumnae of the college and were personally familiar with the best-known paintings in the collection, having seen them regularly on campus while students and again on subsequent visits.

Before any decision was made to sell any part of the college's art collection, in November 2006, a selected group of alumnae was invited to help explore possible options for generating additional financial revenues from the art collection, such as adopting a painting, sharing art, and loaning works. A dozen alumnae, who had a particular interest in the art collection because of their professional and volunteer involvement with the arts, museums, and galleries, participated in meetings held in New York and Washington, DC, with a small group of Trustees. Following the Trustees' decision to sell selected paintings, the committee was unable to reach a consensus in support of the college's position and disbanded. The contacts with this group represented a sincere effort on the part of the college to consult with a knowledgeable constituency.

SELECTION OF PAINTINGS

Eventually, four paintings were selected by the college for sale and were consigned to Christie's in New York for sale at its November 2007 auction.

The paintings selected were *Men of the Docks* by George Bellows, *A Peaceable Kingdom* by Edward Hicks, *Through the Arroyo* by Martin Hennings, and *Troubador* by Rufino Tamayo. The college verified that each of these was owned free from legal restriction of any kind, whether donor imposed conditions or otherwise.

In making the selection, the college was advised by nationally recognized museum directors and consultants with experience in managing art collections held by colleges. The goal was to identify the smallest number of paintings that would raise the greatest amount of money, while preserving the core themes of the collection and ensuring that the college would be left with a coherent and important collection of American art to be used for its intended educational purposes. The selection decisions can be briefly summarized as follows. *Men of the Docks* was a highlight of the collection and the first major painting purchased directly by the college, but it had the highest estimated value. Retaining it in the collection and substituting others of equivalent value would have meant selling more items and reducing the overall value of the collection as an educational tool. *Through the Arroyo* is a painting by a Western artist that could be regarded as lying outside the core of the collection. Similarly, *A Peaceable Kingdom* represents a genre that is not central to the collection. Finally, *Troubador* was the only significant painting by a Latin American artist in a collection otherwise devoted to American artists.

Controversy

Shortly after the proposed sale was announced, a lawsuit was filed in Virginia in November 2007 by several plaintiffs that resulted in the imposition of a temporary injunction against the sale. The injunction was lifted after the plaintiffs were unable to post the full amount of the bond required by the court, but for the three months that the injunction was in place it prevented the college from selling the paintings at the scheduled auction at Christie's (at what proved, in retrospect, to be the top of the market), causing significant unrecoverable financial harm to the college. Following the resolution of the art sale litigation, one painting, *Troubador* by Rufino Tamayo, sold at auction at Christie's in May 2008 at a record price for a painting by a Mexican artist. The global financial crisis in the fall of 2008 had a severe negative effect on the American art market, similar to the decline of the stock market, and effectively put the sale of the other three paintings on hold. These paintings have been held in storage at Christie's for sale at an appropriate time when the American art market improves.[15]

Although the art sale litigation was discontinued, the college was criticized by the AAMD in 2010, as a result of the 2008 sale of the Tamayo and its announced intention to proceed with the sale of the other works at an appropriate time. The college disagrees with the AAMD's assertion of authority over the college's use and disposition of its collection and engaged in a prolonged dialogue with the AAMD, which included meetings with the AAMD Board of Directors and a visit to the college's campus from an AAMD delegation.

Fiduciary Responsibilities and Decisions

The Randolph College Board of Trustees and others in leadership positions at the college have had to make a series of difficult and sometimes controversial decisions in the process of implementing changes that were necessary to remedy the college's financial situation but would not undercut its primary educational obligations. An essential part of that process has been a consistent focus on the educational mission of the college and the obligation of the Board to make decisions in the best interests of the college so that it will continue to fulfill that mission for many years to come. The fiduciary obligations of the Board require the Trustees to pay primary attention to the survival of the college and its role as a liberal arts educational institution, and that is what underlies the decisions that have been made.

The Board has the duty to manage the college's assets so that they will support the college's mission. Taking any action that would require any group of assets to be segregated and preserved in perpetuity, whether by the creation of an express trust or the adoption of a policy that is intended to achieve the same result, would be a very serious step.

In theory, an express trust could be created and selected assets could be conveyed to that trust, but that can only be accomplished in accordance with specific legal requirements.[16] One of the consequences would be to deprive the college of the assets that it might need for its survival, since the full financial value of assets placed in such a trust would no longer be available to the college for use in support of its primary mission. Because of the conflict with the college's mission and the Board's fiduciary obligations that would result, the Board of Trustees has never contemplated, let alone authorized, the taking of any such action with respect to the art collection.

Similar objections would apply to the alternative approach of adoption by the Board of Trustees of a policy (whether based on the existence of an alleged public trust or otherwise) that restricts the use of proceeds of sale from any of its assets. Even if such a policy were not legally enforceable, it would constrain the ability of the college to carry out its primary mission. Such a step would have very serious consequences, and would not be in the interests of the college or current or future students. Randolph College's century-long tradition of collecting contemporary art for educational purposes and its resulting remarkable collection of American art is a significant benefit and serves to distinguish the college from other small liberal arts colleges. It also raises unusual challenges for a college of its size, since the success of the art collection program results in the college having a very valuable asset, at a time when the financial condition of small colleges is under great pressure.

One result of the debate about the art collection has been a renewed appreciation of the educational value of the collection, both for its own sake and also as a stimulus to the creative energies of the students. Randolph College remains committed to the continuation of its Annual Exhibition of Contemporary Art, the development of its art collection, and the use of the collection in support of its educational mission. This commitment is an incentive for the college to distinguish itself more clearly from other art institutions such as traditional museums.

We believe that the decisions taken with respect to the sale of four selected paintings were correct when viewed in the context of the college's situation and taking into account legal and financial considerations and the college's educational mission. Randolph College is pursuing an honorable, legitimate, and fully ethical course that reflects the heritage and traditions of the college. The college's actions have been consistent with its educational obligations, its applicable financial reporting standards, and its historical treatment of its art assets, and support its current and future goals.

The original version of this essay first appeared in *Museums and the Disposal Debate*, edited by Peter Davies (Museums Etc., 2011): www.MuseumEtc.com.

Randolph College

A Sequel, a New Relationship, and More Controversy

Peter Dean and Bradley W. Bateman

The second volume of *A Handbook for Academic Museums: Beyond Exhibitions and Education* (2012) included an essay, "Randolph College: A Study in Governance,"[1] by Peter Dean, a Trustee of Randolph College, and John Klein, then President of Randolph College. That essay (Dean and Klein 2012) discussed the history of Randolph College's art collection and the decision made by the college in 2007 to sell four paintings[2] from that collection and use the sale proceeds to increase the size of the college's endowment. This chapter carries the story further with an account of the sale in 2014 by the college to the National Gallery in London of one of those four paintings, *Men of the Docks* by George Bellows, and a discussion of the issues and controversies that have arisen as a result.

The purpose of this chapter is twofold: first, to describe the process of the sale of *Men of the Docks* and the significance of that event, and second, to explore some of the implications for colleges and universities of acquiring and owning valuable art collections while pursuing an educational mission. This second topic also discusses the tensions that arise at the intersection of academic and museum communities and organizations. Reference is made to Dean and Klein (2012) for additional details and other relevant aspects of the background to this chapter.

A SEQUEL AND A NEW RELATIONSHIP

Randolph College's Art Collection

As the result of a century of acquiring art, first as Randolph-Macon Woman's College and then as Randolph College,[3] the college owns a significant collection of American art. Many paintings were acquired directly by the college from its Annual Exhibition of Contemporary Art, which has been held each year since 1911. Other works have been donated to the college. Thanks to the vision and judgment of those organizing and selecting the annual exhibitions, who were determined to acquire only "the best work" for the college, and the generosity of those who have donated funds to the college for the purpose of art acquisitions, the value of the collection has increased greatly.

The college's purpose in building its art collection was to provide an education in which each student engaged directly with great art. That purpose has not changed, and the collection is still so used in support of the college's mission to prepare "students to engage the world critically and creatively, live and work honorably, and experience life abundantly." However, the increasing size and value of the collection, and the need to employ proper curatorial standards, inevitably led to changes in the location of and access to the paintings. Originally displayed throughout the campus, most of the collection is now housed in the college's Maier Museum of Art, which is used regularly for teaching purposes by members of the faculty and is also open to the public. Randolph College is the owner of all the art and accounts for the collection in its financial statements as a capital asset.[4] The Maier is neither a separate entity from the college nor an accredited museum.

THE PAINTING: *MEN OF THE DOCKS*

One of the first paintings acquired by the college, and perhaps its most celebrated acquisition, was *Men of the Docks*, painted in 1912 by George Bellows. This painting was purchased directly from the artist in 1920 after it had been displayed at the college in that year's Annual Exhibition. It is a bold and dramatic work set on the docks in Brooklyn in winter, where a group of longshoremen are gathered in front of a huge ocean liner with the office towers of Manhattan in the background. It has been described by the National Gallery as follows:

> *Men of the Docks* is the final and largest in a series of Bellows paintings of workers gathered on a frigid winter day on the New York waterfront. Heroically scaled and vigorously painted, part genre painting and part cityscape; it is an outstanding example of the socially engaged, modern realism that was central to American art in the early 20th century.[5]
>
> The wilful awkwardness and brutality with which [Bellows] paints the grey flank of the ocean liner, docked on the Brooklyn waterfront, the thick slabs of pigment that evoke forms and clothing of the workers and the dray horses,

and the careful distinguishing of the workers' various mute expressions evoke something of the raw and unbeautiful energy of the urban experience in what was at the time one of the world's fastest-growing cities. The looming Manhattan skyline opposite, however, is executed in a monochromatic mode. It is this control over the various levels of representation on a single canvas at which Bellows was the American master.[6]

Prior to the 1920 Annual Exhibition, *Men of the Docks* (figure 14.1) was selected for many exhibitions, including New York, Toledo, Columbus, Detroit, Philadelphia, Cincinnati, Chicago, and San Diego. It was apparently one of the artist's favorite works, but he was persuaded to sell it to Randolph-Macon Woman's College at least in part because he was interested in the college's plan to start a collection of original contemporary art, and because of its position as a women's college located in the South (Virginia). As a result he agreed to sell the painting for $2,500. The funds for the purchase were raised by the Randolph-Macon Art Association and included contributions from students at the college, alumnae of the college, and residents of Lynchburg, as well as trustees of the college, who raised half the sum.[7]

Ever since its acquisition, *Men of the Docks* was one of the best known and loved paintings in the college's collection. Generations of students were

Figure 14.1. George Bellows, *Men of the Docks*. 1912.
Randolph Museum

familiar with it from its prominent location in the college library and later from its display at the Maier. Many members of the faculty have used it as a teaching resource for art, history (both social and economic), and other subjects, and it has been included in exhibitions at several museums.

SALE OF *MEN OF THE DOCKS*

Dean and Klein (2012) describe the process that led to the decision by Randolph College to sell *Men of the Docks* and three other paintings in order to raise capital funds for the college's general endowment. These endowment funds are used as permanent capital that will yield an annual source of operational funds; none of the proceeds from the sale of the paintings is to be used for the ordinary operating expenses of the college or to pay down debt. Furthermore, to avoid depleting the value of the endowment, the amount drawn each year is limited in the budgetary process to an amount that represents a sustainable draw on the principal.

Men of the Docks was the most valuable painting in the college's collection. The painful decision to include it in the group of four works that were to be sold was driven by the realization that the sale of one major painting for a high price would enable the college to retain a far greater number of other works in the collection. In the end, the teaching value of a painting is not necessarily commensurate with its monetary value, and the Board of Trustees concluded that the value of the collection as an academic asset would be preserved better by maintaining the quantity and diversity of other works.

The proposed sale at auction in November 2007 was frustrated by litigation that resulted in a temporary injunction. Unfortunately for the college, the process of lifting the injunction and dismissing the litigation in late 2007 and early 2008 coincided with the collapse of the art market following the financial crisis that was developing at that time. Although one of the four paintings, *Troubador* by Rufino Tamayo, was sold very successfully at auction in May 2008, the estimated sale price of the other three, including *Men of the Docks*, was reduced and was not expected to approach previous levels until the American art market recovered.

Although the college did not alter its plans to sell the paintings, it was forced to bide its time for an indefinite period. The paintings remained for sale, but the college was not actively seeking buyers.

This situation persisted until the spring of 2013 when the college was contacted directly by the National Gallery in London with an offer to purchase the painting. This offer was coupled with a proposal that the National Gallery and the college should enter into an academic partnership involving internship opportunities for students at the college, lectures at the college, the possible loan of art between the Maier and the National Gallery, and other features. Following a period of negotiation, the parties agreed on a price of $25.5 million and the legal process commenced.

The contract was signed and the closing was set for the beginning of February 2014. On February 7 the sale was announced publicly when *Men of the Docks* was unveiled to the public at the National Gallery in Trafalgar Square. The sale received a great deal of attention in the press in both the United States and in the United Kingdom and in many other countries. Some of the reasons for this are discussed below.

MEN OF THE DOCKS IN LONDON

Displayed in Room 43, which is one of the galleries devoted to impressionist paintings, *Men of the Docks* hangs comfortably in the company of famous works by Manet, Monet, Pissarro, and Sisley. Reframed and beautifully lit, it holds its own, simultaneously revealing both the artistic influences that these masters, and others such as Goya, had on Bellows and his own vigorous commentary on social and economic conditions of the time. The painting is of an unmistakably American subject—the docks of New York City—but it speaks to larger issues as well. Bellows was a keen observer of some of the less attractive features of life in New York in the early twentieth century and his eye and point of view, as well as his painterly skills, are evident in this painting.

Depicting laborers seeking work on a freezing winter day that hangs on the cusp between misery and beauty, *Men of the Docks* is compelling visually and as commentary, asking important questions about capitalism, equality, and fairness that are as relevant today as they were in 1912. In that respect Bellows can be seen to go beyond the more genteel scenes reflected in the neighboring paintings and to look further below the surface. This perception sharpens the edge of any comparison of his work to the great masters he followed and adds great value to the experience of seeing his work juxtaposed with theirs.

SIGNIFICANCE OF THE SALE

From Randolph College's perspective, in addition to the sale proceeds, which would substantially increase the college's endowment, there are at least four other features of the sale that were recognized by the Board of the college and are worth mentioning.

Sale to a public museum: Although *Men of the Docks* was held by the college as an asset for the use of its academic program, it had been displayed publicly for many years and was well known both to scholars of American art and to residents in the Lynchburg community. Selling the painting to a public institution where it would continue to be on public display was considered to be an important benefit. This was especially true in the case of the National Gallery of London, which is one of the best-known art museums in the world, with a collection that, though smaller in size than some other major museums,[8] is of exceptionally high quality. Its reputation and location at Trafalgar Square in the center of London makes it one of the most visited art museums in the world, with about six million visitors a year, of whom almost one million come from North America. The total number of annual visitors is almost three orders of magnitude larger than the corresponding number of visitors to the Maier.

Although not all visitors to the National Gallery will visit the impressionist galleries where *Men of the Docks* is hung, it is clear that as a result of the sale the painting will be accessible without charge[9] to far more people in a year than would be able to see it at the Maier on the Randolph College campus in Lynchburg over a period of several decades. Even if one only considers the number of visitors to the National Gallery from the United States, many more of them will see the painting in London than would ever see it in Lynchburg.

The National Gallery is a national institution of great public importance in the United Kingdom. With almost two hundred years of history as a public institution, it has an unsurpassed reputation as a major museum, and the college is pleased that *Men of the Docks* will now be displayed in its galleries.

Educational partnership: The willingness of the National Gallery to enter into an educational partnership with Randolph College has generated a valuable opportunity for the college to enhance its educational mission and also demonstrate publicly the college's commitment to the incorporation of arts as an integral part of its curriculum. At the time of the writing the details of the partnership have not been announced, but they will include internships at the National Gallery for students, lectures at the college's campus in Lynchburg by curators and other department heads from the National Gallery, opportunities for students spending a semester at the college's campus in Reading, England, to attend lectures in London, and the possible loan of works between the Maier and the National Gallery. So far as the authors are aware, the National Gallery has no comparable educational arrangement with any other college or university in the United States.

First American painting at the National Gallery: Despite the scope of its remarkable collection, the National Gallery previously had no American paintings on display, and its purchase of *Men of the Docks* represents its first major acquisition of an American painting.[10] This purchase is a departure from the National

Gallery's previous collection policy, which limited its collection to artists from western Europe, and an expansion of that policy to include paintings from artists in other countries that are created in the western European tradition.

The sale to a British institution also means that *Men of the Docks* is the first painting by George Bellows in any public collection in the United Kingdom.

The emergence of the National Gallery as the purchaser of *Men of the Docks* is a happy coincidence of two institutions discovering a mutually beneficial confluence of interests. Randolph College's announcement that it would sell *Men of the Docks* matched the National Gallery's increasing interest in exploring American painting, and in particular the work of George Bellows. In 2009 the National Gallery entered into a collaboration with the Terra Foundation for American Art for the purpose of bringing American art to Britain, and in 2011 it organized an exhibition in London, *An American Experiment: George Bellows and the Ashcan Painters*. The success of that exhibition (which had more than ninety-eight thousand visitors) demonstrated the appeal of Bellows as an artist in Britain, where his work is not well known. This positive development was reinforced by the successful and comprehensive retrospective exhibition, *George Bellows*, that was organized in 2012 by the National Gallery of Art in Washington, DC, and also traveled to the Metropolitan Museum of Art in New York later that year and to the Royal Academy of Arts in London in 2013. *Men of the Docks* was included in that exhibition at all three venues.

Recognition of American art: As an American academic institution, Randolph College is pleased that this transaction brings long-lasting benefits to scholars, students, and lovers of art, especially American art. The acknowledgment of George Bellows as a major artist whose work can hang comfortably in the company of some of the greatest European artists is a recognition of the quality of early twentieth century American painting, and also an excellent demonstration of the links between Bellows and the traditions of western European art. As Dr. Nicholas Penny, the Director of the National Gallery, has said:

> Bellows has almost always been seen in the context of American painting, but the way he painted owed much to Manet, and his depiction of the violence and victims of New York derived from Goya and earlier Spanish art. He will seem as modern and original as ever in the National Gallery, but our visitors—many of them from North America—will understand him in a different way. We are thrilled to have been able to purchase this painting.[11]

Placing an American artist directly in the context of European paintings rather than in an American wing will enable visitors and students to understand better the universal qualities of great art and the lessons that the painting teaches. That is an outcome which any academic institution can and should welcome and support.

Randolph College celebrates the vision and determination of its early leaders that enabled the college to acquire such a magnificent work, and also its stewardship of the painting for ninety-four years. Though those who became familiar with the painting through its long display at the college's campus in Lynchburg must necessarily regret its absence, the fact that the painting is now hanging in one of the world's most renowned museums in a major international city, where it will be seen by millions every year, is a source of legitimate satisfaction. This sale to the National Gallery, which concludes a process begun in 2007, confirms the steadily increasing institutional vigor of Randolph College, and the establishment of an academic partnership adds a new and important relationship to the college's resources. Those associated with the college may feel proud that an international audience will now become more aware of Randolph College and its long stewardship of *Men of the Docks* as this painting takes its place among the masterpieces in the National Gallery. This is borne out by the many favorable comments received from alumnae of the college since the announcement of the sale.

MORE CONTROVERSY

One might suppose that the primary reason to tell the story of the sale of George Bellows's *Men of the Docks* would be to establish a public record of the sale so that future historians can document correctly the provenance of the painting. This would be true for any important painting, but Bellows's star is rising, and as the purchase of this painting by the National Gallery in London demonstrates, he is becoming recognized internationally as one of the leading American painters of the first half of the twentieth century, in the same rank as Edward Hopper. Thus, it seems especially important to have an accurate public record of the sale.

In the case of this sale, however, there is another reason for telling the story of the sale of the painting. Without in any way diminishing Bellows's stature or the importance of this work, it is also important to have an accurate account of the painting's sale because the sale was extremely controversial in certain circles.

AAMD SANCTIONS

About a month after the sale was announced, in March 2014, the Association of Art Museum Directors (AAMD) imposed sanctions upon the Maier Museum of Art at Randolph College. Previously, in June 2011, the AAMD had censured the Maier following the sale by the college in 2008 of one of the four paintings selected for sale in 2007 (Tamayo's *Troubador*) in order to raise funds for the college's endowment and its announced intention to proceed with the eventual sale of the three other paintings. The sanctions imposed in March went beyond a censure and included specific instructions to AAMD members directing them to suspend any loans of works of art and collaborations between the Maier and AAMD member museums. The AAMD is an organization whose membership is limited to individual directors of art museums located in North America that meet certain criteria as to collection size and budget, and other matters. An organization that is headed by an AAMD member is referred to in AAMD documents as a "member museum"; other art museums are referred to generally as "art museums," but it does not appear that term has any specific definition. No one at the college, whether or not associated with the Maier, is or ever has been a member of the AAMD. Despite the ownership of a very fine art collection, neither the college nor the Maier meets relevant AAMD eligibility criteria, nor are they subject to AAMD jurisdiction or oversight.[12]

The entire controversy around the sale by the college of paintings from its collection is conveniently encapsulated in the AAMD's principal argument from its "code of ethics": the proceeds from the sale of art from the collection of any art museum must only be used to buy more art for the collection of that museum. The AAMD's shorthand way of saying this is, "Art is not a fungible asset." This belief is used to justify the AAMD's position that the financial value of art should not be used to support an organization. From this point of view, the sale was controversial because the college sold *Men of the Docks* and transferred the sale proceeds into its endowment to generate income for the future operation of the College.[13]

For those unfamiliar with the AAMD's "code of ethics," the controversy may seem surprising since art is truly a fungible asset for almost anyone who owns it, and its financial value is in fact of great importance. Artists sell their own art to increase their incomes, make investments for their retirement, support their families, and send their children to college. Private collectors sell art regularly in order to have funds for making other purchases, whether it is to buy more art or to buy shares of Facebook or a second home. Businesses, whether large corporations, professional firms, or restaurants, often buy art and use it to decorate their premises, then sell it later to realize gains in the value of the art; they can (and do) use the money to purchase other assets. One can imagine that artists such as Jeff Koons and Damien Hirst would not be making so much art, at such a blistering pace, if art were not a fungible asset. Presumably artists would be very unhappy if art were not a fungible asset. So would auction houses and art dealers.

Thus, the statement that "art is not a fungible asset" is absurd when it is stated in isolation. What the AAMD really means to say is that "Art is not a fungible asset when it is owned by a museum." Given the fact that art is obviously a fungible asset, one might ask why this one class of owners (museums) must look at the objects in their art collection so differently than any other class of owners. Why is art a fungible asset for everyone who owns it except for a museum? The AAMD has not answered this question in a way that is either consistent or convincing.

INCONSISTENCIES

The AAMD's position is inconsistent in a literal sense since it does not object at all to the sale of art from the collection of a museum. It is quite willing to tolerate sales of art from a museum's collection; it is only concerned that the proceeds from the sale do not "escape" for any other purpose than the purchase of yet more art. For example, the AAMD expressly refused to criticize the sale in 2013 by the Pennsylvania Academy of Fine Arts of an important work by Edward Hopper for the purpose of raising funds to purchase contemporary art. In addition, at the time of writing the AAMD has failed to make any comment about the sale by the Georgia O'Keeffe Museum in November 2014 of *Jimson Weed* by Georgia O'Keeffe for $40 million, with the announced intention of using the proceeds for future acquisitions of other works by the same artist. Unlike the sale of *Men of the Docks* the O'Keeffe painting was purchased anonymously at auction and thus is likely to disappear from public view.

From this one can only conclude that, in the eyes of the AAMD, any one painting in a museum's collection is indeed fungible with any other painting that the museum might have a stronger reason for owning. Simply put, the AAMD believes that a museum may sell a Hopper to buy a Bellows, but it may not sell a Hopper to build a new wing in which to house its collection of Bellows paintings.

The AAMD is also inconsistent in its attitude to the use of sale proceeds by academic institutions that sell art. Its position that such proceeds should not be used for general institutional support is ignored when it is convenient to do so. In March 2014 (the same month in which it imposed sanctions on Randolph College) it made no objection to the purchase by the Kimbell Art Museum, itself an AAMD member museum, from Worcester College in Oxford of an important painting by Jacob van Ruysdael, the proceeds of which were used by the seller to fund the construction of student housing. According to the public record, that painting had been donated to Worcester College two hundred years earlier. Even leaving aside issues of donor intent (because the authors have no information on the terms of the gift to Worcester College), one may well wonder how the AAMD can justify such an inconsistent approach.

Sometimes the AAMD has justified its "ethical" stance against the use of sale proceeds for purposes other than acquiring new items by claiming that such use of proceeds might make donors less willing to donate a work of art, or contribute toward the purchase of a specific work of art, on the grounds that such use would devalue their original philanthropy. This is also an inconsistent argument. The AAMD evidently has no problem with the sale of a work of art, whether donated or purchased with a donor's funds (unless the work was accepted subject to an express condition prohibiting sale). It has no edict against the sale of any individual piece of art; its rules are restricted to the use of proceeds (though even those rules are applied inconsistently). If a donor bequeaths a Picasso to a museum that later sells the painting in order to purchase a Damien Hirst sculpture, the AAMD assumes that the donor (or other future donors) will not be upset and that this will have no effect on future philanthropy. But if the museum sells the Picasso to help build a new wing to house a collection of contemporary art, then the AAMD believes that this creates a risk that the donor (or other future donors) will abandon their philanthropy to art museums. Where is the evidence for this distinction?

A DIFFERENT VIEW OF AAMD RULES

The inconsistency explicit in the examples listed above makes it difficult not to conclude that the real issue for the AAMD is something different—maintaining the size of the collections owned by its member museums. A standard criterion for judging museums and museum directors is the size and quality of their collections. What the AAMD members seem to be defending with a series of inconsistent arguments is their own turf. If museum directors were genuinely concerned that potential donors would be repelled by the deaccessioning of works that have been donated (or that have been purchased with donated funds), then they would not allow the sale of those pieces of art at all. Instead, they assume that as long as the funds have been used for the purchase of another work that they deem to be more valuable, interesting, or relevant than the work that was sold, then donors will find this perfectly acceptable and will not be discouraged from continuing to donate.

This analysis reveals that despite the wording of the AAMD "code of ethics," the important issue is not what art has been donated to a museum or what piece of art has been purchased with contributions solicited from donors; what really matters is that the directors control the selection and management of their collections. As long as directors can sustain the size of their collections and control what is done with past gifts, their actions in selling art create no problems under their "code of ethics." This makes it very difficult not to infer that the real purpose of the code is to preserve the power and prestige of museum directors, including their ability to control acquisition budgets.

PUBLIC TRUST

Another argument often used by the AAMD to support its position is based on the presumed existence of a "public trust." By this argument, it contends that the art in a museum is held for the public's use and that selling it, therefore, violates a "public trust," somehow imposed on all art held by the museum, that the art will be held for the benefit of the public, whether or not any of it is actually on display and available to the public. This argument also seems inconsistent. The focus in the AAMD rules on the use of sale proceeds reveals that there is evidently no "public trust" attaching to any one work of art, only a public trust that is presumed to be attached to the fungible, monetized value of a piece of art—the proceeds of sale. If the trust covered the work itself then it could not be sold or otherwise disposed of without express authorization from the creator of the trust, but that step is never taken. This principle has apparently been partly codified in New York state law, in a rule adopted by the New York State Board of Regents that restricts the ability of state-chartered museums to sell items from a collection unless the proceeds are used for new acquisitions,[14] but in no other jurisdiction of which we are aware. The whole concept of a public trust arising in such a context has been criticized cogently as a so-called "ethical principle" (see Donn Zaretsky's recent essay on this topic[15]). It is also inapplicable to Randolph College, which owns its art collection directly and has not subjected it to any form of trust, a fact that the college made clear to the AAMD, long before the sale of *Men of the Docks*.

OTHER FLAWS IN AAMD REASONING

If one moves beyond the inconsistent arguments that the AAMD has offered for its edict against the sale of art from a museum's collection when sale proceeds are used for the general support of the selling institution, one finds, in the case of the sale of *Men of the Docks*, several additional features that make the AAMD's case for sanctioning the Maier Museum seem inconsistent with its own rules, and thus highly questionable.

The imposition of sanctions on the Maier Museum is inconsistent prima facie because neither the Maier nor Randolph College is a member of the AAMD. The AAMD's policy on deaccessioning, which is derived from its "ethical principles," states expressly that the policy applies to member museums.[16] Despite this clear limitation, the operative section that authorizes the imposition of sanctions applies expressly to any "art museum," whether or not it is a member museum.[17] The AAMD rules fail completely to establish, whether legally or otherwise, by what authority it has the right to impose sanctions on someone who is not a member of the organization.

In this case, the sanction is even more inconsistent because the Maier Museum had nothing to do with the sale to the National Gallery. The painting did not belong to the Maier, it was an asset owned directly by Randolph College, and the decisions with respect to its sale were made by the college's Board of Trustees. Personnel at the Maier were not informed of the sale of the painting until it was announced publicly, and the Maier is not a party to the contract with the National Gallery. Thus, the question clearly arises: why sanction the Maier Museum?

EFFECT OF SANCTIONS

The AAMD's decision to sanction the Maier will not alter Randolph College's use of its art collection. To the extent that it inhibits any other museum from borrowing any works from the Maier, or lending works to the Maier, those museums and the scholars, students, and art lovers who would see the works on loan will be the losers. The AAMD's actions undermine rather than promote scholarly activities. Since the National Gallery in London is not a member of the AAMD (whose membership is limited to directors of North American museums), the sanctions do not affect the college's plans for collaboration with the National Gallery.

LEGAL AND GOVERNANCE ISSUES

Beyond the inconsistencies and weaknesses in the AAMD's position, there are also more fundamental questions about whether its position is appropriate or legally valid. The question of whether the sale is appropriate leads quickly to the fundamental question of who bears the fiduciary responsibilities for the management of a museum or a college. Presumably any museums large enough to be members of the AAMD are governed by a board of trustees or board of directors. If they are, then the fiduciary responsibilities for each museum fall on the board and not on the director of the museum who is appointed by the board. For example, as in the recent case of the Delaware Art Museum, when bonds that were sold to raise funds for the expansion of a museum must be paid, it is the museum's board, not the director, that bears the responsibilities for seeing that the bonds are paid. If, as is the case with the Delaware Art Museum, the liquid funds are not available, then it is the board's decision, not the director's, whether to sell works of art to pay off the debt.

This is a matter of basic institutional governance. It is the board of a museum that is responsible for establishing policies for the management of its assets and performance of its obligations. In this context, the inappropriateness of the director of a museum making a declaration of whether any art may be sold, and what can be done with the proceeds of the sale, is glaringly obvious. It is not a director's place to make such a decision, and it is not the business of directors collectively to try to impose binding policies restricting what their governing boards may or may not do. Seen from this perspective, the AAMD's "code of ethics" looks even more like an effort by museum directors to protect their own prestige and power and prevent their boards from doing anything that might compromise that prestige and power.

Understanding the inappropriateness of museum directors taking upon themselves the decisions about what is done with the funds from deaccessioning also helps highlight the inappropriateness of their sanctioning Randolph College for the sale of *Men of the Docks*. The Board of Trustees of Randolph College has a fiduciary responsibility to see that the college provides the best possible liberal arts education to its students. The trustees' decision to sell the painting was based on a difficult decision that having a larger endowment was more important to providing that education than the continued ownership of the painting. Since the college, not an art museum, owned the painting, the board's decision had to be based on its collective judgment on the best way to fulfill the college's mission and meet the board's fiduciary responsibilities.

It is the obligation of the board of a college, and the individual trustees or directors, to fulfill two primary duties of due care and of obedience to the mission of the institution, and to do so in the best interests of the institution. The fact that a college may own art, or even have a museum, whether or not accredited, does not alter the mission of the college or trump the primary duties of the college's board. This is a matter of common sense and also of law. No doubt the existence of subordinate organizations within the structure of a university or college introduces complications in governance. But the tail does not, and cannot, wag the dog. In the end the purpose of a college such as Randolph College is to provide an education to enrolled students. That is a complex and often difficult mission, but it has to take priority over other wishes and goals. The views of the AAMD and other museum organizations cannot alter that reality. This issue, and especially the relationship between parent organizations such as a college and subordinate institutions was explored in greater detail by Mark Gold in the second volume of *A Handbook for Academic Museums: Beyond Exhibitions and Education*;[18] the reader is referred to that essay for additional discussion.

In summary, if museum directors do not have any business telling their boards what to do, still less do they have any business telling a college's board what to do.

ANTITRUST LAW

Finally, there is an unexplored legal question involved in the AAMD's sanctioning of the Maier Museum at Randolph College. For more than a century, federal antitrust laws have prohibited unlawful restraints on trade. Concerted refusals by two or more parties to deal with a third party (boycotts) that have economic effect in interstate commerce are prohibited as per se violations of law. Agreements to take such action can give rise to civil, and in extreme cases criminal, liability.[19] The AAMD's action in imposing sanctions on the Maier and directing its member museums to cease art lending and borrowing activities with the Maier has already caused some museums to withdraw from completing agreements for borrowing paintings from the college. Such actions have economic effect and reduce the revenues of the college, which raises the possibility that the sanctions may constitute a violation of federal antitrust laws.

CONCLUSION

The sale of *Men of the Docks* to the National Gallery in London was a milestone event. The sale enabled the National Gallery to own one of George Bellows's greatest paintings and will allow almost seven million people a year the opportunity to see the painting in the context of the western European paintings that most influenced Bellows. The sale confirms Bellows's status as one of the great American painters of the early twentieth century.

The sale also established a partnership between Randolph College and the National Gallery that will provide numerous educational opportunities for Randolph students: lectures at the college by experts from the National Gallery, internship opportunities in London, and loan opportunities that will enrich exhibitions and classes at the college. The sale also substantially increased the endowment of the college and will, thereby, allow for a larger annual contribution to the college's operating budget, which will enhance educational opportunities and scholarships for students.

But the sale was also controversial. From the college's point of view, the controversy was unnecessary. At a moment when support for art museums is undergoing a sea change with the reduction of much corporate and foundation support, the board of the Association of Art Museum Directors voted to sanction the Maier Art Museum by directing member museums to stop participating with the Maier Museum in exchanges of materials for exhibitions. The AAMD has no jurisdiction over Randolph College or the Maier, and there are serious ethical and legal arguments against its efforts to diminish the educational opportunities available to the students at Randolph. In an environment in which the AAMD fears continued loss of public support for museums, it has made a perverse decision to sanction an institution that had no part in the sale and that is not even eligible for AAMD membership. It remains to be seen whether the AAMD's inconsistent principles about the proper use of funds from deaccessioning will garner public support. It is difficult to understand how such an inconsistent "code of ethics" can be made compelling.

Whether the sanctions will increase philanthropic support for American art museums is unclear. But they have provided abundant publicity for a sale that has otherwise helped Randolph College and its students in manifold ways and represents a great moment in the rise of George Bellows in international stature.

The original version of this essay first appeared in *Museums and the Disposal Debate*, edited by Peter Davies (MuseumsEtc., 2011): www.MuseumsEtc.com.

15

Taking the Barbershop out of the Berkshires

How the Berkshire Museum Case May Set New Precedent

Julia Courtney

The story of Norman Rockwell's 1950 painting, *Shuffleton's Barbershop*, in the collection of the Berkshire Museum since 1958, quickly gained notoriety when it became the subject of great debate as the Berkshire Museum proposed to deaccession and sell the painting to help fund a reinvention of the institution and keep it from closing its doors.

The museum was running a $1.15 million annual deficit in 2017. The canvas, created by Rockwell in 1950, depicts a rural barbershop in East Arlington, Vermont, where Rob Shuffleton worked as a barber, styling up the locals. The subtly enigmatic work, created for the April 29, 1950, cover of *The Post*, is undoubtedly among Rockwell's masterpieces. Executed at the height of the artist's career, *Shuffleton's Barbershop* represents the very best of Norman Rockwell: a technical tour de force that demonstrates the continuing power and resonance of the artist's distinctive vision of American life.[1]

The work is a glimpse into the after-hours life of the quaint New England barbershop, where the owner, Rob Shuffleton, moonlights as a community cello player. Rockwell, who depicts him rehearsing his act, once referred to Shuffleton as "a tonsorial virtuoso who always trims his locks [to] exactly the right length." Shuffleton's Barbershop was a place, as was the little town of Arlington, Vermont, itself, where a world-famous artist could go and be treated like everyone else—which was what Rockwell preferred.[2] Donated to the museum by the artist in 1958, the painting resided in western Massachusetts for over sixty years, and will soon travel first to the Norman Rockwell Museum in Stockbridge, Massachusetts, where it will be on view for eighteen months as part of the recent settlement of a months-long court case.

Then the painting may potentially travel to another Massachusetts museum, before making its way to its new home on the West Coast at the Lucas Museum of Narrative Art in south Los Angeles, slated to open in 2022.[3] Until April 2018, the purchasing museum remained anonymous, to add intrigue to this creative resolution to deaccessioning. Cofounded by famed movie director George Lucas and his wife, Mellody Hobson, the Lucas Museum will also be home to thirteen other canvases and eight studies by Norman Rockwell.

The painting and the Berkshire Museum became a hotbed of controversy in 2017, when the museum planned to deaccession and sell forty artworks from the collection of forty thousand objects, in an effort to ease the museum's financial crisis and keep it from closing its doors. The sale was the first step in a plan designed to help the museum better serve its immediate community through a renovation and change in its mission, largely in response to the young families in the community and membership who reflect the museum's largest audience. According to the museum's website, educational programs that focus on science, exploration, and literacy are a huge attraction.

The forty artworks proposed for deaccession during midsummer of 2017 included Norman Rockwell's *Shuffleton's Barbershop* as well as works by Albert Bierstadt, Augustus Saint-Gaudens, Francis Picabia, Henry Moore, and Edouard Vuillard, which went on view at Sotheby's New York in advance of the intended sale in November 2017. This proposal quickly met with opposition from the local community and professional organizations that regulate the museum world, including the American Alliance of Museums (AAM) and the American Association of Art Museum Directors (AAMD). The sale was halted and an investigation by the Massachusetts Attorney General's Office (AGO) ensued.

The roller-coaster debate from summer to winter 2017 began with the museum's announcement of the sale on July 12, through Sotheby's New York. The museum board maintained that the sale was necessary to raise funds or the Berkshire Museum would have to close within eight years, due to financial strain and the decline in financial support. Community members who opposed the sale formed a grass-roots organization, Save the Art, in response. The pushback, along with objections registered by museum organizations AAM and AAMD, Rockwell's family, and the community prompted the investigation by the Massachusetts Attorney General's Office.

Initially chartered in 1871, the legislature placed geographic restrictions on the Berkshire Museum's collection, then known as the Athenaeum, requiring its display within Pittsfield, Massachusetts. Paper manufacturer Zenas Crane and his family endowed the institution with its land and significant artwork in the early twentieth century.[4]

The *Berkshire Eagle* newspaper in Pittsfield, Massachusetts, which followed the unfolding of the case with a magnifying glass, published the following timeline for the proposed sale of artwork from the museum's collection:

- 2016: Berkshire Museum trustees discuss the institution's future at two board retreats, including possible sale of artworks. Museum files new corporation papers with the Secretary of State's Office. Using language taken directly from state law, the organization states that it holds the right to "sell, convey, lease, exchange, transfer or otherwise dispose of all or any of its property."[5]
- June 2017: Museum board authorizes its President, Elizabeth McGraw, and museum Executive Director, Van Shields, to sign a consignment contract with Sotheby's New York for forty works of art.
- June 22: Museum attorney Mark Gold notifies AGO of the museum's plan to sell forty works of art from the collection in a letter, noting that none of the works have restrictions. Gold suggests auction proceeds could be as high as $75 million.
- July 11: Museum's Collections Committee meets to change its policies, eliminating a requirement that it first offer works to other museums and allowing it to use sale proceeds for operations expenses. The Committee votes to approve deaccession of forty works; minutes released by the museum show no discussion of the issue.
- July 12: Museum officials announce plans to sell forty works from the collection and use proceeds to build an endowment to ensure financial stability and pursue building renovations related to its "New Vision" project to emphasize multimedia and interactive exhibits focusing on science and natural history.
- Late July: Three national museum groups oppose the plan to use auction proceeds for the project and the endowment: the Association of Art Museum Curators (AAMC), the Association of Art Museum Directors (AAMD), and the American Alliance of Museums (AAM).
- Sept. 5: Museum Director, Van Shields, confirms that he withdrew the museum's relationship with the Smithsonian Institution. The affiliation began in April 2013.
- Sept. 20: Massachusetts Cultural Council (MCC) asks museum leaders to halt sale of artworks and suspends fiscal year 2018 funding to the museum. MCC's Executive Director, Anita Walker, calls the museum's plan a violation of the public trust.
- Sept. 22: State Representative Tricia Farley-Bouvier, D-Pittsfield, supports the museum's planned art sale and the people who shaped it, saying, "I stand firmly with the board of the Berkshire Museum."[6]

- Sept. 25: Nancy Edman Feldman resigns from the museum board at its annual meeting. Departure of Carol Riordan, who had abstained from the July 12 vote to sell the art, follows in August. "I resigned because I didn't agree with the strategic direction the museum was taking," said Riordan, the board's Treasurer. "I didn't find it transformative."[7]
- Oct. 13: Pittsfield Mayor, Linda Tyer, supports the museum's "bold transformation" to an institution focusing on science and natural history.
- Oct. 20: A group of plaintiffs, including three sons of artist Norman Rockwell and Pittsfield artist Tom Patti, file a civil lawsuit seeking an injunction halting the sale. The suit names the Massachusetts AGO as a party of interest, compelling that office to file a response.
- Oct. 20: Sotheby's New York publishes online catalogue featuring the sale of works linked to the museum's New Vision project. Sotheby's schedule demonstrates only nineteen of the original forty works have scheduled sale dates.
- Oct. 24: The museum announces that Shields, the museum's Executive Director, will take medical leave for surgery on a heart valve and will be absent through the rest of the year. Nina Garlington and Craig Langlois are named interim Co-Executive Directors during Shields's absence.
- Oct. 26: A second group of plaintiffs, made up of three residents of Lenox, file suit in Suffolk Superior Court also seeking injunction; the cases are combined.
- Oct. 27: New England Museum Association (NEMA) holds a roundtable "think tank" called *The Deaccessioning Dilemma: How Can We Support Standards AND Museums in Crisis?* at the annual NEMA Conference in Falmouth, Massachusetts.
- Nov. 1: Judge John A. Agostini of Berkshire Superior Court holds a hearing of the combined cases. Near the end of the hearing, the lead lawyer for the state asks that, if plaintiffs are found to lack standing, the state be entered as a plaintiff.
- Nov. 7: Agostini denies a request for injunction and criticizes the AGO for the handling of its review of the deaccession and sale.
- Nov. 10: AGO seeks and secures a preliminary injunction from Massachusetts Appeals Court. The thirty-day order bars the art sale, forcing seven of the Berkshire Museum works to be pulled from a scheduled Nov. 13 auction at Sotheby's New York City. Other works are also removed from three different auctions that week.
- Nov. 20: State Senator Adam Hinds, D-Pittsfield, praises museum trustees for taking bold action but indicates that they might need to consider compromise; urges the parties to find common ground.
- Nov. 20: Justice Joseph A. Trainor clarifies that all proceedings in the Berkshire Superior Court are on hold.

- November and early December: The museum and sale opponents file multiple motions with the Massachusetts Appeals Court. The museum seeks speedy trial at the Superior Court level. Opponents support higher-court review.
- Dec. 13: Trainor extends the injunction through Jan. 29. "These delays benefit no one," said William F. Lee of the Boston law firm WilmerHale. "It is ironic that, during this holiday season when the museum is visited and enjoyed by more families than ever, its future is placed in grave jeopardy."[8]
- Dec. 18: Appeals Court denies the museum's request to lift the prohibition on Superior Court action. It also denies the museum's bid to expedite the appeal, which normally takes many months to a year to play out.
- Dec. 26: Shields returns to the museum from medical leave on a part-time basis.
- Feb. 7, 2018: The AGO files a status report to the Appeals Court that the AGO and the museum will unite to seek resolution to the art-sale dispute, which could speed up the process. The public statement pledged cooperation to solve the question of whether museum trustees can sell two paintings (there is disagreement on whether or not the paintings are restricted) by artist Norman Rockwell, and other works.
- Feb. 9, 2018: Announcement of a resolution is made. Professional museum organizations are unhappy with the results. Art will be sold for up to $55 million and proceeds can be used to fund New Vision. The Rockwell, purchased by an anonymous museum, will remain in the public domain, but not in the Berkshires.
- April 5, 2018: Justice David Lowy of the Massachusetts Supreme Judicial Court said in a six-page ruling issued Thursday that the museum had sufficiently established a need to sell the works, which could raise upwards of $55 million, in order to continue operations. The decision clears the way for at least some of the pieces to go up for sale at Sotheby's in New York, and for the private sale of the prized Rockwell painting.
- April 12, 2018: The Lucas Museum of Narrative Art (cofounded by famed movie director George Lucas and wife, Mellody Hobson) reveals that they are the new owner of *Shuffleton's Barbershop* by Norman Rockwell. The Lucas Museum will also be home to thirteen other paintings and eight studies by Norman Rockwell.

As the case neared resolution, the status report issued on February 7, 2018, stated that the joint petition to be filed soon would ask for one or more of three types of court relief, including "equitable instruction," "deviation," or "cy pres." Under what's known as equitable instruction, parties ask a court to provide guidance on how trusts and assets should be interpreted. Under deviation, a court would modify terms of a trust—in this case, the documents that govern how the museum must operate. Or the court could engage in what is called cy pres, a process by which a nonprofit's purpose is allowed to change.[9]

This turn represented an attempt to truly resolve the case and bring forth perhaps unconsidered options that could appease both sides and set a precedent for deaccessioning cases in the museum world. According to summary of the settlement, which employed the cy pres court relief, the AGO and the museum jointly recognized:

- A shared responsibility for the collection of the Berkshire Museum and to the community it serves;
- The Berkshire Museum faces serious financial challenges including a dwindling endowment, a weakening fundraising climate, and an annual operating deficit of $1.15 million—that will force it to close within the next several years absent a substantial infusion of capital of approximately $60 million;
- Fundraising alone will not be sufficient to generate the capital necessary to ensure the museum's survival;
- The AGO, through its investigation, determined that the Berkshire Museum met its demonstrated financial need to deaccession assets;
- A two-year Master Planning Process, including extensive input from hundreds of members of the community, financial guidance from a respected nonprofit consultant, and consideration of alternatives to deaccession, led to development of a plan that will allow the museum to continue fulfilling its mission;
- A shared commitment to ensure public access, especially in the Berkshires, to Norman Rockwell's *Shuffleton's Barbershop*;
- The AGO believes court review is necessary before any sale, and the museum has filed a cy pres petition with the Supreme Judicial Court; and
- The importance of finding a solution that will help this community resolve its differences.[10]

Key terms of the agreement included:

- The Museum filed a cy pres petition, to which the AGO agreed, the petition filed with the Supreme Judicial Court outlines the terms of the settlement.
- If approved by the Supreme Judicial Court, the Berkshire Museum will be authorized to sell artworks to meet its financial need, with the agreement structured so that the museum may reach its financial goal without necessarily selling all forty works.

- This authority extends to the nineteen items the museum acquired before 1932.
- The Berkshire Museum can structure the sale of these works in an effort to raise up to $55 million, specifically:
  - $50 million of the net proceeds to the museum may be used by the museum without restriction;
  - Net proceeds between $50 and $55 million will be held by the museum in a separate fund for the benefit of the museum's collection and to be used for acquisitions and to support the museum's collection, including in connection with the New Vision;
  - Any net proceeds that exceed $55 million will be held by the museum in a separate fund for the benefit of the museum's art collection and to be used for acquisitions and to support the museum's art collection, including in connection with the New Vision.
- A nonprofit US museum has made an offer, obtained by the museum with the support of the AGO, to purchase *Shuffleton's Barbershop* with conditions ensuring the work will remain in public view, including:
  - Within 120 days of finalizing the acquisition of *Shuffleton's Barbershop*, the buyer will initiate a loan of the work to the Norman Rockwell Museum for a period of eighteen to twenty-four months;
  - Following the loan to the Norman Rockwell Museum, the buyer will explore the possibility of loaning *Shuffleton's Barbershop* to other museums in the Commonwealth of Massachusetts, such as the Museum of Fine Arts in Boston or the Worcester Art Museum;
  - The buyer will ultimately display *Shuffleton's Barbershop* in a place of prominence within its museum and will consider periodically loaning the work to museums in Berkshire County and to museums in the United States and around the world;
  - The remaining works will be sold in three groups, or tranches, as determined by the museum, until the museum receives $55 million in net proceeds, including the net proceeds from *Shuffleton's Barbershop*.[11]

The result means the Museum may not need to sell *all* of the forty deaccessioned artworks to avoid financial ruin and the Museum can sell these works in private sale, even for a lower price than would be received through public auction, if that means these works will be accessible to the public.

Both sides had strong arguments for and against the museum's original plan to sell the artwork, which illustrates the challenge of integrating ethical standards with practical, fiduciary responsibility. First, the Berkshire Museum's Board of Trustees contends that without the sale, the museum would

need to close its doors in seven years. The sons of late artist Norman Rockwell, along with supporters from the community who opposed deaccessioning, sought to block the auction sale and keep the paintings at the Berkshire
Museum and in Pittsfield, Massachusetts. They later retreated from litigation,
indicating that they were satisfied with the outcome and achieved the goal of
keeping the Rockwell in the public domain, even if not in the Berkshires.[12]

This inflexibility or unwillingness to deeply consider creative options to
the Museum's financial crisis while tempering ethical concerns demonstrates
a naïveté about the severity of the predicament and prohibits balanced, viable
solutions. It is unlikely that the Berkshire Museum (or any museum for that
matter) staffed with informed administrators and board members would entertain such dramatic measures unless they were truly warranted. That said, it is
the responsibility of professional museum organizations to scrutinize and challenge seemingly impetuous proposals initiated by museum boards, as a means
of checks and balances, so that a more comprehensive solution can emerge.

The AAM, AAMD published a joint statement in protest of the sale of the
Rockwell painting:

One of the most fundamental and long-standing principles in the museum field
is that a collection is held in the public trust and must *not* be treated as a dispos-
able financial asset. This prohibition is upheld by both AAMD and by AAM,
which sets accreditation standards for art museums, science centers, natural
history museums, and historical museums.

AAM and AAMD are communities of museum professionals founded to support museums, large and small, and the diverse communities they serve. Actions
such as those being proposed by the Berkshire Museum undermine the public's
trust in the mission of nonprofit museums—and museums' ability to collect,
teach, study, and preserve works for their communities now and into the future.

Two of the works the museum is currently planning to sell are important
paintings by Norman Rockwell, given by the artist to the people of Pittsfield.
Rockwell entrusted these works to the museum for safekeeping and to share
with the public. The other works proposed for sale are by many noted artists
from America and around the world. If these works were indeed sold, it would
be an irredeemable loss for the present and for generations to come.

Selling from the collection for purposes such as capital projects or operating
funds not only diminishes the core of works available to the public; it erodes the
future fundraising ability of museums nationwide. Such a sale sends a message
to existing and prospective donors that museums can raise funds by selling parts
of their collection, thereby discouraging not only financial supporters, who may
feel that their support isn't needed, but also donors of artworks and artifacts,
who may fear that their cherished objects could be sold at any time to the highest
bidder to make up for a museum's budget shortfalls. That cuts to the heart not
only of the Berkshire Museum, but every museum in the United States.

The Berkshire Museum contends that in order to be a good steward of their institution they must be poor stewards of their collection. We believe those two responsibilities are not mutually exclusive. We are sympathetic to the financial challenges museums of all sizes may face. And we are heartened by the many creative solutions that museums across the country have developed to meet those challenges and uphold the professional standards of the field.

We have been in communication with the Berkshire Museum leadership and we continue to hope that they will reconsider their decision. We stand ready to assist, in any way we are able, to find other solutions to the institution's needs without resorting to the selling of works that can never be recovered.[13]

According to the *Art Newspaper,* potential buyers for *Shuffleton's Barbershop* included celebrities George Lucas and Alice Walton, prominent collectors of Rockwell's work who both have or are constructing private museums. The spokesman for the Lucas Museum of Narrative Art, due to open in two years in Los Angeles, would not initially comment on the Berkshire Museum agreement,[14] but in April 2018, revealed that they were the new owners of the canvas. The $1.15 million deficit that the Berkshire Museum faced inspired a proposal for a dramatic institutional overhaul and prompted an agreement to explore the possibility of similar transactions that would place the works in public institutions, even if they prove less financially lucrative than selling the works at auction.[15]

Brian Allen, art historian and former director of the Addison Gallery of Art at Phillips Academy in Andover, Massachusetts, recently commented in an article published by the international *Art Newspaper*, titled "Auctions Houses Must Share the Blame for University Sell-Offs," that auction houses who help museums to "raid their collections" should be held accountable and stated that formerly they understood this to be a "low down business practice."[16] This area of the deaccession process should be explored more deeply to see if alternate means exist to keep artwork in the public domain, while providing museums in distress with the needed resources. Private clients typically pay more for artwork than nonprofit museums would, but with some additional incentives, auction houses might be swayed to assist museums in matching the artwork they are deaccessioning with a museum that would welcome the new acquisition.

Elizabeth McGraw, the President of the Berkshire Museum's board of trustees, commented, "For the people of Berkshire County who rely on our museum to engage with the arts, history, and science, this agreement is the promise of a long future for our small but extraordinary museum and its collection." A spokeswoman for the Massachusetts AGO advised, "Importantly, the agreement adheres to Massachusetts charities law and sets an important precedent for other museums that charitable organizations must act transparently and seek court approval to modify restrictions and sell charitable assets in accordance with their charitable mission and demonstrated financial need."[17]

In a formal joint statement, the AAM and AAMD commented on the resolution: "While the negotiated agreement with the Berkshire Museum may satisfy legal standards, it falls far short of ethical standards and best practices for museums. This is indeed a sad day for the arts community in the Berkshires and the museum community across the country." The organizations added that they firmly believed the sale of art to fund operational expenses "is a violation of the public trust, and is not the path to financial sustainability for museums. On the contrary: the more museums violate the trust of their donors and the public, the more it will diminish the volume of future donations—both cash and objects—and lead to the need for more such sales."[18]

The efforts by the Berkshire Museum to monetize artworks that led to the Massachusetts AGO's involvement to stop the sale didn't happen overnight. Selling off or "deaccessioning" objects from an institution's collection often "happens after a museum has been on shaky financial ground for quite a while," according to Sally Yerkovich, director of Seton Hall University's Institute of Museum Ethics and author of *A Practical Guide to Museum Ethics*. "It comes at the end of the process."[19] "Things do change. Tastes change, the focus of a museum may change, the financial situation of a museum may change, and the people in charge of a museum don't want their hands or their successors' hands to be tied by strict conditions."[20]

Much of the concern and publicity over the case and the Rockwell painting being transferred into private hands is understandable; however, true apprehension about artwork moving from public institutions into the private domain would also extend to the forty other works, which have mostly been kept out of the limelight; protestors have downplayed them in favor of the more compelling battle of keeping the Rockwell painting in the Berkshires. One could argue that some of the other works are more important from an art historical perspective. For example, works by Hudson River painters Albert Bierstadt and Frederic Church, whose work was included on the list of those to be auctioned, have garnered no specific protests. The two artists were among the best-known and most successful painters of their generation. Bierstadt spent several weeks in Yosemite Valley on expedition for the US Army, completing the plein air studies he later used to compose his most important paintings. He used studies created during all stages of his journey to complete a remarkable series of large-scale paintings that not only secured his position as the premier painter of the western American landscape but also offered a war-torn nation a golden image of their own Promised Land.[21] Frederic Edwin Church's painting *Valley of Santa Ysabel, New Granada*, with an auction estimate of $7 million, though lesser known, is an outstanding example of his work near the end of the luminist movement.[22]

Two charming works by William-Adolphe Bouguereau, also on the list to be auctioned, have hardly been mentioned in the protests surrounding the de-accession and sale. *The Newborn Lamb* and *The Horseback Ride*, with a combined auction estimate of $5 to $6 million, certainly warrant some attention.

Barbizon artist George Inness's canvas, *Mountain Landscape: The Artist at Work in Leeds, in the Catskills with Artist Sketching* (1867–69), exemplifies that Inness was inspired by the idea of divine significance in nature. Similarly, *Magnolia*, a still life by John La Farge, best known for his stained glasswork, is another fine painting.

According to the Berkshire Museum's website, once the Supreme Judicial Court approved the agreement between the Attorney General and Museum, the Museum was permitted to complete the sale of *Shuffleton's Barbershop* to a nonprofit American museum, and to sell thirty-nine other works of art previously deaccessioned through Sotheby's auction house. Once the litigation ended, the Museum will resume its capital campaign and make decisions about its future based on the outcome of both.

In December, the AAM hosted a think-tank style convening of museum professionals, board members, and volunteers at Harvard University, *Don't Raid the Cookie Jar: Creating Early Interventions to Prevent Deaccessioning Crises*. In the Summary Report notes, participants commented that the "temptation to link sale of deaccessioned materials to financial need, may increase in coming years because the growth of collections, overall, is outpacing the ability of museums to support that growth."[23] Although while the convening took place, a Massachusetts Appeals Court judge extended an injunction blocking the sale of collections from the Berkshire Museum and the grass-roots group Save the Art/Save the Museum staged a rally outside the convening venue to protest that sale, the agenda and discussions purposely did not focus on the Berkshire Museum or any other particular case of deaccessioning.[24] Instead, participants brainstormed modes of detection, timelines, and risk factors for intervention for museums in distress, identifying possible "red flags" and intervention methods. Several "pitches" were made at the end of the two-day sessions identifying ways to assist museums: Trustee and Museum Director Training Workshops, Financial Health Dashboard, and a Leadership Training and Trustee Support System. While admirable, these measures can only be applied early in the process of financial decline. It was recognized in the end-of-day debriefing sessions that the gap between the guidelines from AAM's and AAMD's ethics policies and the reality museums face must be addressed. A future convening of professionals to explore new options in the evolving financial landscape like mergers, changes in standards, etc. was suggested and hopefully will transpire.

It will be interesting to see how and if professional standards regarding deaccessioning for museums may change over the next five to ten years. A glimpse into the after-hours life of museum finances may be warranted. And like owner and barber Rob Shuffleton, of Rockwell's famed painting *Shuffleton's Barbershop*, who moonlighted as a cello player, museum professionals, boards of trustees, and supporters may need to "moonlight" by exploring ways to integrate museum ethics with the financial realities that museums are likely to face going forward. This critical discussion has the potential of truly impacting the way that museum deaccessioning is handled in the future.

Notes

INTRODUCTION

1. American Alliance of Museums, *Direct Care of Collections: Ethics, Guidelines and Recommendations* (April 2016): 3.

2. AAM, 5.

3. AAM, 6.

4. van Gelder, Lawrence, *1971–73 Deals Studied*, *New York Times* (Archives), June 27, 1973, pg. 113, accessed on June 27, 2018.

5. van Gelder, 113.

6. van Gelder, 113.

7. van Gelder, 113.

8. van Gelder, 113.

9. Chen, Sue, "Art Deaccessions and the Limits of Fiduciary Duty," *Art Antiguity and Law*, Duke Law Student Paper Series, 2009, pg. 104.

10. Chen, 104.

11. Chen, 104.

12. Jennifer White, "When It's Okay to Sell the Monet: A Trustee-Fiduciary Duty Framework for Analyzing the Deaccessioning of Art to Meet Museum Operating Expenses," *Michigan Law Review* 94, no. 4 (February 1996): 1065.

13. White, 1065.

14. White, 1065

15. White, 1065.

16. White, 1065.

17. Bernie Fishman, Two Cheers for Deaccessioning, Is it Okay to Sell the Monet: Deaccessioning for Museum, Julia Courtney.

CHAPTER 3

1. American Alliance of Museums, *Code of Ethics for Museums*, 2000.

2. American Alliance of Museums Accreditation Commission, *Considerations for AAM Accredited Museums Facing Retrenchment or Downsizing*, 2008.

3. Association of Art Museum Directors, *Policy on Deaccessioning*, 2010.

4. American Bar Association, Business Law Section, Subcommittee on the Model Nonprofit Corporation Law, *Revised Model Nonprofit Corporation Act* (Prentice Hall Law and Business, 1988, Section 8.30[a]).

5. See, for example, Massachusetts Charitable Mechanic Ass'n v. Beede et al., 320 Mass. 601 (1947), cited in Commonwealth of Massachusetts, Office of the Attorney General, *Guidelines on Notice Requirements of G.L. c. 180, §8A(c)*.

6. Sotheby's, *Important Old Master Paintings: The Property of the New-York Historical Society (Sale 6653)*, January 12, 1995 (with auction results laid in); *Important Paperweights: The Property of the New-York Historical Society (Sale 6656)*, January 18, 1995 (with auction results laid in); *Americana and Decorative Arts: The Property of the New-York Historical Society (Sale 6661)*, January 29, 1995 (with auction results laid in).

7. "Rules Governing Pre-Emption for N. Y. State Public Institutions," reproduced in *Legal Issues for Museum Administration*, American Law Institute, 1995.

8. Sotheby's, auction results laid in.

9. Carol Vogel, "Met Museum Pre-empts Sale of Old Master," *New York Times*, January 20, 1995.

10. "$17.6 Million for Historical Society," *Art in America* (March 1995): 29.

11. Beverly Schreiber Jacoby, "Cavaet Pre-Emptor," *Museum News* (January/February 1996): 55.

12. Jacoby, 55.

13. Jacoby, 55.

14. Brooklyn Museum press release, "Brooklyn Museum Announces Landmark Costume Collection Partnership with Metropolitan Museum," December 16, 2008, http://www.brooklynmuseum.org/press/uploads/Costume%20Collection%20Press%20Release.pdf.

15. Judith Thurman, "Closet Encounters," *New Yorker*, May 10, 2010, accessed July 15, 2011, http://www.newyorker.com/magazine/2010/05/10/closet-encounters.

16. Brooklyn Museum press release, 2008.

17. Dianne M. Pogoda, "Curators Mull Future of Brooklyn Museum's Costume Collection," *WWD* 159, no. 119 (June 19, 1990): 3.

18. Brooklyn Museum press release, "The Andrew W. Mellon Foundation Awards $3.925 Million to Brooklyn Museum for Landmark Survey of Its Historic 70,000 Object American and European Costume Collection," March 2005.

19. Carol Vogel, "Brooklyn Museum's Costume Treasures Going to the Met," *New York Times*, December 16, 2008.

20. Norman M. Feinberg, Chair of Board of Trustees of Brooklyn Museum, phone conversation with author, June 17, 2011.

21. Kevin Stayton, Chief Curator of Brooklyn Museum, phone conversation with author, June 6, 2011.

22. Id.

23. Harold Koda, Curator in Charge, the Costume Institute at the Metropolitan Museum of Art, phone conversation with author, July 15, 2011.

24. Id.

25. *American Woman: Fashioning a National Identity*, on view at the Metropolitan Museum of Art May 5–August 15, 2010.

26. *American High Style: Fashioning a National Collection*, on view at the Brooklyn Museum May 7–August 1, 2010.

27. Jan Glier Reeder, *High Style: Masterworks from the Brooklyn Museum Costume Collection at the Metropolitan Museum of Art* (New York: Metropolitan Museum of Art and New Haven: Yale University Press, 2010).

28. "Costume Collections: A Collaborative Model for Museums," symposium held at the Metropolitan Museum of Art, May 21–22, 2010.

29. Jan Glier Reeder is the Consulting Curator for the Brooklyn Museum Costume Collection at the Metropolitan Museum of Art.

30. Vogel, "Brooklyn Museum's Costume Treasures Going to the Met."

31. Brooklyn Museum website, http://www.brooklynmuseum.org/about/mission.php.

32. Kevin Stayton, Chief Curator of Brooklyn Museum, phone conversation with author, June 6, 2011.

33. Carol Vogel, "A Silent Auction for Library's Art," *New York Times*, April 29, 2005.

34. Carol Vogel, "New York Public Library's Durand Painting Sold to Wal-Mart Heiress," *New York Times*, May 13, 2005.

35. Id.

36. Carol Vogel, "Eakins Masterwork Is to Be Sold to Museums," *New York Times*, November 11, 2006.

37. Stephan Salisbury, "Stunned by Sale, But Not Giving Up, City and Arts Leaders Are Ready to Try to Match the $68 Million Price Tag for Eakins' Masterpiece," November 12, 2006, http://articles.philly.com/2006-11-12/news/25407677_1_gross-clinic-thomas-eakins-painting.

38. Carol Vogel, "Philadelphia Raises Enough Money to Retain a Masterpiece by Eakins," *New York Times*, April 24, 2006.

39. Affidavit of James C. Donnelly, Jr., The John Woodman Higgins Armory, Inc. v. Martha Coakley et al. (Supreme Judicial Court Civil Action No. SJ-2013-490), December 10, 2013.

40. Id. at 10.

41. Covenants for the Transfer of Assets of the Higgins Armory Museum to the Worcester Art Museum, November 19, 2013.

42. Judgment, The John Woodman Higgins Armory, Inc. v. Martha Coakley et al. (Supreme Judicial Court Civil Action No. SJ-2013-490), December 20, 2013.

43. Verified Complaint in Equity, Trustees of the Berkshire Museum v. Maura Healy (Supreme Judicial Court Civil Action No. SJ-2018-065), February 9, 2018.

44. Id.

45. Assent to Plaintiff's Motion for Entry of Judgment, Trustees of the Berkshire Museum v. Maura Healy (Supreme Judicial Court Civil Action No. SJ-2018-065), February 9, 2018.

46. Colin Moynihan, "A Struggling Historic Library Says It Needs to Sell Its Art," *New York Times*, November 17, 2017.

CHAPTER 5

1. Important Old Master Paintings and Sculpture, Sotheby's New York, January 31, 2013, lot 107.

2. Id. Glossary of Terms.

3. Id. Lot 107; J. S. Held, *Rubens: Selected Drawings*, London 1959, vol. 1, p. 138, under cat. no. 106.

4. Martin Bailey, "Rubenshuis Director Says Clara Serena Portrait 'Is by Rubens'," *Art Newspaper*, March 24, 2015; *Rubens in Private: The Master Portrays his Family*, Cat. Rubenshuis, Antwerp, March 28–June 28, 2015.

5. Id.

6. Bendor Grosvenor, "Re-discovered: Rubens' Portrait of His Daughter," *Art History News*, March 24, 2015.

7. On the attributions, see Sotheby's 2015, lot 107 (Literature); Walter Liedtke, *Flemish Paintings in the Metropolitan Museum of Art*, New York 1984, vol. 1, pp. 231–33.

8. Id.

9. Id.

10. Id.

11. Egbert Haverkamp-Begemann, in *Olieverfschetsen van Rubens*, exhibition catalogue, Rotterdam 1953, pp. 64–65, cat. N. 43 (as portrait of Clara Serena by Rubens); Liedtke, p. 232, n. 2, as rejecting Rubens attribution in a letter to the museum dated January 30, 1975.

12. Liedtke, p. 232.

13. Id. p. 231.

14. Reinhold Baumstark, in *Liechtenstein The Princely Collections*, exhibition catalogue, New York 1985, p. 324, cat. no. 204.

15. Anne-Marie Logan, *Peter Paul Rubens: The Drawings*, exhibition catalogue, New York 2005, under cat. no. 84.

16. Bailey, 2015.

17. Bendor Grosvenor, "A Sleeper Awakes . . .?" *Art History News*, February 2, 2013.

18. Bailey, 2015 (reporting that the Rubens scholar David Jaffe remains "doubtful" of the attribution).

19. Id.; Grosvenor, 2015; Lorne Manly, "A Painting Sold by the Met Is Declared a True Rubens," *New York Times*, March 25, 2015.

20. *Rubens in Private*, 2015.

21. www.rubenshuis.be/en/page/clara-serena-remain-rubens-house.

22. Horst Vey, "Van Dyck's Two Lost Group Portraits for the Brussels Town Hall," in Hans Vlieghe, *Van Dyck 1599-1999, Conjectures and Refutations*, Turnhout 2001, 65–75.

23. *Van Dyck: The Anatomy of Portraiture*, Frick Collection, New York, 2016, cat. no. 31.

24. S. J. Barnes, N. De Poorter, O. Millar, and H. Vey, *Van Dyck: A Complete Catalogue of the Paintings*, New Haven, 2004; Bendor Grosvenor, "The Empire Strikes Back," *arthistorynews.com*, June 16, 2011.

25. *Anatomy of Portraiture*, cat. no. 32, Ill. P. 130.

26. Id.; G. Gluck, *Van Dyck: Des Meisters Gemalde in 571* Abbildungen, Stuttgart 1931, p. 286.

27. Horst Vey, *Die Zeichnungen Anton Van Dycks.*, 2 vols. Brussels, 1962, p. 269, under cat. no. 197; See also *Anatomy of Portraiture*, cat. no. 32.

28. *Anatomy of Portraiture*, p. 129; Vey in Barnes et al., 2004, p. 396, under no. III.208.

29. Vey in Barnes et al., 2004, no. III.A33.

30. *Anatomy of Portraiture*, p. 133, n. 11; Susan Grundy, "Christie's vs Christie's in the Saint Louis Van Dyck Debate," *Art-Antiques-Design*, September 11, 2014.

31. New York, Christie's, January 27, 2010, lot 177.

32. *Anatomy of Portraiture*, cat. no. 32; Grundy, 2014.

33. *Anatomy of Portraiture*, cat. no. 33.

34. Christie's London, Old Master and British Paintings, July 8, 2014, lot 18. This work too had once been accepted as by Van Dyck but brought only 1,000 pounds when sold at Christie's in 1988 as the work of a follower.

35. Christie's London, Old Master and British Pictures, December 2, 2014, lot 16.

36. John Hawley, review of the Frick exhibition in *caa.reviews.org/reviews/2911#*, College Art Association, December 9, 2016.

37. Deborah Vankin, "LACMA's 50th Anniversary Party Starts Early with Major Donations," *LA Times*, January 20, 2015.

38. Among the many articles on George Harding and his collection see Walter J. Karcheski Jr., "George F. Harding, Jr. and his 'Castle'," in *Arms and Armor in the Art Institute of Chicago* (1995); Jean Lotus, "Behind Art Institute's New Arms and Armor Exhibit," *Cook County Chronicle*, April 3, 2017; William Currie, "Lost Treasures: Harding Museum Has Been Reduced to Pieces and Memories," *Chicago Tribune*, June 6, 1993.

39. Id.

40. Id.; see also *Illinois, ex rel. William J. Scott v. Silverstein*, 76 CH 6446, 86 Ill. App. 3d 605, 408 N.E. 2d 243 (1980).

41. William Currie, "Plan to Auction Two More Harding Treasures Revealed," *Chicago Tribune*, November 20, 1976; Sotheby Parke-Bernet, New York, December 2, 1976, lot 153. The Delacroix is presumably the *Arab at the Tomb* (or *Ben Abou at the Tomb*) of 1838, lent by George Harding to the 1930 exhibition *Delacroix* at the Art Institute of Chicago (cat. No. 12) and now in the Hiroshima Museum, Japan. The Rubens is in the collection of the Art Institute of Chicago.

42. Currie, 1976; William Juneau, *"Judge Halts Harding Museum Auction Plan,"* *Chicago Tribune*, December 21, 1976.

43. John Henry Merryman, Albert E. Elsen, and Stephen K. Urice, *Law, Ethics and the Visual Arts*, 5th ed. (2007): 1211–1217.

44. Merryman, 2007, p. 1216, n. 2, citing Stephen E. Weil, "Breaches of Trust, Remedies and Standards in the American Private Art Museum," in *Beauty and the Beasts: On Art Museums, the Law, and the Market* 160, 183 (1983).

45. Rita Reif, "Auctions," *New York Times*, June 21, 1985; Currie, 1976.

46. Alexandre Ananoff and Daniel Wildenstein, *Francois Boucher*, 2 vols., 1976, no. 222.

47. Id.

48. Sotheby's, New York, June 6, 1985, lot 147.

49. Reif, 1985.

50. Colin B. Bailey, *The First Painters of the King: French Royal Taste from Louis XIV to the Revolution*, Stair Sainty Matthiesen, New York, 1985, p. 102, no. 15.

51. Id.

52. Id.

53. Id.

54. Reif, 1985.

55. Id.

56. *Francois Boucher: Paintings, Drawings and Prints from the Nationalmuseum, Stockholm*, exhibition catalogue, 1984, P.2, p. 17.

57. Bailey, 1985, p. 105, n. 2.

58. *Francois Boucher, 1703-1770*, ed. Alistair Laing, exhibition catalogue, Metropolitan Museum of Art, New York, 1986, cat. no. 40.

59. Bailey, 1985, p. 105, n. 2.

60. Laing, 1986, p. 200.

61. The best of the arms and armor went on view in new rooms at the Art Institute in the spring of 2017. Jean Lotus, "Behind Art Institute's New Arms and Armor Exhibit," *Cook County Chronicle*, April 3, 2017.

CHAPTER 6

1. Robert R. Macdonald, "Ethics: Constructing a Code for All of America's Museums," *Museum News* 71 (May/June 1992): 62–65.

2. Given all of the fuss about deaccessioning, one might be surprised to discover that the word is not mentioned in the American Alliance of Museum's *Code of Ethics for Museums*. The word *deaccessioning* is often used as shorthand for what are, in fact, two separate processes: deaccessioning, the formal removal of an object from a museum's accession records, and disposition, the physical removal of an object from a museum. Indeed, it is the methods chosen for disposing of an object and then, if the object is sold, the use of the funds that were received for the object that incite controversy both within the field as well as with the public. For a discussion of the

process see Martha Morris, updated by Antonia Moser, "Deaccessioning," in *Museum Registration Methods*, 5th ed., edited by Rebecca A. Buck and Jean Allman Gilmore (Washington, DC: The AAM Press, 2010), 101.

3. Edward H. Able Jr., "AAM's Ethics Code Expresses the Shared Values of U.S. Museums," *Museum News* 70, no. 4 (August 1, 1991): 80.

4. American Association of Museums, *Code of Ethics for Museums*, Washington, DC: American Association of Museums, May 18, 1991, p. 13.

5. American Alliance of Museums, *Direct Care of Collections: Ethics, Guidelines and Recommendations*, April 2016, Washington, DC: American Alliance of Museums, p. 4; Alan J. Friedman, "Why Did the 1991 Code of Ethics Fail?" *Curator* 37, no. 1 (1994): 10.

6. American Association of Museums, *Code of Ethics for Museums*, Washington, DC: American Association of Museums, 1994, p. 9.

7. AAM, *Direct Care of Collections*, p. 4; AAM Ethics Committee Correspondence, 1986.

8. International Council of Museums, *ICOM Code of Ethics for Museums* (ICOM: Paris, 2017), p. 13.

9. Burt Logan, Memorandum to AAM Board of Directors, May 1, 2014.

10. AAM Accreditation Commission, "Proposal: Task Force on Use of Deaccessioning Proceeds for Direct Care and Acquisitions," PowerPoint presentation for the May 17, 2014, AAM Board meeting.

11. AAM Accreditation Commission, *op cit.*

12. Direct Care Survey Instrument, American Alliance of Museums' Direct Care Task Force, April 13, 2015.

13. AAM, *Direct Care of Collections*, p. 6.

14. AAM, *Direct Care of Collections*, p. 7.

CHAPTER 7

1. Formerly the American Association of Museums.

2. *Code of Ethics for Museums*, American Alliance of Museums (adopted 1991, revised 1994 and 2000), http://www.aam-us.org/resources/ethics-standards-and-best -practices/code-of-ethics-for-museums.

3. *Accounting for Contributions Made and Contributions Received*, Statement of Financial Accounting Standards No. 116, Financial Accounting Standards Board (June 1993), http://www.fasb.org/jsp/FASB/Document_C/DocumentPage?cid=1218 220128831&acceptedDisclaimer=true.

4. FASB reorganized all of its existing accounting standards into the Accounting Standards Codification (ASC) in 2009, in order to consolidate its standards and make them more easily accessible. All standards specifically for not-for-profit organizations are now contained in Topic 958. While the ASC superseded FASB's previous Statements, including FASB 116, the substance of FASB 116 was not

changed. We will refer to the Standard as "FASB 116" when discussing the Standard's history, original promulgation, and its accompanying material, such as its "Basis for Conclusions."

5. See Marie C. Malaro and Ildiko Pagany DeAngelis, *A Legal Primer on Managing Museum Collections*, 264–65 (3rd ed., 2012); Julie Hart, *An Overview of Field Wide Guidelines on Deaccessioning*, Legal, Ethical and Professional Guidelines for Collections Stewardship Seminar (March 13, 2007), http://southphillyblocks.org/pacscl/docs/deaccession/JulieHartFieldwideGuidelines.pdf; John E. Simmons, *Things Great and Small* 56 (2006).

6. FASB does not take any enforcement action with regard to its standards. However, if an auditor finds a museum to be in material violation of accounting standards, he or she may issue a qualified audit report. A qualified audit may have a number of financial ramifications, such as compromising an institution's eligibility for competitive grants, damaging its credit rating, or placing it in violation of bond covenants. To the best of the authors' knowledge, no museum has ever received a qualified audit for utilizing deaccession proceeds for direct care; however, several museums have been sanctioned by the Association of Art Museum Directors (AAMD) for such use, including the Delaware Art Museum (sanctions ongoing), *Association of Art Museum Directors Sanctions Delaware Art Museum*, Association of Art Museum Directors (June 18, 2014), https://aamd.org/for-the-media/press-release/association-of-art-museum-directors-sanctions-delaware-art-museum; Randolph College's Maier Museum of Art (sanctions ongoing), *Association of Art Museum Directors' Statement on Randolph College and Maier Museum of Art*, Association. of Art Museum Directors (March 12, 2014), https://aamd.org/for-the-media/press-release/association-of-art-museum-directors-statement-on-randolph-college-and); and the National Academy Museum (sanctions suspended), Robin Pogrebin, "Sanctions Are Ending for Museum," *New York Times*, October 18, 2010, http://www.nytimes.com/2010/10/19/arts/design/19sanctions.html?_r=0.

7. Simmons, *supra* note 5 at 56 (emphasis added).

8. Hart, *supra* note 5.

9. Id.

10. FASB 116, *supra* note 3 at 4; see also ASC Master Glossary, "Collections," and ASC 958-360-25.

11. FASB 116, *supra* note 3 at 37 (emphasis added).

12. As compared to the AAMD, which limits membership to the directors of art museums meeting certain criteria. AAMD has promulgated its own *Code of Ethics for Museum Directors* and standards and best practices, but these are specific to art museums, and AAMD's reach does not extend nearly as far as that of AAM: as of early 2016, AAMD has 242 members, while AAM has accredited 1,054 organizations and claims more than 30,000 individual, institutional, and corporate members. See *Membership*, Association of Art Museum Directors (last visited February 24, 2016), https://www.aamd.org/about/membership; "The Alliance Announces Five Newly Accredited Museums and Six Museums Re-Accredited," American Alliance of Museums (November 19, 2015), http://www.aam-us.org/about-us/media-room/2015/the-alliance-announces-five-newly-accredited-museums-and-six-museums-re-accredited.

13. FASB 116, *supra* note 3 at 37.

14. *Code of Ethics for Museums*, American Alliance of Museums (1994).

15. Compare *Code of Ethics* (1994), Id., with *Code of Ethics* (2000), *supra* note 2.

16. Since May 2014, AAM's Direct Care Task Force has engaged in a project to provide "clarity on the use of deaccessioning proceeds, specifically on what is generally accepted as a definition of direct care." The Task Force plans to issue a white paper before AAM's 2016 annual meeting. AAM's intent is not to move away from direct care, but rather to provide guidance as to the meaning and scope of direct care. AAM anticipates that the white paper will clarify the ethical issues surrounding the topic of direct care and provide guidance for museums in their decision-making. See generally *Task Force on Direct Care*, American Alliance of Museums (last visited January 7, 2016), http://aam-us.org/resources/ethics-standards-and-best -practices/direct-care-task-force?utm_source=MagnetMail&utm_medium=Email &utm_campaign=Direct%20Care%20Survey%20Now%20Open.

17. *AAMD Policy on Deaccessioning*, Association of Art Museum Directors (2010), https://aamd.org/standards-and-practices (interestingly, AAMD specifically refers to FASB 116, not the ASC). However, the other major national museum association, the American Association for State and Local History (AASLH), like AAM, allows deaccession proceeds to be used for collections care, stating "[h]istorical resources shall not be capitalized or treated as financial assets," and "[c]ollections shall not be deaccessioned or disposed of in order to provide financial support for institutional operations, facilities maintenance or any reason other than preservation or acquisition of collections, as defined by institutional policy." *Statement of Professional Standards and Ethics*, American Association of State and Local History (June 2012), https:// docs.google.com/viewerng/viewer?url=http://download.aaslh.org/AASLH-Website -Resources/AASLHProfessionalStandardsandEthicsStatement.pdf&hl=en_US.

18. See *AAMD Policy on Deaccessioning*, *supra* note 17. Compare the policy's Preamble and section II, both discussing reasons underpinning and criteria for deaccessioning decisions with the two sentences of section I(B) limiting use of sale proceeds to acquisitions of works. Nor is a discussion or explanation of this limitation offered in AAMD's *Code of Ethics for Museum Directors* (revised 2011) or its *Professional Practices in Art Museums* (2011), both available at https://aamd.org/standards-and-practices#.

19. *AAMD Policy on Deaccessioning*, *supra* note 17 at 3, ¶D.

20. For example, the National Trust for Historic Preservation thoroughly discussed its rationale for the use of proceeds from the disposition of collections objects for direct care as when it proposed to modify its collections management policy to allow for the accessioning of historic structures and landscapes. "When Buildings and Landscapes Are the Collection," National Trust for Historic Preservation (August 19, 2014), http://blog.preservationleadershipforum.org/2014/08/19/collections -enhanced-content/#.VstikCmLRak. Additionally, the AASLH has promulgated a thorough and persuasive position paper regarding the impropriety of capitalizing museum collections. *Ethics Position Paper #1: The Capitalization of Collections*, American Association of State and Local History (June 2003), http://resource.aaslh .org/view/ethics-position-paper-1-the-capitalization-of-collections/.

21. FASB 116, *supra* note 3 at 37.

22. Id. at 4. See also ASC 958-360-25-1 ("[A] not-for-profit entity (NFP) need not recognize contributions of works of art, historical treasures, and similar assets if the donated items are added to collections."); ASC 958-360-25-2 ("Works of art, historical treasures, and similar items that are not part of a collection shall be recognized as assets in financial statements."); and ASC 958-360-25-3 ("An NFP that holds works of art, historical treasures, and similar items that meet the definition of a collection has the following three alternative policies for reporting that collection: a. Capitalization of all collections items[;] b. Capitalization of all collections items on a prospective basis (that is, all items acquired after a stated date)[;] c. No capitalization.").

23. ASC Master Glossary, "Collections." This definition is, nearly verbatim (with only minor grammatical changes), the conditions for noncapitalization stated in paragraph 11 of FASB 116. See FASB 116, *supra* note 3 at 7.

24. FASB 116, *supra* note 3 at 37 (emphasis added).

25. Id. at 42 (emphasis added). Again, note that using proceeds from the sale of collections for activities other than acquisition is not explicitly foreclosed.

26. Id. at 37-38; see also ASC 958-360-25.

27. ASC Master Glossary, "Collections."

CHAPTER 8

1. American Bar Association, Business Law Section, Subcommittee on the Model Nonprofit Corporation Law, *Revised Model Nonprofit Corporation Act* (Prentice Hall Law and Business, 1988, Section 8.30[a]).

2. Marie C. Malaro and Ildiko Pogány DeAngelis, *A Legal Primer on Managing Museum Collections*, 3rd ed. (Washington, DC: Smithsonian Books, 2012), 18.

3. Ibid. at 20.

4. Virginia Hill Worden, Letter to Faculty, Staff, Alumnae, and Trustees, August 17, 2007.

5. Delaware Art Museum, press release, March 26, 2014.

6. Id.

CHAPTER 9

1. Tom Mayes, "Defining 'Direct Care' for Museum Collections," National Trust for Historic Preservation: Preservation Leadership Forum, posted April 15, 2016, http://forum.savingplaces.org/blogs/tom-mayes/2016/04/15/defining-direct-care-for -museum-collections.

2. "Task Force on Direct Care," American Alliance of Museums, updated May 29, 2015, http://www.aam-us.org/resources/ethics-standards-and-best-practices/direct -care/direct-care-task-force.

3. Carole M. P. Neves et al., "Acquisition and Disposal of Collections," In *Concern at the Core: Managing Smithsonian Collections*, 139–202. Smithsonian Institution (2005): first paragraph on 165.

4. M. Vecco, M. Piazzai, "Deaccessioning of Museum Collections: What Do We Know and Where Do We Stand in Europe?" *Journal of Cultural Heritage* (2014): Section 4, page 3, first paragraph.

5. Mychal Brown, "Disposal as an Essential Collections Management Tool: The Legal, Ethical and Practical Case for Deaccessioning in the United States," 104–105. In *Museums and the Disposal Debate: A Collection of Essays*, edited by Peter Davis (2011).

6. "Direct Care of Collections: Ethics, Guidelines and Recommendations," *Museum* (2016): 46.

7. Carole M. P. Neves et al., "Acquisition and Disposal of Collections," in *Concern at the Core: Managing Smithsonian Collections*, 164–202. Smithsonian Institution (2005): 170.

CHAPTER 10

1. "Art History" was added to the department's name in the early 2000s to better reflect the dual nature of the department, which had long offered courses in both Art History and Studio Art. For clarity's sake, I will use the newer name to refer to the department in this article, except in the case of direct quotations from archival materials.

2. See *IMPORTANT EGYPTIAN, GREEK, ROMAN, AND WESTER ASIATIC ANTIQUITIES*, 1978.

3. Coll. No. 81.084.

4. See Gold 2015 and Jandl and Gold 2015.

5. American Alliance of Museums. 2000. "Code of Ethics." https://www.aam-us.org/programs/ethics-standards-and-professional-practices/code-of-ethics-for-museums/.

6. I am grateful to numerous individuals for their assistance with this project, in particular to David Hill at the American Numismatic Society, to Elise Kenney and Dr. Susan B. Matheson at the Yale University Art Gallery, and to Dr. Ulla Kasten at Yale University's Council on Middle East Studies. At Wheaton College, I extend special thanks to the staff of the Marion B. Gebbie Archives and Special Collections, to the Permanent Collection's work-study team, and to the Provost's Office, which supported this research with summer funding.

7. David Hill, "The Newells: Two Big Personalities and an Enduring Legacy," *ANS Magazine* 13, no. 3 (2014): 36.

8. Rick Witschonke, "Better Late Than Never," *ANS Magazine* (Winter 2008), http://numismatics.org/magazine/newellwinter08. See also Hill 2014.

9. Hill, "The Newells," 36. The database for United States Passport Applications 1795–1925, available at familysearch.org, includes numerous passports for Adra Newell, several of which include photographs of her.

10. While researching Adra Newell, many individuals with whom I spoke expressed disbelief that her life or collecting practices were worthy of investigation, often employing the term "just a wife" to describe her.

11. Both women and their parents are buried in the family plot in Green-Wood Cemetery in Brooklyn, NY, as are Adra and Edward Newell and other members of the Nelson family.

12. "United States Census, 1910," database with images, *FamilySearch* (http://familysearch.org/ark:/61903/1:1:MKYK-KJ2 : accessed August 6, 2017), Eliza Nelson, Jersey City Ward 8, Hudson, New Jersey, United States; citing enumeration district (ED) ED 151, sheet 12A, family 250, NARA microfilm publication T624 (Washington, DC: National Archives and Records Administration, 1982), roll 891; FHL microfilm 1,374,904.

13. Adra's great-great-great-grandfather Joshua Nelson fought as a second major in the New York militia in 1776. See *Lineage Book National Society of the Daughters of the American Revolution*, 1912, 65.

14. The family's ties to New Amsterdam are evidenced by Adra Newell's membership in the Society of Daughters of Holland Dames, which noted "with deepest sorrow" her passing in a paid death notice in the *New York Times* on September 9, 1966. This patriotic, hereditary organization only grants membership to individuals who can prove lineal descent to an individual born or residing in the Netherlands or New Netherland prior to 1674, when the Treaty of Westminster was signed, or to an individual who held certain offices or status in New Netherland. See www.holland dames.org.

15. "United States Census, 1860," database with images, *FamilySearch* (https://familysearch.org/ark:/61903/1:1:MC4Z-3WG : accessed April 12, 2016), Samuel C. Nelson, 1860.

16. Mary Depue Ogden, ed., *Memorial Cyclopedia of New Jersey* (Newark: Memorial History Company, 1915), 101, https://archive.org/stream/memorial cycloped02ogde/memorialcycloped02ogde_djvu.txt.

17. "United States Census, 1860," database with images, *FamilySearch* (https://familysearch.org/ark:/61903/1:1:MC4Z-3WG : accessed April 12, 2016), Samuel C. Nelson, 1860.

18. "United States Census, 1870," database with images, *FamilySearch* (https://familysearch.org/ark:/61903/1:1:MND2-RNK : accessed April 12, 2016), Samuel C. Nelson, New Jersey, United States; citing p. 17, family 117, NARA microfilm publication M593 (Washington, DC: National Archives and Records Administration, n.d.); FHL microfilm 552,367.

19. "United States Census, 1880," database with images, *FamilySearch* (https://familysearch.org/ark:/61903/1:1:MN8C01NH : accessed August 13, 2016), Samuel C. Nelson, Jersey City, Hudson, New Jersey, United States; citing enumeration district ED 33, sheet 457B, NARA microfilm publication T9 (Washington, DC: National Archives and Records Administration, n.d.), roll 0784; FHL microfilm 1,254,784.

20. Memorial Cyclopedia of New Jersey 1915, 101.

21. "United States Census, 1870," database with images, *FamilySearch* (https://familysearchorg/ark:/61903/1:1:MNDK-FL9 : accessed April 12, 2016), William A. Marshall in household of David Marshall, New Jersey, United States; citing p. 1, family 4, NARA microfilm publication M593 (Washington, DC: National Archives and Records Administration, n.d.); FHL microfilm 552,367.

22. Ibid.

23. "New Jersey, Marriages, 1670–1980," database with images, *FamilySearch* (https://familysearch.org/ark:/61903/a:a:FZ2R-JY2 : accessed March 31, 2016), William A. Marshall and Grace Nelson, 29 Apr. 1878; citing Jersey City, Hudson, New Jersey, United States, Division of Archives and Record Management, New Jersey Department of State, Trenton; FHL microfilm 494,248.

24. "United States Census, 1880," database with images, *FamilySearch* (https://familysearch.org/ark:/61903/1:1:MN8Z-NY1 : accessed August 13, 2016), Grace Marshall in household of William Marshall, Jersey City, Hudson, New Jersey, United States; citing enumeration district ED 38, sheet 119D, NARA microfilm publication T9 (Washington, DC: National Archives and Records Administration, n.d.), roll 0784; FHL microfilm 1,254,784.

25. "New Jersey State Census, 1895," database with images, *FamilySearch* (https://familysearch.org/ark:/61903/a:a:QL7S-1J7V : accessed July 21, 2017), Eliza J. Nelson, Jersey City, Hudson, New Jersey, United States; citing p. 76, household 111, line #527, Department of States, Trenton; FHL microfilm 888,671. See also, "United States Census, 1900," database with images, *FamilySearch* (https://familysearch.org/ark:/61903/1:1:M9JY-V7S : accessed, August 5, 2017), Eliza Nelson, Precinct 2 Jersey City Ward 8, Hudson, New Jersey, United States; citing enumeration district (ED) 131, sheet 22A, family 448, NARA microfilm publication T623 (Washington, DC: National Archives and Records Administration, 1972); FHL microfilm 1,240,978.

26. "United States Census, 1910," database with images, *FamilySearch* (https://familysearch.org/ark:/61903/1:1:MKYK-KJL : accessed August 5, 2017), Lucy B. Nelson in household of Eliza Nelson, Jersey City Ward 8, Hudson, New Jersey, United States; citing enumeration district (ED) ED 151, sheet 12A, family 250, NARA microfilm publication T624 (Washington, DC: National Archives and Records Administration, 1982), roll 891; FHL microfilm 1,374,904.

27. Thomas William Herringshaw, ed. *The American Elite and Sociologist Blue Book* (Chicago: American Blue Book Publishers, 1922), 370, https://babel.hathitrust.org/cgi/pt?id=uc1.$b540507;view=1up;seq=5.

28. "EDWARD T. NEWEL TO WED," New York Times, March 11, 1909.

29. "United States Passport Applications, 1795–1925," database with images, *FamilySearch* (https://familysearch.org/ark:/61903/1:1:QV5Y-D4QM : accessed September 4, 2015), Adra Marshall Newell, 1923; citing Passport Application, New York, United States, source certificate #338978, Passport Application, January 2, 1906–March 31, 1925, 2363, NARA microfilm publication M1490 and M1372 (Washington, DC: National Archives and Records Administration, n.d.); FHL microfilm 1,737,833.

30. "United States Passport Applications, 1795–1925," database with images, *FamilySearch* (https://familysearch.org/ark:/61903/1:1:QVJP-7XQW : accessed September 4, 2015), Frances C. Newell, 1902; citing Passport Application, New York, United States, source certificate #50432, Passport Applications, 1795–1905, Roll 590, NARA microfilm publications M1490 and M1372 (Washington, DC: National Archives and Records Administration, n.d.); FHL microfilm 1,516,368. See also "New

York State Census, 1905," database with images, *FamilySearch* (https://familysearch .org/ark:/61903/1:1:SPFP-48F : accessed April 3, 2016), Frances C. Newell in household of James J. Keller, Manhattan, AD 25, ED 18, New York, New York; citing p. 11, line 10, county offices, New York; FHL microfilm 1,433,107.

31. Joseph Ciccone, "Young Edward Newell," *ANS Magazine* (Winter 2004), http://numismatics.org/magazine/author/admin/page/20/.

32. Ibid.

33. "United States Passport Applications, 1795–1925," database with images, *FamilySearch* (https://familysearch.org/ark:/61903/1:1:Q24F-JVJX : accessed October 4, 2016), Frederick S. Newell, 1897; citing Passport Application, Wisconsin, United States, source certificate #, Passport Applications, 1795–1905, 496, NARA microfilm publications M1490 and M1372 (Washington, DC: National Archives and Records Administration, n.d.); FHL microfilm 1,513,460. See also "United States Passport Applications, 1795–1925," database with images, *FamilySearch* (https:// familysearch.org/ark:/61903/1:1:Q24F-K1XL : accessed October 4, 2016), Frederick S. Newell, 1899; citing Passport Application, Wisconsin, United States, source certificate #, Passport Applications, 1795–1905, 534, NARA microfilm publications M1490 and M1372 (Washington, DC: National Archives and Records Administration, n.d.); FHL microfilm 1,513,820.

34. Ciccone, "Young Edward Newell," http://numismatics.org/magazine/author/ admin/page/20/.

35. "United States Passport Applications, 1795–1925," database with images, *FamilySearch* (https://familysearch.org/ark:/61903/1:1:Q24F-K1XL : accessed October 4, 2016), Frederick S. Newell, 1899; citing Passport Application, Wisconsin, United States, source certificate #, Passport Applications, 1795–1905, 534, NARA microfilm publication M1490 and M1372 (Washington, DC: National Archives and Records Administration, n.d.); FHL microfilm 1,513,820.

36. Caryn Hannan, ed., *Wisconsin Bibliographical Dictionary* (Hamburg: State History Publications, 2008), 292.

37. "EDWARD T. NEWELL TO WED," *New York Times*, March 11, 1909.

38. Ciccone, "Young Edward Newell," http://numismatics.org/magazine/author/ admin/page/20/.

39. Ibid.

40. Ibid. See also Hill 2014.

41. Ibid

42. Ibid.

43. "Newell, Edward Theodore, 1886–1941. Biographical or Historical Note," American Numismatic Society, http://numismatics.org/authority/newell.

44. Witschonke, "Better Late Than Never," http://numismatics.org/magazine/ newellwinter08/.

45. "Newell, Edward Theodore, 1886–1941. Biographical or Historical Note."

46. Briggs Buchanan, "The Newell Collection of Oriental Seals: An Important Addition to the Yale Babylonian Collection," *The Yale University Library Gazette* 43, no. 2 (October 1968): 91, http://www.jstor.org/stable/40858181.

47. Adra M. Newell, "Last Will and Testament," August 10, 1953, 2. Archives, American Numismatic Society.

48. Buchanan, "The Newell Collection," 91.

49. "Newell, Edward Theodore, 1886–1941. Biographical or Historical Note."

50. "NOTICE TO THE AMERICAN NUMISMATIC SOCIETY AND COPY OF SELCTION BY ADRA M. NEWELL PURSUANT TO ARTICLE VI OF LAST WILL AND TESTAMENT, CONSENT ACKNOWLEDGMENT, RECEIPT AND DELIVERY." Surrogate's Court: Suffolk County, No. P-96/1941, 1-2. Archives, American Numismatic Society.

51. "List of Items at the American Numismatic Society Selected by Mrs. Newell," prepared by Samuel Marx, Inc. 1941. Archives, American Numismatic Society.

52. See "List of items . . ." 1941: 54 and 57.

53. Hill, "The Newells," 38.

54. Ibid.

55. Ibid.

56. Hill, "The Newells," 38–39.

57. Hill, The Newells," 41.

58. Sebastian Heath, "Arras Coins at the ANS," *ANS Magazine* (Winter 2004), http://numismatics.org/magazine/arraswinter04/.

59. Hill, "The Newells," 41.

60. Hill, "The Newells," 38.

61. Ibid.

62. Hill, "The Newells," 41.

63. Unless otherwise noted, all unpublished documents cited in this chapter are housed in the Gebbie Archives at Wheaton College or in other college offices.

64. Harry Hoffman to Wheaton College President, July 13, 1953.

65. Ibid.

66. Howard Meneely to Harry Hoffman, July 16, 1953.

67. The first record of a passport issued to Adra Newell was dated January 22, 1914. Repeated searched of the "United States Passport Applications, 1795–1925" digital database found no passport issued to her prior to this date, although she must have had a passport during her honeymoon travels. Either record of her passport from 1909 was lost or she was added to Edward's passport at the time of their marriage, as was common practice at the time. Adra is listed on Edward's passport for both 1919 and 1921.

68. No record has yet been found of any member of Adra's immediate family having been issued a passport prior to her marriage to Edward, although her mother traveled with the couple at least twice, once in 1914 and again in 1921. Grace Nelson Marshall was issued a passport on November 24, 1919 to accompany Adra and Edward on their travels to Greece and Italy. That record indicates that she was issued a passport in 1914 when she spent time from March through May in France and Italy, when Edward and Adra also spent time in Italy. She also travelled with them in 1921. See database for "United States Passport Applications, 1795–1925," available at familysearch.org, for passports issued for Grace Nelson Marshall in 1914 and 1921.

69. See database for "United States Passport Applications, 1795–1925," available at familysearch.org, for passports issued for Edward and Adra Newell in 1914, 1919, 1921, and 1923.

70. "United States Passport Applications, 1795–1925," database with images, *FamilySearch* (https://familysearch.org/ark:/61903/1:1:QV5B-JMHZ : September 4, 2015), Edward Theodore Newell, 1919; citing Passport Application, New York, United States, source certificate #142278, Passport Applications, January 2, 1906–March 31, 1925, 992, NARA microfilm publications M1490 and M1372 (Washington, DC: National Archives and Records Administration, n.d.); FHL microfilm 1,637,059.

71. Newell, "Last Will and Testament," August 10, 1953, 1.

72. Kelekian founded and operated galleries in Cairo, Constantinople, London, New York City, and Paris. Given the extent of her travels, it remains unclear in which—if not all—of these locations Adra Newell purchased objects. See https://www.freersackler.si.edu/wp-content/uploads/2017/09//Kelekian-Dikran.pdf, published February 29, 2016.

73. Newell, "Last Will and Testament," August 10, 1953, 3.

74. John S. Khayat to Wheaton College President, August 7, 1967.

75. John S. Khayat to William C. H. Prentice, September 7, 1967.

76. Most of the portraits and a few of the landscapes remain part of the Collection to this day. See Malouin and Niederstadt 2009.

77. While the Japanese prints and plaster casts remain in the Collection, the scientific instruments and study collections are managed by faculty in the Biology Department.

78. The familial portraits serve a similar role to this day. A portrait of Mrs. Wheaton near the end of her life hangs in the main lobby of the college's Wallace Library while portraits of the Wheatons as a young couple are prominently displayed in the President's House, their former home.

79. See http://wheatoncollege.edu/arts/permanent-collection/wheaton-collection-of-japanese-prints/.

80. In 1924, Mrs. Thomas O. (Mary Rich) Richardson generously donated dozens of paintings, primarily American and European landscapes, 17 of which remain extant. The Elizabeth Wright Shippee Memorial Art Rental Collection was founded in 1937 and eponymously named for a Wheaton senior who died in a car accident in October 1936. Primarily comprised of reproductions with some original drawings, etchings, engravings, and lithographs, the rental collection was active from 1937 through 2002; many found-in-collection objects now located on campus are from this rental collection. See Malouin and Niederstadt 2009.

81. Found-in-collection (or FIC) objects continue to be identified to the present day, particularly when buildings are renovated or faculty and staff retire and clean out their offices.

82. To learn more, please visit www.wheatoncollege.edu/arts/permanent-collection.

83. Now Professor of Art History and Gallery Director Emerita, Dr. Murray retired in 2010.

84. "Wheaton College Permanent Collection Collections Management Policy" (May 2014), 1.

85. For example, an archival photograph from the 1930s depicts students working with a group of ancient ceramic vessels, all of which are listed in the collection database as belonging to the Newell Bequest. This is highly unlikely, given that Mrs. Newell appears to have little knowledge of the College until decades later and that the works do not fit the description of ceramics in the 1967 appraisal conducted by Samuel Marx, Inc. It is now believed the vessels were part of a collection once housed in and managed by the Classics Department.

86. John D. Bishop, May 22, 1971.

87. The AVC was also regularly referred to as the Visiting Committee in Art.

88. "Visiting Committees," *Intercom*, October 13, 1961, 4–5.

89. Renovated between 2000–2002, Watson Fine Arts, as it is commonly known, continues to house the Art History faculty, as well as the college's Beard & Weil Galleries and the Permanent Collection Storage and Study Rooms. It is also home to the Music and the Theatre & Dance Departments, Wheaton's two theatres, the Office of the Arts, and a textile-focused makerspace. As part of the renovation, a purpose-built studio building was added to Meneely Hall, creating Mars Arts & Humanities, which now houses the Studio Art faculty.

90. Mary L. Heuser, "Draft—Report of the Visiting Committee in Art," November 4, 1961, 4.

91. "Visiting Committees," 5.

92. Ibid.

93. Mary L. Heuser, "Report of the Business Meeting of the Visiting Committee in Art," October 27, 1964, 3.

94. Ibid.

95. Susan Rainey, "Minutes of the Meeting of the Visiting Committee in Art," April 12, 1969, 3.

96. Mary L. Heuser, "Minutes of the Meeting of the Visiting Committee in Art," October 12, 1967, 3.

97. Ibid.

98. Heuser, "Minutes," October 12, 1967, 4.

99. Heuser, "Minutes," October 12, 1967, 5.

100. Art Visiting Committee, "A Preliminary Report of the Meeting of the Visiting Committee in Art," October 21, 1967.

101. Agnes Mongan to William C. H. Prentice, October 25, 1967.

102. William C. H. Prentice, November 2, 1967.

103. Heuser, "Minutes," October 12, 1967, 3.

104. Lucile E. Bush, "Art Department Report to the President's Report—1963–1964," 3.

105. In a letter to then President Emerson, AVC Chairman Faison pointed out that the college had an obligation to care for the artwork in its possession and to consider it as a collection even though "it is clear that the works of art owned by Wheaton have no such status at present." June 20, 1975, 2.

106. Heuser, "Minutes," October 12, 1967, 4.

107. Heuser, "Minutes," October 12, 1967, 3.

108. Art Visiting Committee, "A Preliminary Report," October 21, 1967, 2.

109. Ibid.

110. Heuser, "Minutes," October 12, 1967, 5.

111. Art Visiting Committee, "A Preliminary Report," October 21, 1967, 2.

112. Newell, "Last Will and Testament," August 10, 1953, 11.

113. J. David Bishop, May 5, 1978.

114. Newell, "Last Will and Testament," August 10, 1953. Gallery Archives, Yale University Art Gallery.

115. Coll. nos. 1967.34.1–12.

116. Coll. no. 1967.34.17.

117. Coll. no. 1967.34.25.

118. Coll. no. 1967.34.24.

119. Moussa M. Domit, "Memorandum to: Professor Hallo," June 14, 1967. Gallery Archives, Yale University Art Gallery.

120. Coll. nos. 1967.154.1–2.

121. Coll. no. 1967.154.3.

122. Coll. no. 1967.154.5.

123. While the bequest made to the Met and Yale have been confirmed, an inquiry to the New York Historical Society found that the society had no request of a bequest from Adra Newell.

124. Samuel Marx, Inc. "Bequeathed to Wheaton College at Norton, Mass." 1967.

125. Ibid.

126. An Asian art expert, Faison served in the US Navy Reserves during World War II and was later assigned to the Office of Strategic Services' Art Looting Investigation Unit where he assisted the effort to return looted artwork.

127. Jacqueline Crowell Silvi, "Art Visiting Committee Meeting Minutes," October 28, 1972, 1.

128. Silvi, "Meeting Minutes," October 28, 1972, 2.

129. Ibid.

130. S. Lane Faison Jr. to William C. H. Prentice, October 1, 1972, 2–3.

131. S. Lane Faison Jr. to William C. H. Prentice, October 1, 1972, 2.

132. William C. H. Prentice to S. Lane Faison Jr., October 13, 1972, 1.

133. Ibid.

134. Silvi, "Meeting Minutes," October 28, 1972, 3.

135. S. Lane Faison Jr. to William C. H. Prentice, December 21, 1972, 1.

136. S. Lane Faison Jr. to William C. H. Prentice, December 21, 1972, 3.

137. S. Lane Faison Jr. to William C. H. Prentice, December 21, 1972, 2.

138. S. Lane Faison Jr. to William C. H. Prentice, December 21, 1972, 1.

139. Ibid.

140. Ibid.

141. "Art Department Meeting Minutes," October 14, 1969.

142. Anne J. Neilson, "Meeting Minutes," Wheaton College Board of Trustees, June 8, 1974, 4.

143. William C. H. Prentice to Thomas McCormick, May 18, 1971.

144. Anne J. Neilson, "Minutes of the Meeting of the Executive Committee," Wheaton College Board of Trustees, June 13, 1977, 1.

145. S. Lane Faison Jr. to Alice F. Emerson, August 9, 1977, 1.

146. S. Lane Faison Jr. to William C. H. Prentice, October 1, 1972, 2.

147. Ibid.

148. Alice F. Emerson to S. Lane Faison Jr., August 1, 1977, 2.

149. William C. H. Prentice to Thomas McCormick, May 18, 1971.

150. Jacqueline Crowell Silvi, "Art Visiting Committee Meeting Minutes," December 2–3, 1977, 2.

151. Alice F. Emerson, "Memorandum to the files," December 20, 1977.

152. S. Lane Faison Jr. to Alice F. Emerson, December 20, 1977, 1.

153. Eunice Work to John E. Park, September 28, 1931.

154. "Doves and Dolphins on Greek Coins," *Wheaton News*, April 30, 1932, 1.

155. "Miss Heather Young Engaged to Marry Ensign Cyril Gsell," *The Rye Chronicle*, March 5, 1953, 12.

156. Murray Friedman to Arthur D. Raybin, November 9, 1966.

157. Ibid.

158. Arthur D. Raybin, "Memorandum to Mr. Prentice, Mrs. Bishop, Miss Marshall, Business Office, and Alumnae Office," November 11, 1966.

159. J. David Bishop, handwritten note dated May 28, 1978, on 1966 memorandum by Arthur D. Raybin.

160. Raybin, "Memorandum," November 11, 1966.

161. Doris Taylor Bishop to Mrs. Cyril C. Gsell, November 22, 1967.

162. Ibid.

163. For example, see William C. H. Prentice to J. David Bishop, July 23, 1973.

164. Dorothea Wender to Alice F. Emerson, November 20, 1978.

165. See J. David Bishop and R. Ross Holloway, *Wheaton College Collection of Greek and Roman Coins* (New York: American Numismatic Society, 1981).

166. See the eponymously named catalogue.

167. Jayne Giniewicz, "Glass Sold At Auction," *Wheaton News*, February 8, 1979, 3.

168. The exact number of objects sold remains unclear as several lots contained multiple objects, such as Lot 19 "GROUP OF VESSEL FRAGMENTS" and Lot 166 "COLLECTION OF GLASS AND STONE BEADS."

169. Giniewicz, "Glass Sold," 3.

170. Coll. no. 2003.478.

171. See http://www.getty.edu/art/collection/objects/221867/unknown-maker-opaque-red-bowl-near-eastern-syro-palestinian-8th-9th-century/.

172. *Important Ancient Glass from the Collection formed by the British Rail Pension Fund* (London: Sotheby's, 1977).

173. Giniewicz, "Glass Sold," 3.

174. "Compendium/Fund File '98," 1998.

175. Coll. no. 1967.007.

176. Coll. no. 1967.002.

177. Heuser, "Minutes," October 12, 1967, 4.

178. Coll. no. 1981.084.

179. S. Lane Faison Jr. to William C. H. Prentice, December 21, 1972, 3.

180. Coll. no. 1985.033.

181. Coll. no. 1993.133.

182. Coll. no. 1983.010.

183. Coll. no. 2005.013.

184. Coll. no. 2009.001.001–013.

185. Coll. no. 2013.006.

186. "Compendium/Fund File '98," 1998.

187. According to their 1921 and 1923 passports, Adra and Edward Newell planned several trips to Palestine. During one of these visits, they presumably acquired the *Amber-Colored Pitcher* and *Deep Green Jar* identified as Palestinian in origin and offered as Lots 131–132 in the Sotheby Parke Bernet sale. See Barag 1970 and 1971.

188. Elsbeth B. Dusenbery, "ANCIENT GLASS IN THE COLLECTIONS OF WHEATON COLLEGE," *Journal of Glass Studies* 13 (1971): 9.

189. Mary L. Heuser to S. Lane Faison Jr., March 30, 1972.

190. *Collection/Reflection: A History of Wheaton's Permanent Collection*, curated by Kayla Malouin, Class of 2010, in the Spring 2010 semester; *Turning the Page: The Evolution of Artist's Books* curated by students enrolled in ARTH 335: Exhibition Design in the Fall 2010 semester; *The Art of Intellectual Community: Early Modern Objects and Pedagogy*, curated by students enrolled in *100 Years, 100 Objects*, curated by students enrolled in ARTH 335 in the Fall 2012 semester; *Tracing the Thread*, curated by students in ARTH 335 in the Fall 2014 semester; *It's Elemental: Water*, curated by students in ARTH 335 in the Fall 2016 semester.

191. When Watson Fine Arts was renovated between 2000–2002, what was previously known as the Watson Gallery was enlarged to include two exhibition spaces and renamed the Beard & Weil Galleries.

192. *Egyptian and Roman Antiquities in the Permanent Collection* was curated by Felicia Bartosiewicz, Class of 2009, and Lauren Salois, Class of 2010, while Whitney Alves, Class of 2010, curated a display of lighting devices.

193. These were offered by the Art/Art History, the Classics, and the French Studies Departments.

194. See Audrey Martin, "Wheaton students do some sleuthing for Attleboro Arts Museum," *Attleboro Sun Chronicle*, February 8, 2018.

195. Kayla Elizabeth Allen, Class of 2015, Madi Cook-Comey, Class of 2019, Christine Evers, Class of 2019, and Allison Meyette, Class of 2018, contributed to this project, which was supported by a Hood Grant for Faculty-Student Summer Research in 2013 and a Mars Grant for Faculty-Student Summer Research in 2017.

196. Coll. no. 1983.009.

197. While access to the Collection Storage Room is restricted, tours are offered several times each year as part of Admission Visiting Days, Homecoming, or Commencement/Reunion Weekend. Donors are also occasionally offered private tours of the Collection Storage Room, accompanied by College Advancement staff. All tours

are supervised by the Curator of the Permanent Collection and limited to groups of 12 or fewer participants.

198. Coll. no. 1990.001.

199. S. Lane Faison Jr. to William C. H. Prentice, December 21, 1972, 3. Faison attributed the quote to his mentor Henri Focillon (1881–1943), a French art historian.

200. S. Lane Faison Jr. to William C. H. Prentice, October 1, 1972, 3.

201. S. Lane Faison Jr. to William C. H. Prentice, December 21, 1972, 3.

CHAPTER 11

1. The legal concepts discussed in this essay are offered for reference and discussion purposes only. This essay does not purport to address every conceivable legal issue or subissue. Given the variable nature of the relationships between rights holders in digital works and the variety of types of digital works, there is no one-size-fits-all solution to the legal issues involved in digital collections management. Readers faced with specific questions or concerns involving digital acquisitions, accessions, or deaccessions should consult with legal counsel.

2. "Smithsonian American Art Museum's Third Annual 'SAAM Arcade' to Feature 40 Independent Games," June 28, 2017 (see https://newsdesk.si.edu/releases/smithsonian-american-art-museum-s-third-annual-saam-arcade-feature-40-independent-games, accessed December 31, 2017).

3. "@ at MoMA," Inside/Out: A MoMA/MoMA PS1 Blog, posted by Paola Antonelli, Senior Curator, Department of Architecture and Design, https://www.moma.org/explore/inside_out/2010/03/22/at-moma/, last accessed December 31, 2017.

4. Marie C. Malaro and Ildiko Pogany DeAngelis, *A Legal Primer on Managing Museum Collections*, 3rd ed. (Washington, DC: Smithsonian Books, 2012), 59.

5. Although beyond the scope of this essay, if the digital work will be collecting any personal information or other data from users (i.e., museum visitors when the work is exhibited), it might be a good idea to consider the potential privacy and data security obligations the museum may be undertaking and include the use of third-party service providers in that analysis.

6. An interesting question to consider: if the term is less than perpetual, can the work be accessioned into the collection, or does this further strain the traditional concept of ownership such that the work would be more appropriately considered a loan than an acquisition?

7. This essay assumes that the donor or seller is either the artist or the gallery representing the artist. If the donor is neither the artist nor the gallery, they may be reluctant to provide the following recommended provisions. Nonetheless, it is advisable to try to secure these since the museum will otherwise have very limited avenues of protection. In this case, the museum might also inquire as to any representations and warranties offered by the artist or gallery to the donor and request that the donor agree to pass those to the museum in the Donor Agreement.

8. The legal provisions here are offered for reference and discussion purposes only. Given the variable nature of the relationships between rights holders in digital

works, some of these recommendations may be unreasonable or impractical. For that reason, simple reliance on a single form agreement is also not recommended for digital acquisitions. Consult with an attorney to determine whether and to what extent these legal provisions apply to the museum acquisition.

9. Marie C. Malaro and Ildiko Pogany DeAngelis, *A Legal Primer on Managing Museum Collections*, 3rd ed. (Washington, DC: Smithsonian Books, 2012), 249.

10. For example, in the case of video games, a video game console could easily become a necessary part of the accession as an integral part of the historical relevance and significance of the work.

11. For example, cultural heritage objects subject to removal and return pursuant to the Native American Graves Protection and Repatriation Act of 1990.

CHAPTER 12

1. M. Yolen Cohen, "The Unsung but Revolutionary Art Institutions of Massachusetts," May 12, 2014, http://www.huffingtonpost.com/malerie-yolencohen/the -unsung-but-revolution_b_5310430.html.

2. New York Trust Co. v. Eisner, 256 U.S. 345, 349 (1921).

3. See Peter Suciu, "American Experimental Helmets from WWI," *Military Trader*, November 30, 2011, http://www.militarytrader.com/military-trader-news/american -experimental-helmets-from-wwi; Charles McGrath, "Dressed to Kill from Head to Toe," *New York Times*, October 5, 2012, at C25, http://www.nytimes.com/2012/10/05/ arts/design/met-show-recalls-bashford-dean-armor-curator.html?pagewanted=all; see also generally Bashford Dean, *Helmets and Body Armor in Modern Warfare* (Yale University Press: 1920).

4. Benedict Crowell (Ass't Sec'y of War, Director of Munitions), *America's Munitions: 1917-1918*, at 224, Washington: Government Printing Office (1919).

5. Sara Wermiel, "A Steel and Glass Office Building and Industrial Art Museum in Worcester: Development and Historical Significance of the Higgins Armory Museum Building" at 8 (a report prepared for the Higgins Armory Museum), January 2014, http://www.higgins.org/WermielHAM.pdf (quoting William F. Holland, "Office Building of Steel and Glass," *Steel* 88 [January 22, 1931] at 35).

6. Multiple letters between Jefferson Warren (Director of The John Woodman Higgins Armory) and Norman Rockwell, August 1961 September 1962 (Higgins Armory Museum archive); see also cover, *Saturday Evening Post*, November 3, 1962, image available at http://www.saturdayeveningpost.com/2013/04/12/ art-entertainment/norman-rockwell-art-entertainment/rockwells-that-dont-look-like -rockwells.html.

7. Letter from Groucho Marx to John W. Higgins, December 3, 1953 (Higgins Armory Museum archive).

8. The "Monuments Men" were a joint unit of Allied Forces, formed from leading museum directors, curators, and art historians, to protect Europe's art treasures during and after World War II. They have recently been memorialized in a book and a block-

buster Hollywood movie, both called *The Monuments Men*. The character played by George Clooney in the movie is based on WAM's George Stout.

9. Kary Ashley Pardy, "An Institutional History of the Higgins Armory Museum and Its Relationship with Worcester, Massachusetts," University of South Carolina, master's dissertation, at 8 (2013), http://scholarcommons.sc.edu/cgi/viewcontent .cgi?article=3523&context=etd.

10. See, e.g., Mary Louise Higgins Wilding-White, "John Woodman Higgins Armory, Inc.: Important Yearly Events Outlined" (c. 1986), Higgins Armory Museum archives.

11. See, e.g., Ibid.; see also Minutes of the [Higgins Armory] Fin. Cte. Mtg (October 18, 1978), Higgins Armory Museum archives.

12. See Mass. Gen. L. ch. 180, § 8A(c); see also *Mass. Charitable Mechanic Ass'n v. Beede*, 320 Mass. 601 (1947).

13. See Geoff Edgers, "Founder's Kin Fights to Stop Higgins Armory's Closure," *Boston Globe*, March 27, 2013, http://www.bostonglobe.com/arts/theater-art/ 2013/03/26/final-vote-higgins-armory-closing-deal-raising-debates/l2FfLPKX6la V7q2lyHslyM/story.html.

14. See Steven Foskett Jr., "Incorporators Vote to Merge Collection, Close Higgins Armory December 31, 2013," *Worcester Telegram and Gazette*, March 27, 2013, http://www.telegram.com/article/20130327/NEWS/303289992/0.

15. Copies of these documents are a matter of public record and are available from the authors on request.

CHAPTER 13

1. Peter Dean was a Trustee of Randolph College (2006 to 2016) and John E. Klein was President of Randolph College (2007 to 2013). *[Edited 2018]*

2. References to the "college" refer equally to Randolph-Macon Woman's College and to Randolph College.

3. Professor Smith was Professor of Art at Randolph-Macon Woman's College from 1893 to 1928. Upon her death she left funds to the college for the purpose of building a permanent collection. None of the four paintings that the college has sold or plans to sell was acquired with the funds left by Professor Smith.

4. Louise Jordan Smith, "Art in Education," *Proceedings of the Third Capon Springs Conference for Education in the South* (St. Augustine's School, Raleigh, 1900), 41.

5. Minutes of the Twentieth Annual Meeting of the Alumnae Association of Randolph-Macon Woman's College, May 30, 1919 (Bulletin of the Alumnae Association of Randolph-Macon Woman's College, 1920), 30.

6. Randolph College mission statement. The college's motto is *Vita Abundantior (A life more abundant)*. This concept has been a cornerstone of the college's educational philosophy from its beginning, and is reflected in the college's mission statement. The principles expressed in this statement include a continued focus on

the importance of the visual and other arts as a vital component of an undergraduate education.

7. See www.maiermuseum.org for more information, including a history of the building.

8. Ellen M. Schall, "The Liberal Art of Collecting," in *American Art: American Vision,* (Randolph-Macon Woman's College, 1990), 22. This publication was the catalogue produced for the 1990–91 exhibition of paintings from the college's collection that toured Richmond, Chicago, Tampa, and Atlanta. Ms. Schall, now Ellen Schall Agnew, was then the director of the Maier.

9. Schall, "'Liberal Art," 22–23.

10. The most recent are a set of Operational Policies (which includes a Collection Management Policy, an Ethics Policy, an Acquisitions Plan, an Exhibition and Program Policy, and a Facility Use Policy) published in 2002. These have not been adopted by the Board of Trustees.

11. The Maier is listed on the AAM website as a member, but it is not listed as an accredited museum.

12. FASB No. 116, Paragraph 11: "An entity need not recognize contributions of works of art, historical treasures and similar assets if the donated items are added to collections that meet all of the following conditions:

(a) Are held for public exhibition, education or research in furtherance of public service rather than financial gain
(b) Are protected, kept encumbered, cared for and preserved
(c) Are subject to an organizational policy that requires the proceeds from sales of collection items to be used to acquire other items for collections.

13. See, for example: Ethics Position Paper #1, "The Capitalization of Collections" (American Association for State and Local History, 2003); William G. Tompkins, "Should Museums Capitalize Their Collections," *Museum News* (January/February 2004).

14. The Maier is an institutional member of the AAM, but that does not require compliance with the AAM's accreditation standards. The AAMD's membership consists of individual directors of major museums, and a member museum is one that is headed by an AAMD member. No one at the college is eligible for membership in the AAMD.

15. *Men of the Docks* will be on display in 2012–13 as part of the major retrospective exhibition of George Bellows's work organized by the National Gallery of Art in Washington, and continuing at the Metropolitan Museum of Art in New York and the Royal Academy of Art in London.

16. For a recent and relevant example of a failure to take the necessary steps to create a trust, see the 2011 decision of the High Court of Justice in England in *Young and another v HM Attorney General and Others* [2011] EWHC 3782 (Ch) (December 19, 2011). Although the case was decided under English law, the principles are similar to US law. The court held that, because no legally recognized trust had been created, the irreplaceable Wedgwood collection of pottery assembled by Josiah Wedgwood and

Sons Ltd. and transferred in 1964 to the Wedgwood Museum Trust Ltd. was held as a general asset of the Wedgwood Museum Trust and therefore could be sold to satisfy creditors of that company when it became insolvent.

CHAPTER 14

1. Stefanie S. Jandl and Mark S. Gold, eds., *A Handbook for Academic Museums* (MuseumsEtc, 2012), 522–51.

2. *Men of the Docks* by George Bellows, *A Peaceable Kingdom* by Edward Hicks, *Through the Arroyo* by Martin Hennings, and *Troubador* by Rufino Tamayo. *Troubador* was sold at auction in May 2008. The college continues to hold the two remaining paintings for eventual sale.

3. Unless the context otherwise requires, references to the "college" refer equally to Randolph-Macon Woman's College and to Randolph College.

4. This accounting method is one of two alternative methods that are expressly permitted under Statement of Financial Accounting Standards No. 116 *Accounting for Contributions Received and Contributions Made*, issued in 1993 by the Financial Accounting Standards Board. See also IRS Form 990, Part IV, line 8 and Schedule D, Part III.

5. Press release National Gallery, February 2014.

6. Chris Riopelle, National Gallery, Curator of Post-1800 Paintings, quoted February 2014.

7. Roberta D. Cornelius, *The History of Randolph-Macon Woman's College* (University of North Carolina Press, 1951), 228–29.

8. The National Gallery's collection consists of about 2,300 paintings.

9. The National Gallery has no entrance charge.

10. So far as the authors are aware, the National Gallery has only one other painting by an American artist: *The Delaware Water Gap* by George Inness (1857), which was bequeathed to the Tate Gallery in 1939 and transferred by it to the National Gallery in 1956. This painting is rarely displayed.

11. Press release National Gallery, February 2014.

12. In addition to the AAMD there are other associations and organizations in the United States whose membership consists of museums or individuals connected with museums; some of these are principally made up of university and college museums. These include the American Alliance of Museums (AAM), the College Art Association (CAA), and the Association of Academic Museums and Galleries (AAMG). Some of these organizations have also issued statements to the effect that the college's sale of *Men of the Docks* violates their policies. For reasons of brevity this essay concentrates only on the policies and actions of the AAMD, which is perhaps the most prominent of such organizations.

13. See Dean and Klein (2012) and footnote 4 for the background to this decision, and also a discussion of the relevant accounting principles adopted by Randolph College.

14. Section 3.27 of the Rules of the NY Board of Regents. These rules do not apply to all New York museums, only those that operate under a state charter.

15. Donn Zaretsky, "There's No Such Thing As the Public Trust, and It's a Good Thing, Too," in *Legal Issues for Museum Professionals*, Rowman & Littlefield, (October 2014). See also Dean and Klein (2012).

16. AAMD Policy on Deaccessioning, June 9, 2010 (AAMD Policy).

17. AAMD Policy, Section VIII—Sanctions.

18. Mark S. Gold, "Trustees of Parent Organizations: Just Doing Their Job," in *Handbook for Academic Museums: Beyond Exhibitions and Education* (MuseumsEtc, 2012), 508–21.

19. Sherman Act, 15 U.S.C. §1.

CHAPTER 15

1. www.Artdependence.com, *Shuffleton's Barbershop* by Norman Rockwell, accessed February 14, 2018.

2. www.Artdependence.com, *Shuffleton's Barbershop* by Norman Rockwell, accessed February 14, 2018.

3. Larry Parnass, "Lucas Museum Buys *Shuffleton's Barbershop*," *Berkshire Eagle*, April 12, 2018.

4. Larry Parnass, "Berkshire Museum Art Sale Timeline," *Berkshire Eagle*, Saturday, December 30, 2017.

5. *Berkshire Eagle*, December 30, 2017.

6. *Berkshire Eagle*, December 30, 2017.

7. *Berkshire Eagle*, December 30, 2017.

8. *Berkshire Eagle*, December 30, 2017.

9. Larry Parnass, *"AG, Berkshire Museum Seeks Court Resolution to Art-Sale Dispute,"* *Berkshire Eagle*, February 6, 2017.

10. Berkshire Museum Case Summary, February 8, 2018.

11. Berkshire Museum Case Summary, February 8, 2018.

12. Larry Parnass, "Rockwell Sons Drop the Berkshire Museum Suit; Other Plaintiffs File with the SJC," *Berkshire Eagle*, February 15, 2018.

13. https://aamd.org/for-the-media/press-release/statement-on-the-berkshire-museum-proposal-to-deaccession-works-of-art, accessed February 16, 2018.

14. James Miller, "Berkshire Museum and Massachusetts Attorney General Reach Deal to Sell Works," https://www.theartnewspaper.com/news/berkshire-museum-and-massachusetts-attorney-general-reach-deal-to-allow-sale-of-works, *Art Newspaper*, February 9, 2018, accessed February 16, 2018.

15. Miller, February 9, 2018.

16. Brian Allen, "Auction Houses Must Share the Blame for University Sell-Offs," *Art Newspaper*, February 5, 2018.

17. Miller, February 9, 2018.

18. Miller, February 9, 2018.

19. Daniel Grant, "Should Museums Be Allowed to Sell Donated Works of Art?" *Observer*, January 24, 2018.

20. Daniel Grant, "Should Museums Be Allowed to Sell Donated Works of Art?" *Observer*, January 24, 2018.

21. National Gallery of Art, "Biography of Albert Bierstadt," https://www.nga.gov/collection/artist-info.6707.html, accessed February 16, 2018.

22. Metropolitan Museum of Art, "Biography of Edwin Church," https://www.metmuseum.org/toah/hd/chur/hd_chur.htm, accessed February 16, 2018.

23. *Don't Raid the Cookie Jar: Creating Early Interventions to Prevent Deaccessioning Crises Summary Report*, American Alliance of Museums, December 2017.

24. *Don't Raid the Cookie Jar: Creating Early Interventions to Prevent Deaccessioning Crises Summary Report*, American Alliance of Museums, December 2017.

Index

About the Editor and Contributors

Julia Hollett Courtney has over twenty years of experience in the museum field. She earned an MEd in art education from Lesley University in Cambridge, Massachusetts, and a master's degree in art history and museum studies from Harvard University. Courtney was the Curator of Art for the Springfield Art Museums in Springfield, Massachusetts (Michele and Donald D'Amour Museum of Fine Arts and the George Walter Vincent Smith Art Museum) from 2006 to 2016. She edited and contributed to *The Legal Guide for Museum Professionals* (Rowman & Littlefield, 2015) and has conducted scholarly research and written on the collections as well as researched, organized, and designed numerous exhibits that have received national and international attention.

Courtney is a freelance writer, editor, and artist and has contributed to *Antiques and Fine Art* magazine and many art catalogues. She is a member of the American Alliance of Museums, New England Association of Museums, Association of Art Museum Curators, and the Museum and Arts Law Committee of the Section of Science and Technology Law of the American Bar Association.

ABOUT THE CONTRIBUTORS

Bradley W. Bateman is the tenth president of Randolph College, a position he has held since 2013. He spent the bulk of his teaching career (1987–2007) at Grinnell College, where he was the Gertrude B. Austin Professor of Economics, before becoming the provost at Denison University (2007–2013). Bateman is a historian of economic thought who has published widely on John Maynard Keynes, as well as on the religious foundations of economics

255

in America. He is the author of *Keynes's Uncertain Revolution* (1996) and co-author (with Roger Backhouse) of *Capitalist Revolutionary: John Maynard Keynes* (2011). He is the co-editor of sever books including *Keeping Faith, Losing Faith: The History of Religious Belief and Political Economy* (2008).

Darlene Alexis Bialowski has worked in the museum field for over twenty years. She is Principal of Darlene Bialowski Art Services LLC, a firm that provides collection management services to private collectors, artists, cultural organizations, and museums since 2007. Her firm also performs appraisals of fine and decorative arts for a variety of purposes including insurance schedul-ing, estate distribution, damage and loss, and charitable contribution.

Bialowski holds a bachelor of brts in anthropology and an associate degree in the administration of criminal justice from the American Uni-versity, Washington, DC; a paralegal certificate from the University of New Hampshire; a certificate in appraisal studies in fine and decorative arts (New York University); and is a graduate of the Winterthur Institute (2014). She is the former registrar for the Springfield Museums in Spring-field, Massachusetts, a consortium of five museums of varied disciplines. She is an Accredited member of the Appraisers Association of America; holds the position of President of Red Arch Cultural Heritage Law and Policy Research Inc.; is a former chair of the Registrars Committee of the American Alliance of Museums; and is a member of several museum and historical property associations. Bialowski has contributed to the museum field over the years with presentations at various regional, national, and international conferences as well as for the general public. She has pub-lished articles for the museum profession and for the *Journal of Advanced Appraisal Studies*.

Lori Breslauer currently serves as General Counsel for the Field Museum of Natural History in Chicago, Illinois. She provides legal advice and counsel to the Museum on a broad and diverse range of matters including collections management, cultural property, exhibitions, education initiatives, business affairs, intellectual property, and insurance. Breslauer earned her JD from Northwestern University School of Law and her BS from Purdue University with highest honors. She has worked at the Field Museum since 1994.

Catherine Colinvaux is the former President of the Board of Trustees for the Worcester Art Museum (where she was deeply involved in the Higgins Armory integration) and continues to serve on the Board. Previously, Col-invaux was a senior partner of a national law firm where she represented both plaintiffs and defendants in large-dollar, multijurisdiction disputes, including serving as one of the lead property insurance counsels for all aspects of the 9/11 attack on the World Trade Center. Colinvaux received her BA *magna cum laude* from Harvard and Radcliffe Colleges and her JD *cum laude* from Harvard Law School. She has been recognized by *Massachusetts Lawyers Weekly* as a "Top Woman in Law," by Massachusetts Super Lawyers® as a Top 50 Woman Lawyer, and she is included in *The Best Lawyers in America©*. In 2013, Colinvaux retired to focus on not-for-profit work.

Peter Dean was a Trustee of Randolph College from 2006 to 2016. He participated in the decision making process that resulted in Randolph-Macon Women's College becoming co-educational and changing its name to Randolph College, and later in the college's decision to raise money for its endowment fund from the sale of selected paintings from its art collection. He was also directly involved in the sale of *Men of the Docks* to the National Gallery in London.

Dean is a lawyer based in Atlanta where he is of counsel in the law firm of Eversheds Sutherland (US) LLP, practicing in the areas of commercial, business, and energy law, and also advising clients on governance issues. He is a graduate of the University of Cambridge (Trinity College) and was called to the Bar of England and Wales as a member of Lincoln's Inn. He is admitted to the Bars of New York and Georgia and has practiced law in the United States since 1975, first in New York with a Wall Street law firm from 1975 to 1983, and in Atlanta since 1983.

James C. Donnelly Jr., Esq., is a partner at Mirick O'Connell DeMallie & Lougee LLP in Worcester, Massachusetts, focusing on business disputes and litigation. He has been a Trustee or Incorporator of the Higgins Armory Museum since 1986 and President from 1994 to 1997 and from 2010 to present. He is Treasurer and a member of the Board and Executive Committee of the American Antiquarian Society, a nationally renowned historical research library. He received a BA from Dartmouth College in 1968 and a JD *cum laude* from Boston College Law School in 1973, where he was Editor in Chief of the *Annual Survey of Massachusetts Law*. He has been selected for inclusion in *The Best Lawyers in America©* in the field of corporate governance and named a Massachusetts Super Lawyer®.

Ashley Downing is the Museum Curator at the DuPage County Historical Museum in Wheaton, Illinois. She received her BA in anthropology from Illinois State University and her MA in anthropology from Northern Illinois University. Downing has spent several years working with collection material and the deaccessioning conundrum at the DuPage County Historical Museum and at the Tinker Swiss Cottage Museum in Rockford, Illinois.

Sarah Ebel is Assistant General Counsel for the Field Museum of Natural History, where she provides advice and counsel on a wide variety of legal issues, specializing in intellectual property matters and accessibility compliance. She graduated *summa cum laude* from DePaul University School of Law, where she was president of the Art and Cultural Heritage Law Society. Prior to law school, Ebel was a museum professional, earning an MA in American material culture from the Winterthur Program at the University of Delaware.

Bernard P. Fishman was born in New York City and educated at Columbia and the University of Pennsylvania. For three years he worked in Luxor, Egypt, as an epigrapher at Chicago House, the University of Chicago's research institute. Since then he has directed five museums, most recently the Maine State Museum, where he has been director since 2012.

He is the author or editor of numerous publications, including *A Story of Maine in 112 Objects* (2018). He is the cofounder of Photoarchive3D, an archive of thirty-five thousand historic stereo-view images used for educational programs presented in 3D.

Mark Gold is a partner in the law firm of Smith Green & Gold LLP in Pittsfield, Massachusetts. He holds an undergraduate degree in Economics and International Studies from The American University, a law degree from Georgetown University, and a master's degree in museum studies from Harvard University. His practice includes business and corporate law, venture capital and traditional financing, and nonprofit and museum law. Gold has done considerable research and has published numerous articles on deaccessioning, legal issues for museums, and governance and has participated in panels on those topics and others at meetings of the AAM and regional museum associations. He was coeditor of the three-volume *A Handbook for Academic Museums*, published in 2012 by MuseumsEtc, and authored two chapters of *The Legal Guide for Museum Professionals*, edited by Julia Courtney. He is a member of the Board of Directors and Treasurer of New England Museum Association.

Stefanie S. Jandl is an independent museum professional with expertise on strengthening the teaching role of academic museums within their campus communities. She has over twenty years of museum experience that includes academic outreach, exhibition planning, and collections management. She was the Andrew W. Mellon Associate Curator for Academic Programs at the Williams College Museum of Art in Williamstown, Massachusetts. At WCMA Jandl helped build the museum's Mellon-funded academic outreach program to make the WCMA collections, exhibitions, and programs a vital interdisciplinary academic resource for Williams College faculty and students. She was the coeditor, with Mark Gold, of the three-volume series *A Handbook for Academic Museums*, published by MuseumsEtc. With Mark Gold she coauthored "The Practical and Legal Implications of Efforts to Keep Deaccessioned Objects in the Public Domain," included in *Museums and the Disposals Debate*. She has written for *Gastronomica* and has published on Man Ray and various topics on food and art. She has a BA in political science from the University of Southern California and an MA in the history of art from Williams College.

John E. Klein served as the ninth President of Randolph College from 2007 to 2013. He assumed that position in 2007, following the decision that the College should become co-educational. During his presidency, Klein successfully led the College through its transition and significantly improved the College's finances. Before joining Randolph College, he was Executive Vice Chancellor for Administration of Washington University in St. Louis, serving as chief operating officer. Prior to that, Klein had a successful twenty-eight-year international business career with Bunge, Ltd., a global agribusiness company, becoming CEO of Bunge North America at the age of thirty-nine and serving in that position for eighteen years. He received an AB from Princeton University and a JD from the University of Michigan Law School, after which he practiced law with the law firm of Sullivan & Cromwell in New York City before joining Bunge. With a lifelong interest in art, Klein and his wife Susan are members of the American Art Forum of the Smithsonian American Art Museum, are Bryant Fellows of the American Wing of the Metropolitan Museum of Art, and have each served on the board of the St. Louis Art Museum.

Katherine E. Lewis concentrates her legal practice at the New York law firm of Meister Seelig & Fein in areas of information technology and new media. She works with museums, cultural organizations, and other not-for-profit organizations, as well as for-profit businesses in the technology and entertainment industries. Prior to entering private practice, Lewis worked as an attorney-advisor with the Smithsonian Institution's Office of Contracting for several years, advising and negotiating intellectual property and technology transactions for a variety of museum purposes, including digital media and interactive experiences, software development (including web and mobile applications), software as a service platform and products for public and internal use, collection digitization, content and member management services, commissioning, and acquisition agreements for digital works.

Lewis began teaching Museums and the Law at Harvard's Extension School in Spring 2018 and is Co-Chair of the Museum and the Arts Law Committee of the American Bar Association's (ABA) Section of Science and Technology. She serves as Secretary of the Section of Science and Technology, Board Member of the National Conference for Lawyers and Scientists, and Trustee of the Bronx Museum of the Arts. Lewis is a frequent speaker for ABA programs as well as regional and national museum associations on legal issues facing museums, specifically as they relate to intellectual property and information technology. She earned her juris doctorate and master of laws in intellectual property at the University of New Hampshire School of Law, graduated from the University of Connecticut with a bachelor of arts in art history, and is licensed to practice law in New York, Massachusetts, New Hampshire, and Washington, DC.

An anthropologist by training, **Leah Niederstadt** teaches courses in museum studies and visual culture in the Art/Art History Department at Wheaton College (Norton, Massachusetts), where she also serves as Curator of the Permanent Collection. She holds postgraduate degrees from the University of Michigan and University of Oxford, and her research focuses on contemporary expressive culture in Ethiopia and on the management and use of academic collections.

Trained at Harvard as an architect and engineer, **Michael O'Hare** came to Berkeley after holding teaching positions at MIT and Harvard's Kennedy School, and at Arthur D. Little Inc., Boston's Museum of Fine Arts, and the Massachusetts Executive Office of Environmental Affairs. His research history has included many topics: biofuels and global warming policy, environmental policy (including the "NIMBY problem") and facility siting, arts and cultural policy, public management, and higher education pedagogy. O'Hare was the principal investigator for Berkeley's contract research for the California Air Resources Board for implementation of the Low Carbon Fuel Standard, and recently published on fuel policies for global warming reduction, especially biofuels, their "indirect land use change" and food price effects, and the importance of time and uncertainty in relating fuel carbon intensity to warming policy.

He has been editor of the Curriculum and Case Notes section of the *Journal of Policy Analysis and Management*, is currently an associate editor of the *Journal of Public Affairs Education*, and has published frequently on quality assurance and best practices in professional teaching. Since coming to Cal he has done applied research for government and nonprofit clients on diverse topics including funding of the state Fish and Game Department, surface mining reclamation, nuclear waste disposal and high-speed rail siting, and revitalizing county fairs. He is a regular faculty member of the school's midcareer executive programs and has had visiting positions at Università Bocconi, the National University of Singapore, and Université Paul Cézanne (Aix-Marseille).

Christopher J. Robinson is a partner at the art law boutique firm of Cahill Cossu Noh & Robinson LLP and practices art law and intellectual property law, as well as general commercial litigation. He started his art career as a PhD candidate at the Courtauld Institute of Art in London, followed by nearly twenty years as an art dealer in New York, including six years as an independent dealer in old master and nineteenth-century drawings. He received his JD from Fordham University School of Law in 2001, where he served as Editor in Chief of *Law Review*.

His clients for both litigation and transactional matters include dealers, artists, art advisors, museums, auction houses, appraisers, art foundations, collectors, restorers, developers, and publishers. He is outside legal counsel to the Private Art Dealers Association and the New Art Dealers Alliance, and he has spoken frequently on art issues, in particular on stolen art, consignment fraud, forgeries, copyright and moral rights, public art, dealer transactions, and artists' rights. His student note on *The "Recognized Stature" Standard in the Visual Artists Rights Act*, 68 Fordham L. Rev. 1935 (2000) has been widely cited in court opinions and legal literature. He also has extensive experience in copyright, trademark, unfair competition, and false advertising, as well as libel defense and the First Amendment.

Sally Yerkovich is Director of Special Projects at The American-Scandinavian Foundation, where she oversees all fellowships and grants programs. Yerkovich is also Professor of Museum Anthropology at Columbia University and Director of the Institute of Museum Ethics and Professor in the Museum Professions Program at Seton Hall University. She serves as the Chair of the International Council of Museums Ethics Committee as well as the Professional Standards and Ethics Committee of the American Association of State and Local History. Author of *A Practical Guide to Museum Ethics*, her work, which draws upon more than thirty years of leadership experience in museums, is increasingly engaged with how museums will face the ethical challenges of the future.

.

Lightning Source UK Ltd.
Milton Keynes UK
UKHW02n2136010918
328119UK00003B/101/P

9 781442 270817